WHEN FAITH
MEETS FAME

WHEN FAITH
MEETS FAME

INSPIRING PERSONAL STORIES
FROM THE WORLD OF TV

GuidepostsBooks®
New York, New York

When Faith Meets Fame

ISBN-13: 978-0-8249-4714-9
ISBN-10: 0-8249-4714-2

Published by GuidepostsBooks
16 East 34th Street
New York, New York 10016
www.guidepostsbooks.com

Distributed by Ideals Publications, a Guideposts company
535 Metroplex Drive, Suite 250
Nashville, Tennessee 37211

GuidepostsBooks and *Ideals* are registered trademarks of Guideposts, Carmel, New York.

ACKNOWLEDGMENTS
Every attempt has been made to credit the sources of copyrighted material used in this book. If any such acknowledgment has been inadvertently omitted or miscredited, receipt of such information would be appreciated.

All material that originally appeared in *Guideposts* magazine is reprinted with permission.

"Brought Up Right" was adapted from *Trying to Get to Heaven: Opinions of a Tennessee Talker* by Dixie Carter. Copyright © 1996 by Dixie Carter. Reprinted with permission from Simon and Schuster Adult Publishing Group.

Scripture quotations on pages 15, 106, 174, 205, 230–233 are from *The King James Version of the Bible.*

Scripture quotations on pages 273 and 280 are from *The Holy Bible, New International Version.* Copyright © 1973, 1978, 1984 International Bible Society. Used by permission of Zondervan Bible Publishers.

Scripture quotation on page 58 is from *The Holy Bible, New King James Version.* Copyright © 1997, 1990, 1985, 1983 by Thomas Nelson, Inc.

Scripture quotation on page 262 is from the *Revised Standard Version of the Bible.* Copyright © 1946, 1952, 1971 by Division of Christian Education of the National Council of Churches of Christ in the U.S.A. Used by permission.

Scripture quotation on page 285 is from *The Living Bible.* Copyright © 1971 by Tyndale House Publishers, Wheaton, IL 60187. All rights reserved.

Library of Congress Cataloging-in-Publication Data

When faith meets fame : inspiring personal stories from the world of tv.
    p. cm.
  ISBN-13: 978-0-8249-4714-9
  1. Television actors and actresses—Religious life. 2. Television journalists—Religious life.
I. Guideposts Associates.
  BV4596.T45A8 2007
  791.45092'273—dc22
                        2006024517

Jacket design by The DesignWorks Group, Sisters, Oregon
Interior design by Marisa Jackson

Printed and bound in the United States of America

10 9 8 7 6 5 4 3 2 1

TABLE OF CONTENTS

ANGELS ALONG THE WAY ★ 85

FACING LIFE'S STORMS ★ 125

LISTENING TO YOUR HEART ★ 171

PREFACE

There were five thousand or so of that newfangled invention called the television in the United States in 1945, about the same number of subscribers that signed on for an unusual little magazine that launched that year called *Guideposts*. I don't think anyone could have foreseen the role either would play in postwar America. By 1955, millions of households owned TV sets and *Guideposts* was well on its way to its millionth subscriber. Today *Guideposts*, America's favorite magazine, reaches ten million readers a month. TV? Virtually every American has access to one. In a very real sense, *Guideposts* and television grew up together.

Norman Vincent Peale, who founded *Guideposts*, became a kind of TV star himself after his book *The Power of Positive Thinking* hit the best-seller list in 1953. He and his dynamic wife Ruth even had their own show for a while and were featured on numerous others. And many of Dr. Peale's sermons from Marble Collegiate Church on Fifth Avenue in New York City were broadcast on television. The new populist medium was transforming our culture back then, much like the Internet is doing today.

Guideposts and TV shared several interesting affinities. Both were smaller versions of bigger media: *Guideposts* was pocket-sized and, of course, television was called the "small screen" for a reason. Unlike their big siblings, they lent themselves to a more intimate experience. The stars on television were more real; we felt as if we knew them personally, and they returned week after week, sometimes night after night, often in a live "real time" format (imagine that!) right in our living rooms. It was only natural then that when these stars wanted to talk about their lives off camera, they came to *Guideposts* to tell their true, first-person stories of hope and inspiration. It was a match made in heaven, you might say, and through the years we have featured more celebrities from the world of television than we have from stage, sports and film combined.

Readers love these stories for one important reason: They are moved and empowered by hearing celebrities talk about facing the same challenges they themselves face in life—making a marriage work, understanding their children, reaching out to the disadvantaged or simply being able to tell a friend you are sorry for something you did. Like all of us, TV stars must learn how to put their faith to work in their daily lives, to find meaning and value beyond the material rewards of success. And, as we all know, that can be an amazing and exciting adventure for anyone.

I'm a little blown away when I look at the roster of authors in this book: Art Carney, Donna Reed, Dick Van Dyke, Hugh Downs, Fred Rogers, Brooke Shields, Al Roker, Rachael Ray and Brian Williams, just to name a handful. Giants of their craft who are also everyday people facing the world with hope and optimism and faith . . . people like you and me. And that's the secret of *Guideposts* and television: They bring people together through the extraordinary power of shared experience.

So go on. Turn the page and share with these remarkable people their unforgettable experiences.

Edward Grinnan
Editor-in-Chief
Guideposts

WHEN FAITH

MEETS FAME

INTRODUCTION

It's hard to imagine a world without television. It has such a foothold in our lives: providing the news from around the corner and around the globe, entertaining us with tales fictional and true—and often somewhere in between. TV fills a room with light, color and sound, brightening our moments and showing us stories of life. With the variety of sights and sounds that have come into our living rooms over the past sixty years, we've witnessed some powerful moments on our TV screens. But there are untold stories behind the camera—hope-filled and inspiring stories—from actors, newscasters and crew who have entertained and informed us. Stories from people who made their dreams a reality, found success, and stayed true to who they were and what they believed. Stories of people who know that fame is nothing without faith.

Dr. Allen B. DuMont invented the cathode-ray tube, a mechanism that brought television into American homes. In the October 1952 issue of *Guideposts*, he gave some advice to a sixteen-year-old paralyzed boy named Billy Weatherford, who asked out of his own heartbreak and pain: "Dear God, why do I have to be the way I am? Why can't I walk like the other guys I know? Why does everything seem to be just out of reach?" ·

Dear Billy,

    I asked myself the same question forty years ago, when I was a little younger than you—eleven. It's a hard question, but many of us have found an answer the hard way.

Perhaps you like sports. I did. As a boy, I fancied myself a good athlete. Babe Ruth hadn't started to hit home runs then; he was just a kid in an orphanage. Joe DiMaggio wasn't even born. But fellows like Ty Cobb and Christy Mathewson were doing all right. I hoped to be in the big leagues myself one day, hitting home runs and winning games.

One day I came home from school, aching all over. It was polio, the same crippler that strikes down so many youngsters like you. For a year I lay in bed while doctors worked to save my life. They feared that I would never walk again.

It didn't seem fair that this should happen to me, but what I am most thankful for, Billy, is that I didn't just quit. I tried painting, reading and did puzzles. One day my parents brought me some radio equipment to tinker with, a few crystals and a microphone. The stuff fascinated me.

At the end of my year in bed, I had built my own radio set. All of the energy I had before for sports and boats was now concentrated on radio. Here is the important point, Billy. I might never have become interested in radio if I hadn't been stricken with polio. Sometimes what seems like a great tragedy may, indeed, lead one into the type of activity where he or she will find his or her greatest happiness and success.

During this period my mother prayed for me night and day. We are lucky to have the prayers of those close to us. Perhaps the answer can't be complete recovery. If not, then perhaps the answer is something that will be even more important to us years later.

I came out of my polio experience with a limp that has been with me all my life. My energies then centered on radio, which was the best thing that could have happened to me.

At the age of fifteen, I obtained a license to serve on a ship as a wireless operator. The following summers, during school vacations, were spent on passenger and freight steamers doing this work I loved.

One thing I learned, Billy, was to toughen and condition myself to do well what things I could do. If our scope of movement is limited, then our complete concentration and all our abilities should be focused on doing the one thing we can do best.

Another thing, Billy. Don't let people tell you, "It can't be done." If you want to walk again more than anything else, keep telling yourself that you will walk again. Fix this thought in your mind. Repeat it to yourself over and over again. Someday you will walk again!

All kinds of people are always saying, "It can't be done." Even engineers, and they ought to know better! When I started to work with Westinghouse back in 1921, the building of radio sets was hampered by poor methods of tube construction. No one seemed to think the problem could be licked, except a few of us who hated the sound of the word *can't*.

Ten years later I was a production vice president for another company; television was just a laboratory curiosity— a hope and a dream. I felt the answer lay in the development of the cathode-ray tube, a complicated mechanism, Billy, that translates impulses from the TV station into the picture you see on your TV set. When my coworkers disagreed with my ideas, I quit this company and decided to go into business myself making cathode-ray tubes.

To set up my own business, I converted my basement-garage into a laboratory. That first year I used all my savings, borrowed on my insurance, mortgaged our home and even borrowed from friends.

Interestingly enough, the company that I left went out of business during that same period. I would have been much worse off if I had held on to so-called security rather than taken a chance on opportunity. For this cathode-ray tube—developed by our company—helped make television a billion-dollar industry today.

But material success isn't the most important thing, Billy. Doing creative work that will enrich and benefit humankind is much more so. The development of faith in yourself, in people and in God is all important.

So that is the answer to your prayer, "Why do I have to be the way I am?"

Some of humankind's greatest achievements have come from people who can't hear or see or talk or walk. By closing the door to one way of life, God may be opening the door to a new opportunity. As it was for me and for many others, Billy, and as it might be for you, tragedy can be a great blessing.

Sincerely from the heart,
Allen B. DuMont

Dr. DuMont recognized the spiritual truth that limitations can be blessings that lead to success. From one man's vision that television could go beyond the laboratory and into people's homes, to the dreams of individuals drawn to work in TV, this collection offers touching insights like Dr. DuMont's from those we have invited to enlighten and entertain us. The men and women who light up our TV screens offer glimpses into their hopes, fears and triumphs.

Meet real folks who turn loneliness into creativity, despair into triumph, selfishness into giving, fear into grace. Actors, newscasters, on-air chefs, producers and crew members who work behind the scenes share stories of their successes and the faith that carried them there. Faith was the compass that pointed them toward their goals and dreams. Each person in these pages incites wonder at the strength of the human spirit and provides marvelous evidence that when we trust in Him, God will help us through anything.

BEGINNINGS

You could get strength just from sitting next to Dad in church. When the minister would read from the Bible, Dad would lean forward a little, as though this especially he had to hear. Watching his face, we children could see that the ancient words were food to his spirit, strength to get him through one more week.

DONNA REED

PETER JENNINGS

Listen

My parents' house was often full of interesting and newsworthy people. My father, Charles Jennings, was a broadcaster and a pioneer in Canadian radio. He knew so many people, from the foreign minister to the local grocer, and he would often invite them to our house for lunch together. My father talked to everybody. But most of all he loved to listen.

He told me "every person has a story, you just have to take the time to listen to it." To this day I can't pass a street corner without listening to somebody—and I have tried to pass the joy of it on to my children.

I left school at seventeen, intent on being a journalist. In 1964 I landed a job as an ABC News reporter in New York. I learned one of the most important parts of a reporter's job is listening—it's how you get beyond the obvious to the heart of what people are saying.

In the late 1960s, I became a foreign correspondent. I worked all over the world. But it was always the stories I heard from ordinary people—and often from people I least expected—that opened my eyes.

I became anchor of *World News Tonight* in 1983. One day a young reporter told me about an interview she had just done with a woman who had survived a plane crash. "I asked her how she made it through the accident," the reporter told me, "and she said, 'God got me through it.'"

"Yes, but what really got you through it?" the young reporter followed up.

Our young reporter had expected a particular response, but her perspective was different from the woman's. "That woman already told you what got her through the crash," I told her. "You had the real answer, but you weren't listening carefully enough, so you missed it."

Journalists have a responsibility to fairly convey the many sides of a story. To do this, we must first and foremost be observant. That means listening. It means listening to what someone has to say even if it doesn't fit into a thirty-second sound bite. It means sticking around for the second day of a story to hear what else people say. And it means listening for other people's perspective and never assuming that they share the same one you do.

As the world gets smaller but more diverse, I am more than ever convinced that listening to everybody everywhere doesn't just help you to be a better reporter. It helps you hear the world.

DONNA REED

The Courage to Face Today

Not long ago my younger son Timothy—he's twelve now—came in to me with his homework assignment. Timmie had to read and try to understand all the stories on the front page of our newspaper.

"Oh dear!" I gasped out loud.

"What's the matter, Mom?" Timmie asked, surprised, and I hastened to cover up the momentary despair I felt. There, splashed boldly across the page, were frightening headlines about many of the things that are wrong with our world today. There were reports about a hydrogen bomb explosion, about a murder, a car crash, a divorce. *Oh, Timmie,* I thought to myself, *must you learn about all of these things? What a world to bring you up in!*

Timmie had provided that moment of pause that must come often to parents who try to be responsible and knowledgeable citizens and yet, who want to give their atom-age children a sense of security.

It is easy to believe that our children don't think much beyond baseball or when-they'll-be-allowed-to-wear-lipstick or what's-for-dessert? Actually, however, children are but small adults; they, too, worry about the terrors of atomic war; they, too, can see the dark shadows with which our days are edged.

Again and again my husband Tony Owen and I have discussed this problem. We have not wanted to keep the realities of the world from our two boys and two girls, but for a long time we have had a sense of failure about finding the formula for what we call the courage to face today. Then, recently, Penny Jane, our older daughter, now fifteen, asked a question that eventually gave us our answers.

We were talking about the world today, when Penny Jane said, "Mom, what did you have to worry about in your day?"

Children have a way of making you feel not old, but ancient, as though your youth and usefulness were centuries behind. I had to laugh at her question. "Well," I said, and then my mind began to go back, and all of a sudden it did begin to seem like a long time since my girlhood. Sitting there in the comfort of our lovely Beverly Hills home I began to talk about how I, too, was one of four children and how we lived on a farm near Denison, Iowa.

My family on both sides had pioneered in that state before I was born. As children all of us had chores to perform. I could and did milk the cows and drive the tractor, bring in water from the pump and coal and wood for the stove; to this day I can bake my own bread. The most obvious difference between my childhood and our children's is not that I lived on a farm, but that back in Iowa during the terrible pressure of the Depression years we were quite poor.

I doubt that any people in America suffered more than some of the Midwestern farmers of the early 1930s. These people, our friends and neighbors, were struck with a series of Job-like afflictions. Times were bad everywhere, of course, and there was little money, but on top of this came the drought that withered crops and parched the earth only to be followed by the wind that swept the dry topsoil into great, dark choking dust storms. Family after family loaded their belongings into rickety automobiles and left. . . .

Poverty, need, these are awful things to have happen to you, but even worse, I think, to watch in others. I remember the sounds of our animals crying for food and water. I remember how a little girl from a nearby farm came to say that she would not be playing with me anymore because her family was going away. She didn't know where they were going; they were simply leaving, giving up.

When I think back to those harsh days, I think mainly in terms of my parents, and the anguish I felt inside as I saw them up early and late to bed, day after day, laboring hard with no returns. As children we had few toys and I always yearned for a bicycle which I never got, but I can't recall these things as having been very important to me when I knew so well the inescapable realities of our situation. We might have left the farm, too, if it had not been for Dad.

His name is William Mullenger and he is a stubborn man. He would not give up. One by one we had to sell our livestock. One by one our neighbors deserted their farms and each time my father would say to us calmly but with undeniable vigor shored up by his faith: "It will not always be this way."

I used to wonder how Dad could be so sure when so many others were not. And then, on Sundays, I'd get a glimpse of the answer. On Sundays Dad would pile Mom and the four kids into that old car we drove for fifteen years and we'd rattle to the Methodist church in Denison. You could get strength just from sitting next to Dad in church. When the minister would read from the Bible, Dad would lean forward a little, as though this especially he had to hear. Watching his face, we children could see that the ancient words were food to his spirit, strength to get him through one more week.

Our minister used to read a lot from those books of the Bible that rang with hope. Only recently I searched through the Bible to see if I couldn't find some of the familiar passages and there, in Isaiah, I came across some verses that brought back the whole experience of parched farms and poverty as clearly as though I were there again, sitting in the pew next to Dad. Just listen to these words:

"When the poor and needy seek water, and there is none, and their tongue faileth for thirst, I the Lord will hear them . . . . I will make the wilderness a pool of water, and the dry land springs of water" (Isaiah 41:17–18).

These are the things that my father heard and believed.

Dad was a family man, a real family man. "If there is family strength," he used to say, "that old Depression's not going to get us." And the Depression did pass and it did not get us. Eventually I graduated from high school and with sixty dollars in my purse I left Denison for Los Angeles where I could live with my aunt and go to college.

When I explained to Penny Jane that we had our worries, too, in the far, far away days of my youth, and when later I went delving into the old prophet Isaiah, I was well on the way to discovering how we parents in 1962 can prepare our children to cope with the atomic age. I came to the root of the matter when I began to think about faith, the faith that our family now was renewing in church on Sundays. In essence it was the same as when our family went to church in Denison: the knowledge that God still lives and rules and can handle our problems whatever they may be—if we let Him.

I do not believe that the world changes as much as we choose to think. In my father's day there was the Depression; the suffering then was real and affected millions of people. Before my father's time my forebears in Iowa faced the rigors of nature. All of our ancestors in distant ages have known plague and destruction in one form or another. Yet, centuries before my children, even centuries before Christ, Isaiah spoke about God's power extending beyond Israel to all other nations and unto all generations.

In words not surpassed anywhere in the Old Testament, Isaiah spoke of hope and the kingdom of God on earth. And that's the way it happens: faith and courage are like torches passed from old to young.

Today represents new times, yes. New problems, new fears, but one basic and beautiful thing links us with the past and with the future. That thing is faith, our belief in God and His adequacy.

Dad had that faith when he said about our poverty, "It will not always be this way." With Him we know that if we fail today, tomorrow offers its triumphs.

JIMMY DURANTE

The Chain around My Neck

It's so tough down there on the Lower East Side in New York where
I was born, we always think any kid who walks around with two
ears is a hopeless sissy. In other neighborhoods the truant officer
chases the kids. In our neighborhood we chase the truant officer. On
the level, it's a real rough neighborhood.

Later when I start playing the piano in Coney Island joints, I'm
rubbing elbows with gangsters, gunmen, bootleggers and kidnappers.

None of that stuff dusts off on me hard enough to stick. For that
I owe a lot to many people, but mostly to four special ones. To
remind myself of what I owe them, and because I love them, I carry
on a chain around my neck four little gifts they give me. I wear them
so long they're like part of my flesh. I know they're part of me that
isn't flesh. They're like four commandments that aren't listed with the
big ten.

Every morning I put my fingers on the chain around my neck
and I feel rich. I mean you can probably buy the four things and the
chain for fifty cents and still get change. But I feel rich for what they
give me in my heart.

One of these gifts is a medal of the Madonna. My pop give me
that. He was a barber, and when I'm a kid he lets me lather up the
faces of his customers. It's his hard-earned dollars, and there were
never a lot of them, that learns me how to play the piano. Bartolomeo

Durante, the barber, the kindest, gentlest man I ever know. In giving me the medal he teaches me the art of giving. If his customers don't have the price, he'd cut their hair anyway. To the day he died he wants to give away everything he has.

When he gets too old to barber he lives with my sister Lillian in Brooklyn, and he walks down the streets and passes out all the money he has to anyone who needs it. It gets so bad he can't carry any money with him. So I send it to Lillian and make her his banker.

You know, I don't think I ever see him mad a minute in his whole life. I'd like to be like him.

"Watch the friends you pick," he always says to me. "Some will steal your heart and your thoughts. Avoid them. You only pick the ones to whom you can give your heart and your thoughts."

I always try to.

The second gift on the chain around my neck is a medal of the Crucifixion. My wife Jeanne give it to me when we was married in 1921. We was married for twenty-two years. She died in 1943. Lord have mercy on her.

Her medal of the Crucifixion always reminds me of the art of forgetting and forgiving. Even how I met her reminds me of forgiving.

She came from Toledo, Ohio, and she's a very pretty girl. Pretty inside as well as outside. And she's a great singer. What a pair of pipes she has.

I'm working in an uptown joint in Harlem then, the Alamo, and she drops in looking for a job. The boss eyes her, and says: "Let's hear you sing. Go ahead, Jimmy, play the piano for her."

I resent that because I'm busy—I don't know what I'm busy

about. But I feel busy. So I play a few blue notes and clinkers. She stops, and she's real angry, and she says: "You are probably the worst piano player in the world."

"Them are the conditions that pervails," I say.

First she busts out laughing, and then she lights up the room with the shiningest smile I ever see.

So what do I do? I marry her.

Jeanne knows people and how weak-minded they get, and watching her heart work I learn what forgiveness is. One day she entrusts an acquaintance with some money. A slight loan, you might say. And when it's time to return it, the money isn't there. So the guy says he's sorry and tells her why he hasn't got it. Jeanne never asks him again.

"I feel resentment when I ask and he refuses," Jeanne says. "I don't want to feel resentment, so I'll never ask him."

I never want to feel resentment, so if anyone owes me anything I never ask either.

Jeanne is always telling me: "If anyone does something wrong to you they'll be more unhappy about it than you will. So forget and forgive."

I'm not proud—it takes a lot of time and trouble to keep even the smallest nose in the air.

The third thing on my chain is a St. Christopher's medal. To me it's the art of friendship. Through the years I learn it from my friends Eddie Jackson and Lou Clayton. Lou is around us still even though he died. But a stranger I still don't know and the St. Christopher's medal keep reminding me of what friendship means.

I get the medal about six years ago. I'm ready to start a seventeen-day grind of one-night stands across the country on a bond drive tour when Lou Clayton takes me to the doctor for a checkup. The last X-ray shows a polyp in my lower stomach.

So I'm elected for surgery. No tour. No radio. Nothing. But Al Jolson, Bob Hope, Red Skelton and Frank Morgan took turns doing the radio show for me. That's what success really is, to have friends of that sort. Do the best you can. Stick with your friends. Pray they'll stick with you. The rest is in God's hands.

If I don't have that operation, that polyp could have gone malignant and I am in real trouble. God is really with me.

When they give me that shot in the arm, right before I go into the surgery, and I'm just about getting subconscious I feel someone touching my neck. When I wake up from the anesthesia I see this St. Christopher's medal around my neck and I ask the nurse: "Where does this come from?"

And she says: "Right before we took you up a nice lady with gray hair, dressed very nice, comes in, and kneels down, and says a prayer, and then slips this around your neck, and then she begs the doctor: 'Please doc, take good care of him,' and then she runs out."

Anyway I can never forget this stranger with the St. Christopher's medal.

Before my mother dies, over twenty-five years ago, she gives me a little beat-up cross. That's the fourth gift on my chain. She wore it all her life, and when she gives it to me she says: "Never take it off, and God will always be with you."

It isn't true that I start each day with a song. That's second. I start each day with a prayer. That I get from Mom. She teaches me the art of believing. That's probably the greatest of the four commandments on my chain.

Oh, she teaches me all the commandments, all right, my mother.

A saint. God have mercy on her soul. One time, I think I'm about five years old, I'm walking down the street with her, and we pass a vegetable pushcart. I just snitch a piece of corn; all the kids do. Two blocks later Mom turns around and sees the corn and asks me: "Where did you get it?"

"Off the pushcart," I says.

She hauls me by the ear for two blocks all the way back to the pushcart and makes me explain to the peddler and give it back. I am highly mortified. But that's her way of teaching me the commandments.

As a kid she tells us: "Without believing, you're nothing." And she points to one of the tough guys on the block: "He hasn't got God in his heart," she says. And she turns to a good guy like my father and says: "This one, he has God in his heart."

And we always follow her to church, without her asking, to find where God is. Even after she dies I still follow her.

For a while there's a time when I think I'm too busy to follow her, and during this time I'm helping Father James Keller; he's head of the Christophers. I am helping him make a movie, and he asks me: "Going to church regular?"

I got to admit I miss here and there. "I been very busy," I alibi.

"You find the time," Father Keller says. "You find time for everything else."

He's real severe about it. Would you believe it? And there I am doing a picture for him for free.

But after that, when I think I'm too busy, I touch the beat-up little cross on the chain around my neck, and remember to follow my mother to where God is.

And you know the nicest thing about following my mother to where God is? I always feel it's like walking out of darkness into the sun.

DIXIE CARTER

Brought Up Right

W hen I say in my concert act, as I often do, that my childhood was idyllic, I usually get a laugh. There's always someone in the audience who expects I must be setting up a joke because the word idyllic sounds over the top. Well, not for me.

Growing up in McLemoresville, Tennessee, population around two hundred, my brother and sister and I had handmade clothes, and fresh orange juice, milk and butter. We had bedtime stories and warm laps to rock in. But the luxurious aspect of all these things was that they were evidences of love.

In summer we ate from the garden. Daddy and Gina, as we called our mother, made a game out of gardening with us. Daddy came home from the family store (H. L. Carter and Son, "A Good Place to Trade") just as early as he could so there was still enough daylight for us to go out and work together. I remember how we used to pull warm ripe tomatoes off the vine and sit on the back porch with a sticky salt shaker, salting and eating, leaning way out over the grass so that the juice wouldn't run down onto our clothes.

My mother and father were so good-looking they were shiny. They were crazy about each other, always laughing together, having a good time, Daddy grabbing Gina in the kitchen, singing to her like Bing Crosby and waltzing her around the house. Daddy used to tease and say he had the easy part of rearing us, because my mother was the disciplinarian during the day, and he got to come home from the store in the evening and spoil us.

He was often the one to read us our bedtime stories. Our favorites were the Uncle Wiggily stories, which Daddy read quite dramatically, using different voices for different characters. When the "skillery scalery alligator" was about to get Uncle Wiggily, and my younger sister Midge and I yelped in fright, Gina protested indulgently, "Don't be so graphic! These children will have nightmares."

The summer I was two years old I was taken next door to stay with my grandparents because my mother's heart was acting up and she was put to bed, flat on her back, not to move. Daddy called and asked his younger sister to come help take care of me. She looked like a redheaded Barbara Stanwyck, with beautiful white teeth and a wild reckless laugh. That summer my aunt, always at the piano, taught me to sing.

The trick was getting me to be still enough to learn the words, so she arrived at the solution of setting me on the staircase and blocking my way until I had assimilated that afternoon's verse. Our first number was "Put on the skillet, put on the lead, Mammy's gonna make a little shortnin' bread." She sang the line through and waited for me to finish with the last word. As soon as I caught on to the game and sang all the words with her, she sat me up on the piano bench beside her and played while I sang.

After my nap I got to see my mother. I remember standing by her tall four-poster bed and looking up at her, lying still and pale. She became cheerful and smiling when she saw me, and somebody held me up to kiss her. Then I leaned against the arm of the rocking chair, crossed one leg over the other and delivered the song for the day:

"She'll be coming round the mountain" or "Give me one dozen roses." Years later I read what Kahlil Gibran wrote: "The song that lies silent in the heart of a mother sings upon the lips of her child." I thought of my mother and that time.

I grew up in the Methodist church. My family were, both sides, religious people. My mother's side were Baptists, but when she and my father married, she offered to join his church. She did not, however, change what she believed about doctrine. When my sister and I were baptized as adolescents, we were sprinkled at the Methodist church on Sunday morning, and for good measure immersed at the Baptist church by the Baptist minister later that afternoon.

It was scary to me, going down into that chilly water with my Sunday dress on and having a handkerchief held over my mouth, then stepping out cold and slick as an otter, dripping and embarrassed. But it gave my mother such obvious relief and joy that it was well worth my discomfort.

I often hear bright people say they don't want to force religion on their children; they'll let them grow up and then decide. Decide based on what? No one can decide what they feel about something with which they have no acquaintance. Lack of a religious grounding in the early years is, to my mind, a deprivation.

My maternal grandmother Hillsman had daily Bible readings for us at breakfast and prayers following the readings. The prayers were hard to understand, because just as soon as she started to pray, she would be overwhelmed with gratitude for God's goodness and begin to weep.

She spent summers with us, and sometimes she called us children with great urgency: "Halbert Leroy Carter Jr.! Dixie Virginia

Carter! Melba Helen Carter!" When we ran to answer her summons, we would like as not be met with "Stop! Look at God's beautiful sunset!"

I will never forget seeing her stand out on the porch in the worst of summer thunderstorms, quoting aloud, "God moves in a mysterious way, his wonders to perform; he plants his footsteps in the sea, and rides upon the storm," as the elements raged around her. I remember how she took my baby sister out of my mother's arms when Midge went into convulsions. She walked with Midge while the ambulance took forever coming, and when Uncle Jack, who was there for the summer, said, "What can I do, Mama?" she answered emphatically, "Get down on your knees and pray, Son Jack."

My other grandmother, Mama Carter, lived next door to us. She was the kindliest person I have ever known. She looked to me like I thought angels probably looked. If she heard me say that now she'd probably add, "It would have to be a plump angel." She kept her house in perfect order, cooked three meals a day and had time to read the Bible morning and evening, and read it through each year. She never raised her voice to me except once, when I was eleven and she had begun spending the bad-weather months living in our house with us.

One Sunday morning I got up and came downstairs early, consumed with my desire to see if I could replicate Becky Presson's spectacular performance in the talent contest the night before. I tore into "You Gotta See Mama Every Night." Every note, word, gesture, jerk and wiggle of Becky's was seared into my brain. I was reproducing it verbatim, working up steam. On this particular morning I wanted to scald the air with my performance. I was somewhere around "I don't like the kind of a man who works on the installment plan" when

Mama Carter appeared, disbelief and revulsion writ large on her brow. She wasted no time in notifying me that she never wanted to hear me singing a song like that on the Sabbath again.

Wise people say that happiness isn't having what you want but wanting what you have. By that standard Mama Carter was one of the happiest women I've ever known. She derived a lifetime of pleasure from what was at hand; she loved her family and doted on them, especially us children. She knew all the birds by their songs and all the constellations. She loved being able to tell what the weather was going to be like and helping us to find the Big Dipper and the Little Dipper, and she genuinely enjoyed her daily ritual of rinsing out the cow's water tub and refilling it with cool, crystal-clear water.

Those of us who felt safe for the first twenty years or so of our lives ought to be giving thanks every minute. We ought to be thankful for the sanctity of a place walled and roofed with love. I knew that my brother, sister and I were treasures beyond price. We had chores to do and Bible lessons to learn and music to practice and mosquito bites and sprained ankles and spankings, but we were beloved and safe. It was idyllic.

DONNA DOUGLAS

Becoming a Beverly Hillbilly

I stood looking around the airport in Newark, New Jersey, trying not to panic. It was the early 1960s. I was a young girl just arrived from Baton Rouge, Louisiana, hoping for an acting career in New York City. I'd made a terrible mistake.

An acquaintance had promised to meet me at the airport. But nobody told me that three airports served New York City! I'd originally had tickets to La Guardia, but at the last minute the ticket agent switched me to another flight. He didn't mention I'd be arriving at a different airport.

Believe me, I was afraid. But I had been brought up in the church. I remembered that the Bible says, "Faith is the substance of things hoped for, the evidence of things not seen." To me, in plain language, that means faith is when you trust God, even though you can't see what's a-coming around the corner.

So I said a little prayer and I sat down to wait. I was thankful that when I didn't show up at La Guardia, my friend figured out what had happened and was able to track me down. I had never been so happy to see anybody in my life. I didn't know it at the time, but that was just one of the many "comers" that would be upcoming in my life.

A few days later, alone in my hotel room, I was just about out of courage. I'd come to New York to find work. But how did I expect to find a job in Manhattan? I hadn't gone to college and had never had an acting lesson in my life. I'd done a speck of modeling—in Louisiana. I could throw a mean curve ball (I'd even been approached about playing semipro softball), and had some experience fishing and milking cows, but these were far from talents that would get me hired as an actress. On top of that, people teased me about my Southern accent. I, of course, thought they were the ones who talked funny. Back home in Louisiana, everyone had a drawl like mine.

Fortunately, some photographers decided to give me a break and hired me to do ads for catalogs and magazines. This led to a few TV commercials where I smiled a lot. But I never said a word.

Finally I got a call to audition for a TV game show. The job was as an "elbow grabber," one of the hostesses who brings the contestants out and presents them to the host. If I got the position I'd have steady work, "bread-and-butter money," and national exposure. And once again, I wouldn't have to say a word.

The day of my audition, I was shown to the office of the show's producer—and was thrown for a loop by what came next.

"We're looking for a certain kind of girl," he said. "Are you willing to, ah, do some extra work after hours?"

Warning bells went off in my head.

"What . . . what does that mean?" I asked.

"Would you be willing to go out with one of our sponsors?"

"Would the sponsor be married?" I asked.

"What does it matter? You'd just be going out to dinner."

"No, sir," I said emphatically, "I couldn't do that."

The producer shifted in his chair. Disappointment overwhelmed me. I'd heard there were girls who were willing to do anything to get work. I had tears in my eyes. "Mister," I said, standing up, "I don't want your job. It's not that important to me." And I walked out.

I was mighty surprised when I heard I got the job. It turned out there'd recently been a big exposé of dishonest game shows, and the producer had to be very careful about everyone he hired. He'd been trying to find a girl who wouldn't do anything questionable.

Not long after that, I was asked to go to California to do a screen test at Paramount. The folks back home couldn't believe it when I told them I got a movie contract. But since I had little experience and was no good at bluffing, I got only small parts. I wanted to better myself, so I took acting and speech lessons from a coach who taught me to act and talk like anyone from a working girl to a refined lady.

So I hoped I was ready when I went off to be interviewed for a pilot for a new television series. I wanted this part so much; it seemed like everything I'd worked and prayed for.

When I did my reading, the producer smiled and told me I seemed like a real possibility for the part. She said she'd get back to me as soon as possible. I couldn't speak; I just nodded my head up and down. I was so thrilled I thought my heart would pop wide open.

On my way home, I was scheduled to take my car in for an oil change. I'd arranged for the mechanic at the garage to drop me off at home, then take my car back to service it. He was at the wheel and I was in the passenger seat as we waited at a red light—when a large Bentley rammed into us from behind.

The mechanic was okay, but I ended up in the hospital for seventeen days. During that time, the producers of the television pilot interviewed more than five hundred girls for that part. They selected six for screen tests—and I was one of them. It was wonderful news, except for the fact that I was supposed to show up for a screen test in three days.

This was sure one corner I couldn't see around.

"Please, God," I prayed from my hospital bed, "let me have a chance at this."

Woozy but determined, I went to that screen test. On my way over, I couldn't help thinking of all the sophisticated actresses I was up against—ones who had a lot more experience, and none of whom were wobbly from an accident.

At the studio, the producer Paul Henning explained the series to me more fully. "And for the screen test," he said, "we've got a special request."

I nodded, desperately hoping I'd be able to remember my recent elocution lessons and theatrical training.

"We'd like you to read the part," he said, "using a Southern accent."

I couldn't believe it! The camera started rolling and I read the part in the down-home voice I knew the best—my own Louisiana drawl.

The producer smiled. He seemed pleased. But then the smile left his face. "There's one more thing," he said. "Can you milk a goat?"

I looked to the side of the set, and sure enough, there was a little nanny goat! One look told me she had the same equipment as the cows back home.

"Sure, I can milk that goat!" I said.

That nanny goat was the first of more than five hundred "critters" I worked with during the nine years I played Elly May Clampett on *The Beverly Hillbillies*.

There have been ups and downs in my life. But time and again I've found it to be true that if you give God your best, He'll meet you where you are and use whatever you have to offer.

Even when you can't see what's a-coming around the corner.

TIM RUSSERT

Big Russ

On Election Day 2000 I sat on the *NBC Nightly News* set with Tom Brokaw, trying to make sense of the electoral college map. I'm supposed to be the big expert, the network's chief political correspondent, and even I was having trouble understanding what it meant. Would our new president-elect be George W. Bush or Al Gore?

I paused and thought of my dad, Big Russ, watching TV back home in Buffalo, New York. Keep it simple, he'd say. The first candidate to get 270 electoral votes wins.

I ignored all the computer printouts and reached for a legal pad. In bold print I wrote the names of the states still being contested and how many electoral votes each had. Then I held up the pad to the camera. I could almost hear Big Russ's approval. Now I get it.

We all search for heroes in life. I didn't have to look far for mine. Someone once asked me, "If you could interview anyone who ever lived, whom would you choose?" I thought about Jesus Christ, about Lincoln. But I answered, "My dad."

The older I grow, the smarter my dad seems to get. Hardly a day goes by when I don't rely on something he has taught me. "Your nose to the grindstone and hope for the best" is one of Dad's favorite sayings and it sums up his character perfectly.

Dad never went to college. He left home to serve in World War II, where he was terribly injured in a fiery plane crash. He returned to south

Buffalo to marry and raise a family. Like many in our neighborhood, he worked two jobs. Days, he toiled for the sanitation department. He'd come home for dinner, take a nap and then drive a newspaper delivery truck. Weekends, he'd spend a few hours with his buddies at the American Legion hall.

Dad admired accomplished people. But he was never ashamed of himself or his jobs. What shamed him was a person who didn't take his work—or his family, faith or education—seriously.

I remember my first summer home from college. Dad used his influence and got me a job working a garbage route. I needed the money. I couldn't afford to return to John Carroll University without it.

As the junior crewmember I was given the worst job: dragging the containers to the curb, then lifting them over my head and emptying the contents into the compactor. It was tough physical labor. And, frankly, on the hottest days it smelled. But I did my job without complaint. I had to. My dad had told me, "If you embarrass yourself, you embarrass our family."

At night I'd come home sore and filthy, and stare in wonder at my dad. Soon I'd be back at school, turning pages in textbooks. He labored for years, never once hinting how hard he had it. He never missed a day—at either of his jobs. One morning he drove past us while we were working our route. The driver called out to him, "Hey, Big Russ, your kid's okay." To this day, I think it's the proudest I've ever made him.

When I returned to campus, it was with a new appreciation for the qualities I admire most in people—lessons I learned first from Dad and then from the Jesuit priests who taught me at Canisius High School: faith, hard work, discipline, accountability, responsibility.

It was no secret in our household that I planned to go to law school. Dad approved. "Education is the key to everything," he said. "Who knows? Maybe you'll become a judge." But for the first time in my life, I made a decision he questioned. Instead of joining a law firm, I joined Daniel Patrick Moynihan's successful 1976 New York Senate campaign.

Politics was always a big topic at the dinner table. Like most Irish-Catholic families in south Buffalo, we revered President Kennedy. I even touched him once, when he came through town in a motorcade.

But, somehow, Bobby Kennedy meant even more to me. He seemed to be a different kind of politician. He was a person of privilege who spoke out for those who had no voice—minorities, working people, children, the elderly. His message was simple and connected not just with my generation, but with people like Dad. "America is a great country," Bobby said, "but it could be even better." Maybe the reason I admired him so much was that his idealism and sense of fairness reminded me of Dad.

Moynihan made me feel the same way. He was the smartest person I knew. At the time of the election, he was U.S. Ambassador to the UN and a professor at Harvard. And yet, like Bobby Kennedy, he had a common touch and an unfailing sense of decency. Like me he was the son of a workingman.

Being around Moynihan was great, but I felt out of place on his staff. Most of his aides were serious, high-powered Ivy League graduates whose idea of a good time was a two-hour argument over the details of a tax bill. Alone with the senator, I told him I wasn't sure if I fit in. "I think a little differently from these guys. I have a Jesuit education and a law degree, but half the time I have no idea what they're talking about."

Moynihan laughed. He put his arm around me and said, "Let me tell you something: What they know, you can learn. But what you know, they will never learn. Remember, none of these guys has ever worked on a garbage truck."

He was telling me exactly what Dad always had: Be who you are. In fact, it was no surprise to me that after they met, Moynihan and Dad hit it off like old pals. "Now I understand why you took this job," Dad said.

I thought of them both that Saturday back in 1990 when I was nervous about appearing on *Meet the Press* for the first time. One of my guests was then-Senate Majority Leader Bob Dole, a tough, seasoned political pro from Kansas. I phoned Dad.

"Be yourself," Dad urged. "Pretend you're talking to me. Don't get too fancy. Ask questions that my buddies at the American Legion post would want to know about."

I went home and read everything I could on Senator Dole's political positions. No way was I going to go on air knowing anything less about the issues than he did. Then I tried to look at each matter from the perspective of Dad and his pals.

That fall people in Washington were concerned about the budget deficit and its effect on taxes. My first question to Senator Dole was: "If you were back in Russell, Kansas, this morning in the coffee shop and someone said, 'Senator, you're going to tax my food, you're going to tax filling up my gas tank, you're going to tax buying an automobile—and now I read you're giving a tax cut to those who make over fifty thousand dollars. And I ask you one question: Why shouldn't those who make under fifty thousand dollars have a tax cut?'" I could almost see the guys back at the American Legion leaning in close to the set. Senator Dole looked at me. "I think you ask an excellent question, Tim."

Thanks, Dad, I said to myself, for teaching me to be my father's son.

FAMILY FIRST

*This was the answer to the mystery
that had driven Deborah and me
to want a child so much. Love without limits,
just like God's love for all His children.*

AL ROKER

BOB SCHIEFFER

Career Move

In the fall of 1978 I was riding high, living in Washington, DC, covering the White House during the week and anchoring the Saturday edition of *CBS Evening News.* I was coming into my own as a reporter at the news organization where I had wanted to work all my adult life, and I couldn't imagine changing jobs with anyone. Until my boss, Bill Leonard, called me one day from his office in New York City, that is.

CBS was starting a new morning news show and Bill said he wanted me to anchor it. At first I said no. I liked what I was doing just fine. Besides, it meant moving to New York.

"You know that Walter Cronkite will be retiring in a year or so," he said. "And Dan Rather and Roger Mudd are the leading candidates to replace him. But it's not a done deal.

"You're an outside possibility. *The Morning News* is a good place to show us what you can do. Who knows, you might wind up with Walter's job someday."

I knew that was a long shot at best, but you just don't turn down a chance to get the best job in journalism. I'm a quick decision maker. If something feels right, I just do it and don't look back. So I said yes, negotiated myself a raise and verbally shook on it. I couldn't wait to get home and tell my wife Pat the good news. I figured she would be as happy as I was.

I couldn't have been more wrong. She was crestfallen.

"What about us?" she said. "Did you give any thought to me or the girls?"

I was as taken aback by her reaction as she had been by my news. She and a friend had just started a business, a toy store, and it had become a huge success. Our daughters, Susan, ten, and Sharon, eight, were good students whose world revolved around their friends and their school.

Pat was right. I hadn't thought of them. I had agreed to move our family to New York without even asking them, believing they would be as happy about my promotion as I was. It hadn't even occurred to me that I had turned their world upside down. But a deal was a deal.

The next week Pat got over her shock and agreed it was probably something we needed to do, but her initial disappointment was nothing compared to the girls' reactions. I told them at dinner on Thanksgiving Day.

"I don't know why you're telling us now," Susan screamed. "This is nothing to be thankful about."

She left the table, flung open the front door and ran into the yard. Crying, she began rolling around in the wet grass. Back at the table, her sister sobbed.

I had never felt worse. Nevertheless, I began the assignment the following January, living in a residence hotel on the Upper East Side of Manhattan. Pat and the girls remained in Washington until school was out. In order to be with them as much as possible, I would spend Sundays in Washington, then fly to New York on the last plane out that night. On Monday I would wake up at 3:30 AM in order to be in the office by 4:00 AM to begin writing the broadcast, which aired at 7:00 AM. Midweek I'd fly back to Washington to have dinner with the family, then catch the last flight back to New York. I would return to Washington on Friday and stay overnight, then fly back to New York on Saturday to anchor the *Evening News*, return to Washington Saturday night and repeat the same schedule in the next week.

It was more than exhausting. I needed so much coffee to stay awake before the show that I couldn't sleep afterward. I became irritable and had a hard time focusing on the most simple tasks and decisions. I was suffering from sleep deprivation, but at the time I didn't know what was happening to me. Alcohol had never been a problem in my life, yet more and more I found myself relying on a drink to sleep.

To make it worse, the show wasn't working. It was patterned after our popular Sunday morning broadcast, which had long features about nature and art, but what worked on a lazy Sunday didn't work during the week when people were busy. Nor did I know much about being a host. I was a hard news guy, used to chasing scoops. Anchoring a feature show didn't fit me or my personality, and it showed.

When Pat and the girls finally moved to New York that summer they settled in quickly. Pat loved the city, and as children do, Susan and Sharon adjusted and soon had plenty of new friends. I was the one who was unhappy. I was going to work so early in the morning I seldom saw my family, even though we were living in the same apartment. It was as if I were on Moscow time and they were on New York time.

A weariness unlike anything I had ever experienced came over me. Some of it came from the irregular sleep patterns, but I now understand that much of what I felt was a gnawing fear that for the first time in my life I was about to fail. I had always made a success of whatever I'd done. I believed that with faith and hard work I could accomplish anything. I didn't like this job, but I was determined not to fail so I stuck with it.

Then one day as I was walking home, I passed a restaurant just as a man stumbled out the door. He appeared to be drunk. He lurched into the street and was almost run down by a cab.

I recognized him as one of the most talented and respected men in broadcasting. Friends said he had been devastated years earlier when CBS had originally chosen Walter Cronkite to anchor the *Evening News*. He thought he deserved the job. The boozy lunches became longer and more frequent, and over the years he had become a bitter, frustrated man.

As I watched him stagger away, I said to myself, "Whatever happens, whoever gets Walter's job, I will never let that happen to me."

I walked home. I had been there no more than a half hour when the phone rang. It was my friend, Lane Venardos, a CBS producer.

"Have you heard the news?" he asked. "They just announced that Dan Rather has been picked to succeed Walter Cronkite."

That was it. The contest was over. I had been given my shot and I lost. Dan would replace Walter, and I was happy for him. That night I decided what I needed to do was get back to Washington and do what I did best: be a reporter.

This time I talked it over with Pat and then we talked about it with the girls. We had been in New York just twenty-one months. By then the girls had come to love the city, but it didn't take us long to persuade them to return to Washington and their lifelong friends.

I left New York believing I had failed for the first time in my life. As the years passed I understood that those long hours on the *Morning News* had given me the opportunity to hone my broadcasting skills. I learned to ad-lib and conduct live interviews, skills that would later serve me well as moderator of *Face the Nation*.

Far more valuable was what I learned about being a father and a husband. I took the job in New York because it was a big promotion for me—a chance to get the job I had always wanted. But I learned in the most painful way that a big promotion for Dad isn't always a big promotion for the family. Sometimes it can be the opposite.

We became a much closer family after those days in New York. We started to talk, and we're still talking. My daughters have grown into fine young women, and now there are grandchildren.

And what about that dream job that once seemed so important?

Maybe there is a job someplace that brings the kind of happiness Pat and I have come to know with our children and grandchildren. If there is such a job, I hope someone takes it.

I don't want it. I found something a lot better.

DICK ENBERG

A Father's Love

I always loved and admired my father. He was a good provider, working hard for us during the week in a Detroit factory and the rest of the time on our forty-acre fruit farm. But good and solid as he was, for me he had one shortcoming: He was not a demonstrative man.

I can remember how frustrating that was when I was a kid. In our small Michigan town, I was a starting player on the high school varsity football, basketball and baseball teams, but rarely did he congratulate me on a victory or a good game. Even when I scored twenty-two points in one basketball game, all Dad said was, "How many points did the man you covered score?"

Years later, when I was living alone in California, leading the harried life of a TV sportscaster, Dad, who had been living alone on the farm back in Michigan, came to live with me. He planted fruit trees in my backyard and cared for them like the cherry, apple and plum trees back home. He could fix anything, and I'd tell him what a master carpenter he was. But still there was little praise from him about me and my work.

Then came his long, fatal struggle with cancer. Throughout those difficult months, I longed for an open hug from him whenever I told him I loved him, or at least a quiet, unsolicited "I love you, son." But even on his deathbed Dad was as taciturn as always.

Later, however, I began to think about Dad and me. Maybe he had been quick to criticize and slow to compliment me, but he'd been there—for every game. And then one day, cleaning out his bedroom, I came across a half-dozen shoeboxes. Inside were hundreds of audiotapes, carefully labeled, filed and stored. They were marked with things like "Louisville vs. UCLA Basketball, 1978," "Rams vs. Cowboys, 1973." These were tapes of the games I had broadcast, tapes Dad had secretly made by placing the microphone of his small recorder next to the radio or television speaker.

We know how important it is to hear our loved ones tell us that we are loved. But shouldn't we also be aware of the unspoken words of love? Those tapes told me how much my father cared. And I thought of our Heavenly Father, Whom we never see or touch, but the evidence of Whose caring is everywhere. All those years with Dad, I just needed to look for the signs of love.

JOHN WALSH

The Story behind the Picture

C an one fall so deep into despair that all hope is lost? Can a tragedy be so agonizing that there can be no recovery?

It depends.

I was in such despair. I suffered such tragedy. And I found that, yes, there is a way out. It is not easy or simple. But there is a way.

One July afternoon in 1981, my wife Reve went shopping at the Hollywood Mall with our six-year-old son Adam. While she looked for a lamp advertised on sale, he asked to watch the adjoining TV display. Eight minutes later when she returned, Adam had disappeared.

Reve called me at work. I rushed to the center, where the police had already launched a search for "a small boy in a red baseball cap."

"Don't worry," everyone reassured us, "he'll turn up."

But Adam didn't turn up. And those first torturous hours stretched into days and nights of searching, waiting, jumping at the phone's first ring.

Adam was our only child; we had waited six years for this precious boy with the freckled snub nose, shy crinkly smile and trusting hazel eyes. He had been taught to respect adults and would never leave us without our permission.

How could a child disappear within a few minutes? We felt certain that he had been stolen.

The days and nights merged into a blur as we haunted the police station and put up posters with Adam's picture everywhere. We suffered knowing that he was out there somewhere, held by someone with a sick mind.

My firm, in which I was a consultant in hotel management and design, offered a five thousand dollar reward. Newspapers, radio and TV stations broadcast our personal pleas for Adam's return. Every night we left all our window lights on. Every night I stumbled through swamps and woods with search parties, crying out in the dark: "Adam, it's Dad. We love you!"

Our local police were working hard in the search, but other law agencies said it was "outside our territory" or "we can't get to it until next week." In desperation I turned to Senator Paula Hawkins who put me in touch with the FBI.

The agent I talked to on the phone said there had to be a ransom note and some clear evidence that Adam had been carried over state lines for the FBI to become involved.

"But that's crazy," I pleaded, "he could be thousands of miles away by now. Can't you even get an alert out?"

"We cannot get officially involved," he said matter-of-factly. "We hope you understand."

"No," I shouted, "I don't understand!" I hung up the receiver and slumped against the wall in frustration.

At home I banged my fist on the table. "The FBI will go after a stolen car," I shouted, "but not a stolen child!"

Reve tried to soothe me with the reminder that we were to appear on *Good Morning America*: Our many appeals had drawn their interest. "Maybe we'll get some leads," she said.

The evening before the show, after we checked into our New York hotel, two women approached us in the lobby. "Mr. Walsh," one said, "we have missing children too." They said that over one million children disappear a year; one hundred thousand of them never show up again, presumably murdered, lost forever.

"Please speak for all of us," they begged me.

But what could I do? I knew nothing about being a spokesman: All I wanted was my son back.

That night, in our hotel room, I was awakened by the phone. The Hollywood police were asking if we had our son's dental records.

"Yes, we do. Why?" I asked, heart pounding.

"A small boy's remains have been found in a canal 150 miles north of Hollywood," continued the voice. They would let us know the next day.

We did not sleep that night; but we did appear on *Good Morning America*, where we told our story. Back in the hotel we waited by the phone. Finally the call came; the dental records matched.

Raging in pain, I flung a lamp across the room, screaming: "This damn world! What animal could have done this?" Finally, Reve and I collapsed into each other's arms sobbing.

We stumbled through the following days like robots. At the funeral, Adam's schoolmates sang and presented us with a banner they had made: "If his song is to continue, we must do the singing."

But Reve and I were inconsolable; we could only turn inward, fleeing to a friend's out-of-the-way cabin where we couldn't eat, couldn't even talk to each other. *Where is God in all this?* I wondered. I felt He had abandoned us.

Numb, Reve and I returned home. We were shocked at what we found. My mother and brother, who had stayed at our house, had phoned to say that many viewers of *Good Morning America* had written. But we had no idea how many until we stepped into the garage. It was filled with canvas mailbags, more than twenty thousand letters!

People had reached out to us from all over the nation.

"I could not hold back from comforting you," one stranger wrote.

"I was shocked and sorrowed to hear of your tragedy," wrote another.

Through most of the night Reve and I read those letters; it was some of the best therapy we had.

Many letters came from parents of missing children. They were people who had given up their lives—and often all their money—in searching, and still they had no idea if their children were alive or not.

I thought back to the two women who had pleaded with us at the hotel in New York. So did Reve, for almost as if she were speaking to herself, Reve said: "Maybe . . . maybe we could do something to help."

"Speak for us, Mr. Walsh," the two women had said. I thought of the many invitations I had received to speak before groups and on television since the *Good Morning America* show. Maybe we could do something.

Reve and I decided that we would open a center through which we could try to help parents protect their youngsters. It would be called the Adam Walsh Child Resource Center.

One afternoon while lugging some of the mailbags to the new office we'd rented, a young man introduced himself.

"I'm Jay Howell, an aide of Senator Hawkins, and I'm here seeking your help."

He explained there were two bills, one before the U.S. Senate, sponsored by Senator Hawkins and Senator Arlen Specter, another in a House subcommittee sponsored by Congressman Paul Simon of Illinois. Both called for a computer tracking system to help locate missing children.

"But the legislation is in trouble," he said. "Some government agencies are against it: they want to keep this kind of thing a local police matter."

I winced, remembering how I tried to get the FBI's help. "But what do you want me to do?" I grunted, heaving another bag into the office.

"Give your testimony in Washington, DC, before the Senate sub-committee now considering the bill," he said.

"How do I do that?" I argued. "I'm no politician."

"Just tell your story," he said.

I hesitated. "My wife and I are trying to get back to normal," I said. "I . . . we'll let you know."

I said that to get him on his way. I could work in the center and do some talking, but I had no intention of getting involved in any governmental lobbying.

Besides, I was in no condition to become involved in anything. I was throwing up constantly and had lost twenty-five pounds. Our family priest assured us that Adam was with Jesus, but that didn't help. At night I'd awaken, thinking I heard him calling for me. In the past, whenever he fell and hurt himself, I was always there to make it better. I was his hero. Now, I couldn't help him.

People would try to console me by saying it was God's plan. "What do you mean?" I'd respond angrily, "[That] God plans for a six-year-old child to die like that?"

How could God, an all-powerful Being, permit the murder of children? The clergymen I talked to couldn't answer this question satisfactorily for me.

Then one afternoon I was talking with the county's medical examiner, Ronald Wright, who did autopsies on crime victims.

"How do you handle all of this, Ron?" I asked. "You have to deal with the bodies of people who've been tortured, split open, murdered. How do you keep your sanity and believe that God is in control of this world?"

"John," he said, "I have a deep belief in God but I'm not going to give you a sermon. But, just as I believe in God, so do I believe in the existence of good and evil on this earth. We are told this in the Bible."

He shook his head. "The acts of evil are incredible; they're all around us, overpowering."

He tapped a pencil on his desk in emphasis as he explained his motivation to me. "But I do this job because I believe that I can hold back some of the evil. Through this work I can help convict killers and put them away where they can't harm others. We have to fight evil."

He looked straight into my eyes. "And I am telling you, John, that you have the ability to fight wickedness. I know you. I have seen you on the talk shows and know what you can do.

"The choice is up to you," he emphasized. "You can fall by the wayside like many parents of lost children and become hopeless and helpless. Or you can fight, helping all of us hold back the evil."

I sat looking at this caring man. He wasn't a priest or minister but I believed he spoke of God.

Weeks later in Washington, DC, I testified before the Senate sub-committee on behalf of missing children. "Thousands are out there now pleading for Daddy or Mommy to save them," I said. "We don't ask for a national police force but simply for a centralized system so the FBI can help when local police can't follow up a lead. Is this too much to ask from a great society?"

From then on I traveled day and night, from TV show to TV show, sandwiching in visits to Washington, DC.

My work at home suffered. But in Washington the children's bill was in trouble. It lay dormant in the House subcommittee for months. I went there, haunting the offices of House members, sometimes waiting as long as two hours to speak to one.

"I'm not here for an offshore oil drilling law," I'd tell a Congressman who would listen. "I'm talking about your children. And it's time you started to pay attention to the fact that nothing is being done for those who are missing."

I learned that most legislators didn't understand the problem and some had even been given the wrong facts. A year and a half passed with still nothing done.

We learned that there was a rift in the House of Representatives' subcommittee concerning the bill's wording.

A local newswoman called me one night to report that Reve and I had evidently been making waves in Washington, for an anonymous government official, in referring to us, said: "That couple down in Florida can go pound salt."

"Do you want to comment on that?" asked the reporter.

"No," I said wearily, "let that statement speak for itself."

That night I sadly went into Adam's room and lay down on his bed. At least I could tell him about his new baby sister, Meghan, who had just been born. He had wanted a little sister.

"She's beautiful, Adam," I whispered into the night, "she has a smile just like yours. I wish you could see her." Adam seemed very close to me. "I wish I knew two years ago what can happen to children, Adam. I would have taught you differently and would have done something about it." That awful feeling of guilt swept over me again. "Am I still your hero, Adam?" And then . . . it seemed to me that he was nodding yes, and smiling about his new baby sister.

I rose from the bed. "I will pound salt," I almost shouted.

Back in Washington, I worked with a new surge of strength. Jay Howell urged me on. I talked to every lawmaker I could get to. I pursued one Congressman who was against the bill down the halls, buttonholing him in the elevator.

"The children have no lobby, no vote," I pleaded. "All they need is some kind of clearinghouse so their parents can go to their FBI field office for help."

The legislator said he would think about what I said.

A week later the news came: the bill passed. The Missing Children Act would become a law of the United States.

A few months later, a four-year-old boy, David Rattray, was kidnapped in Vero Beach, Florida. Thanks to the Missing Children Act, fifty FBI men were on the case within a short time and in two days they had narrowed the search down to a man they cornered in a golf-course parking lot. In the scuffle, the man shot himself in the head. When they opened his car trunk, there was little David, alive.

Not long after that we received a letter from David's mother.

> Dear Mr. and Mrs. Walsh,
>
> I know this letter is long overdue, but it is so hard to know what to say. My son David was kidnapped but today he is home and safe. . . . It was because of your courage and efforts that the FBI was able to be in on the case within hours of the kidnapping.
>
> Thank you for helping save our son. I hope and pray that you shall be filled with much happiness and peace.
>
> Pamela Rattray

Today Reve and I continue our work through the Adam Walsh Center not only to alert parents in helping protect their youngsters but also to lobby for new legislation to help make our country a safer place for them.

Yes, there is evil in this world. But we can overcome it. God wants us to fight it in every way we can. And whenever I get tired and depressed, which happens often in this work, I only have to reread Pamela Rattray's letter about her son.

I think God would like what we're trying to do. I'm sure Adam does.

DEBORAH NORVILLE

In Good Times and Bad

What anchors an "anchor"?

Television is a high-pressure business. And when you're an anchor on a national program like the *Today* show, the pressure can be intense. When you're working at breakneck speed, researching stories and interviewing people, when you're in the public eye and fair game for whatever the press decides to print about you, it's easy to lose your own center of gravity.

What keeps me grounded? What anchors this anchor? I found out last fall when I joined the *Today* show.

In some ways, I'd been preparing for the workload of the *Today* program ever since I decided to pursue a career in television news. As a student at the University of Georgia in Athens, I'd drive back and forth from campus, where I was majoring in broadcast news, to Atlanta, where I was working weekends as a reporter at WAGA-TV. During the sessions of the Georgia General Assembly, I'd work ten-and twelve-hour days during the week, covering the legislature for public television, and the same long hours on the weekend for WAGA. But it paid off with an offer of a full-time reporter's job in Atlanta.

In 1981 I moved to WMAQ-TV in Chicago, where I reported on just about everything, including some reports I was especially proud of about battered wives, abused children and child pornography. Five years later, I was asked to join NBC as the anchor on *NBC News at Sunrise*.

Anchoring *Sunrise* was a wonderful opportunity (with the less than wonderful wake-up time of 2:30 AM!) to provide the nation with its first news of the day. As time went by, I'd sometimes be asked to fill in for members of the *Today* program when they were on assignment or vacation. Often that meant signing off *Sunrise* at 6:58 AM and sprinting down the hall to Studio 3B for two more hours of morning television.

When I was asked by my bosses to become a regular on *Today*, it seemed like a natural step after thirteen years in television news. But then the rumors started. The press portrayed me as a conniving woman out to get Jane Pauley's job—never realizing that the chance to work with Jane was one of the big attractions for me.

I was shocked, then hurt, then devastated. Reporters telephoned my friends and former colleagues asking for the dirt about me. One magazine even used my name as a derogatory verb, saying someone had been "Norvilled" out of a job. It was my family's name, a family I was proud of. I broke down and cried. My biggest break had become my biggest heartbreak. Suddenly the best of times were the worst of times.

I'd never dealt with negative press before. I read the stories and thought, *What an ugly person,* and then I realized, *That's me they're talking about.* It was during those dark moments that I saw what was truly important in my life. And I recognized that television news ranked pretty far down the list.

For one thing, I realized what a blessing my husband was. I'd always known that it was a pretty remarkable thing that Karl Wellner and I had even met—and Karl's strength during my rough times was just another sign to me that the Lord had a hand in our meeting. Aided by just a bit of Swedish tradition!

Five years ago, I visited Sweden, where my mother's family had once lived. There I learned of a Swedish tradition that young girls observe on Midsummer's Eve. Legend has it that if an unmarried girl picks seven kinds of wildflowers and sleeps with them under her pillow, she'll dream that night of the man she'll marry.

Well, I picked plenty of wildflowers. None of them made it under my pillow, but the next day some people at a Midsummer party mentioned a friend of theirs, a Swedish businessman living in New York City. Six weeks later, he happened to be in Chicago and looked me up. Karl Wellner and I were married two and a half years later.

I think I couldn't have made it through those tough months on *Today* without Karl. Our motto is *We're in this together, through thick and thin.* As busy as he is with his own career, he always finds time for me—and vice versa. Every day, each of us knows what the other's schedule is. When I know he's got an important meeting, I pray for him, as he does for me.

Another anchor for me has been my family and my Georgia roots. I come from Dalton, Georgia, a town of about twenty thousand in the foothills of the Blue Ridge Mountains. My family has always been hardworking. Dad still runs a carpet-supply company. My mother had been a manufacturing executive before she married Daddy and became part of his company. All my sisters are married and pursue their own careers.

We Norvilles are pretty close-knit. My dad and three sisters and Grandma still live in Dalton. I'm the only one who lives up North. Every time I go back home and we get together, my father says, "You're all growing up and going your separate ways. This is probably the last time we'll all be together." But six months later, there we'll be together again—with Daddy saying the same thing.

It is probably no surprise to you that my family is a source of my strength. But you might be surprised by another anchor I have— a sewing machine.

It's a little portable Kenmore that Santa Claus put under the tree for me fourteen years ago, and it's been a big part of my life ever since. Momma's mother taught her to sew, and her mother taught my grandmother.

I'm not sure Momma taught us so much to keep the tradition alive as to keep us out of her hair. On Saturdays when she'd be working at the office, she'd sit us in front of her portable machine with plenty of fabric scraps to make Barbie doll clothes. I'm sure she never guessed that a sewing machine would open so many doors for me.

When I was a senior in high school, I entered the Junior Miss competition on a lark. But I was at a loss for the talent requirement. I knew I wasn't much of a singer, and although I played the flute in the band, I'd never do a solo. So I sewed! And modeled the clothes I'd made. And horror of horrors! I won the local competition and then the state competition, which brought me to the national finals in Mobile, Alabama.

For nationals, I jazzed up my "talent" as much as I could, enlisting a magician to help with some tricks. This time, in a poof of smoke I would go from wearing a skirt and blouse to an evening gown. It got me through the competition, but not into the winner's circle—which was just as well. Because as I watched the TV crew covering the pageant, I saw something much more intriguing than the competition. I discovered I wanted to work in television.

And as I've traveled the country with my television career, the little Kenmore has traveled with me. When Karl and I were married, I sewed all six bridesmaids' gowns. When we moved into our new apartment (in the midst of the *Today* furor), I kept my mind off the press by keeping my hands busy sewing bedspreads, pillows, dust ruffles and kitchen curtains. It's amazing how much relaxation and solace that little sewing machine has given me.

But my greatest comfort has been the anchor of my faith in God.

My mother died when I was a senior in college, after a long battle with rheumatoid arthritis. Neither she nor Daddy were pushy parents, but they always made sure we knew we were capable of doing just about anything—if we worked hard at it. Perhaps that's why one of the verses she highlighted in her Bible always seems to stick with me: "I can do all things through Christ who strengthens me" (Philippians 4:13).

As a family, we're not boisterous about our faith, but we do go to church and all of us have a personal relationship with God. Sometimes I think my mother's mother has a direct line to Him. We still laugh about the time a couple of offbeat missionaries knocked on Grandma's door wanting to know where she stood with the Lord. Grandma invited them in, gave them a cup of coffee and before they left, quoted enough Scripture to convert them.

Church in Dalton was just a natural part of growing up. Not to attend Sunday school would have seemed odd. I remember going to church and then rushing to have lunch at the country club. It was always a game to see which services had let out first: By the way people were lined up at the buffet you could tell whose minister had been longest-winded that day.

Perhaps because my faith has always been so much a part of my life, as natural as brushing my teeth in the morning and reading the day's newspaper, I never realized what a solace it would be during those rocky first months on *Today*. Almost daily, that verse would repeat itself in my head: "I can do all things through Christ who strengthens me."

Not too long ago, I was trying to explain this to Karl. I repeated to him that little fable "Footprints," in which a man looks back at two sets of footprints moving forward side by side in the sand. One set belongs to the man, the other to the Lord walking beside him. Suddenly, one set of footprints stops.

"When things got rough," the man says to the Lord, "why did you desert me?" And the Lord replies, "I didn't desert you. During those hard times, I carried you."

The Lord did carry me, and He still does. He helps me to keep my focus on those things that are important.

What's important? It's not the praise one might see in the newspapers—nor the criticism.

It's my husband, my family, my faith and the knowledge that I am trying to live my life the way the Lord guides me, that I'm fair and honest, and that perhaps somewhere along life's way, I can help others.

What anchors an anchor? For this anchor, it's the belief that God is always with us . . . carrying us through the difficult times, as well as the good.

CHRIS SCHENKEL

The Man Who Cared

I could see the racers hurtling behind us toward the starting line. I was broadcasting the 1971 Indianapolis 500 race from the pace car. Riding in the convertible with me were astronaut John Glenn, Tony Hulman, who owns the Indianapolis Speedway, and Eldon Palmer, an automobile dealer. Eldon was driving.

The reference point at which Eldon was to get off the track and let the racers speed by us was a flag. But—where was it? The flag was hidden in the crush of people and pit crews who wanted to be at the starting point.

Eldon pulled off, braking hard from our track speed of 130 miles an hour. But it was too late. We were headed right for the stands full of photographers. Eldon had the presence of mind to swing sideways. He crashed into the stands at a speed of sixty miles an hour. We were only bruised and sprained, and although some people in the stands were hurt, there were no fatalities in what looked like a certain-death situation.

When I got home, my wife Fran and our children greeted me with tears of gratitude. Tina, then fifteen, asked, "Dad, what did you think of at that awful moment?" Ted, twelve, wanted to know, "Did you think of us?" And Johnny, seven, demanded, "Did you pray, Dad?"

I had to tell them truthfully, "All I could think of was that stand full of people."

Tina broke the silence. "Well, that's prayer too."

Later I got to thinking about that. I got to thinking that that was a definition of prayer my father would have agreed with.

To Dad, all of life was a prayer. That doesn't mean he didn't pray in church because he did. The population of Bippus, Indiana, when I was growing up, was three hundred. It's still three hundred and the same three churches are still standing. Ours, the Evangelical and Reformed Church, was the most important place in our lives, outside of home. Dad taught Sunday school there until he was seventy-four. We had prayers at home too, morning and evening, along with Bible-reading and hymn-singing.

But when formal worship stopped, Dad's prayer life was just beginning. Work was a kind of prayer with him. For many years he and my mother worked a farm in Bippus, where they raised their six children. In addition, Dad ran a feed-and-grain business. He loved to work and expected his sons to love it too. We children were up at 6:00 AM to feed the animals and milk the cows before school—and home right after school for afternoon chores too.

Dad never could understand when I'd go fishing down at Pony Creek—couldn't understand how anyone could sit still that long. Those were Depression days with a big "D." The cream from the cows we milked was sold to buy groceries. Once a week mother took all of us into town to buy them. I'll never forget the ritual of the Milky Way. There was money enough to buy just one of those candy bars. It was carefully cut into six pieces.

But while work and frugality were part of Dad's prayer life, it was people—all people—who were at the heart of it.

Our church had an orphanage in Fort Wayne, and mother persuaded farm families to take in youngsters during the summer months. We always had one or two of the Fort Wayne kids living with us in July and August. In the summertime, Mama cut the Milky Way seven or eight ways.

When things were particularly bad for the customers of his feed-and-grain store, Dad continued to carry them on his books and never asked for money. Yet I don't remember anyone who ever failed to pay his bill even if it took a long time.

It was the same way with relatives and friends in need whom he helped. He hated gossip; he would walk away from groups where people were being run down.

Dad later became an officer in the local bank, and when the younger bankers were about to refuse a loan to a farmer who really needed it, Dad would say, "You're here to help people, aren't you?" The farmer got the loan. Somehow it never turned out to be a bad loan.

Father hired people during the Depression. The shabbier, the more down on their luck they were, the quicker he seemed to hire them. If we noticed their shabby appearance and talked about it, he'd say, "Better have a look at their pain too. Maybe you won't be so ready to criticize."

One of them was Dave King, who did odd jobs about town. Dave looked like he always slept on a park bench. He was considered lazy and the kids called him the town character. One day Dave came by and asked Dad for a job. My brother Phil and I, who were there at the time, laughed. Dad's stern look squelched us. He gave Dave a job driving a truck. He worked for Dad for twenty years.

Not long after Dave was hired, I was working a team of big draft horses on the farm. I don't know what started it but, as I drove them off the land onto the road, the horses reared up and took off like they were on a racetrack. I was scared out of my wits, trying desperately to hold on to the little seat and keep myself from being thrown off head-long under the horses' hooves or the wheels of the wagon.

Dave saw what was happening and came roaring up behind me in his truck. Then he sped right by me.

"You idiot!" I screamed. "Where are you going?"

But a few minutes—an eternity—later, I saw him ahead, standing right out in the middle of the road, in front of the onrushing horses. Dave had driven far enough ahead to a place where he figured the horses would begin to tire. He stood right out there in front of them yelling, "Whoa! Whoa!" When they eased down, he leaped at the reins and held on until he slowed them to a walk, then to a stop.

Later that night Dad said quietly to me, "Still think my hiring Dave was a big joke?"

Many of those lessons in living and getting along with people I've tried to apply to my own life as I went through school and then into broadcasting. I began in radio at age fifteen with some high school basketball games when I persuaded the local telephone man to connect a line from the high school gym to a public address speaker in front of the drugstore in Bippus. My first paying job came between my freshman and sophomore years at Purdue University with a station in Muncie, Indiana.

After my graduation from Purdue, I spent four years as an infantry officer, then began training to broadcast horse races at Narragansett Park in Rhode Island by cleaning the stalls, walking the hots (cooling off the horses after their workouts) and making color charts so I'd know every stable and its jockeys. My father did not question me as to why a man with a college degree was doing all that dirty work. He thought it was great and said I was to give thanks to God for having the chance to learn my profession so thoroughly.

From Narragansett I went to New York to cover the football games for the New York Giants and I also learned to announce boxing and bowling events. Later came opportunities in college football, professional basketball, the Olympics and major golf tournaments.

But throughout the many experiences I've had in sportscasting, I've never forgotten my father's spirit of caring for other people. Caring about the players, the coaches, the officials helps me resist the temptation to put down an athlete who makes a poor play, for example. It helps avoid hurting someone who needs encouragement much more than negative criticism.

And come to think of it, maybe that attitude of caring, which I feel today, was one more thing my father was praying for.

SOLEDAD O'BRIEN

The Church across the Street

My parents named me Maria de la Soledad: Spanish for the Blessed Virgin Mary of Solitude. It's really no surprise, considering that faith has always been an essential part of my family's life. You might even say that's what brought my parents together. My parents were both immigrants—my mother from Cuba, my father from Australia—studying at Johns Hopkins University. And they both attended daily Mass at the church near campus. Every day my father would offer my mother a ride. Every day, she declined. Finally she said yes. One year later, the day after Christmas, the two of them were married.

My parents took care to instill their beliefs in my five siblings and me. Every Sunday morning at 7:30 AM all eight of us would pack into a pew at church. Our reward was Dad's breakfast special: eggs, bacon, sausage, fresh orange juice and—my favorite—chocolate-covered, cream-filled doughnuts from the local bakery. We would eat and talk, then spend the rest of the morning together reading the Sunday newspaper. When I think about those Sundays with my family, I remember how safe, happy and loved I felt. How good the world seemed.

My Sunday ritual changed dramatically when I began a career in television news. I worked most weekends. Occasionally I would get to church on Saturday evenings, but it was never quite the same. I missed the music and ceremony of Sunday morning Mass.

By the time I was coanchoring the *Weekend Today* show at NBC, my husband Brad and I had two young daughters, Sofia and Cecilia. Because of my work schedule, we were able to attend Mass as a family only at the girls' baptisms. I wanted faith to be central in their lives, yet logistically it seemed impossible.

Still, I felt a pull back to my spiritual roots, a yearning that only intensified after September 11 and the war in Iraq began. Like many people, I was searching for a deeper purpose in my life. Hundreds of my journalism colleagues, including my cohost, David Bloom, were embedded with coalition troops in the Middle East. Every day I read about air strikes, ambushes, civilians and soldiers dying. *What kind of world are our girls growing up in?* I wondered. How could I give them the same sense of security I had as a child?

On Sunday, April 6, 2003, the telephone rang at 1:00 AM, waking me up even before my usual 3:30 AM alarm. I picked it up. An NBC operator asked me to hold for my boss.

At that moment I knew. Something happened to David. All week long we'd been reporting that the troops were approaching Baghdad. Rumors that Saddam Hussein might launch a chemical attack had run rampant. Everyone at the studio was worried about David and our other colleagues on the front.

My boss got on the line. "Soledad," he said, "David is dead."

"What happened?" I asked. Did the tank David was in get hit? Had his unit been ambushed?

"He had an embolism," my boss said.

David had been sitting in a tank for hours. Doctors thought that may have led to the fatal blood clot.

Five hours later, Katie Couric, Matt Lauer and I were on the air, telling the nation that David was dead. I could hardly believe what we were reporting. David was my colleague and a friend. Memories of him flooded my mind. The tireless journalist. His reports were clearly some of the best filed from the front in Iraq. David often brought his three young daughters to see him on the set. We had at least half a dozen two-dollar bets we made over the most arcane facts. It was hard to imagine someone so completely full of life suddenly being gone.

The only consolation was that David died doing something he loved. At his funeral in New York at St. Patrick's Cathedral, one of his friends read a letter David wrote to his wife just hours before his death. "Yes, I'm proud of the good job we've all been doing here, but in the scheme of things it matters little compared to my relationship with you, the girls and God." David's words struck a chord in all of us. It made a big impression to know that in the end he was thinking about his family, his faith.

A few months later, when my contract renewal at NBC was coming up, that thought came back to me. I faced a big decision. An opportunity at CNN had presented itself. I was offered the weekday position cohosting *American Morning*—a more challenging job, a longer day. I spent several weeks weighing the pros and cons. Brad and I discussed what impact the new job would have on our family, and what it would mean for my career. I loved my job at *Today*, and the people I was working with. Yet the job at CNN was a great opportunity.

After fifteen years with NBC, I joined CNN. The first few weekends after I started my new job were eye-opening. Brad and I spent those days enjoying the summer in the city with the girls. Walking around Central Park with my family I realized I wanted to find someplace where Sofia and Cecilia could play outdoors, swim in lakes. A place where we could take them on walks in the woods.

Upstate we found a beautiful little cottage with a wraparound porch. Across the street was a lovely old church. Our first Sunday there, we walked over and settled into a pew—Sofia leaning on Brad's shoulder, Cecilia nestled in my lap. It reminded me of my own childhood.

At coffee hour afterward, the pastor gave us a warm welcome and invited our girls to join the Sunday school class. I was thrilled to hear about all the activities we could get involved in—feeding the homeless, giving Christmas presents to underprivileged children, building homes for the poor in Nicaragua. We met our neighbors. It didn't take long for the girls to start running around with their new playmates.

With two toddlers in tow, Brad and I joke that if the church weren't right across the street, we'd always be late. Seriously though, Sunday morning Mass is again important in our lives, and it highlights exactly what's essential in life—my family and my faith. I still worry about the world our girls are growing up in. But I know they'll have a strong spiritual foundation to rely on—just as I had all those Sunday mornings ago.

MARTHA BYRNE

Closer to Home

K idnapped five times, married five times. I've been tortured, had my children taken from me and in my late twenties I discovered my long lost twin sister. No sooner did we meet than the two of us were trapped for days at the bottom of a well. Not long after that she was poisoned, and died on her wedding day. Not only did I mourn her death but I had to do the dying as well (I played both parts). You see, I've done all these things as an actress on the daytime television drama *As the World Turns*, a career that's given me enormous satisfaction. But much of it would never have happened if it weren't for an important conversation I had a dozen years ago when the world felt very lonely to me.

The acting started when I was ten. My best friend, Allison Smith, had read about an open call for the Broadway musical *Annie*, and was excited about it. "Let's go to the tryouts," she said enthusiastically.

"I'll ask my mom," I told her.

We lived across the bridge in New Jersey, and Mom agreed to take Allison and me into the city just on a lark. She figured we'd do the audition and we would get it out of our systems. Then we could go out for a nice lunch afterward.

The huge theater was overrun with girls our age—all of them vying to be one of the orphans living "a hard-knock life." Girls singing "Tomorrow, tomorrow . . ." and practicing dance steps in the halls. A few even wore bright red wigs. Some of the girls had professional headshots, typeset résumés and mothers who pushed and bragged.

You know what? Of those seven hundred girls, only two were picked: Allison and me. We were in the show. Suddenly my mom was driving us to the city six days a week for shows. Allison and I were funny and cute and singing our lungs out. It was . . . fun. I was a professional actress!

From *Annie* I went on to make commercials and TV shows, and eventually I landed a long-running part on the soap opera *As the World Turns*. I loved acting, but I loved my life at home even more—playing Monopoly with my brother and sisters, renting videos or just making each other laugh. Sunday morning was really special. That's when we all went together to the pretty little church down the street. At seventeen I won an Emmy. My whole family came with me to the award ceremony at Radio City Music Hall.

"Now if you really want a career," people said, "you'll have to go to Hollywood. That's where you need to be seen." That's where the prime-time television shows were cast and the big movies made. That's where the big agents worked and the big studios were. That's where the big breaks happened.

I had just recently graduated from Immaculate Heart Academy in New Jersey when I announced to my parents and siblings that I was California-bound. I said good-bye to my colleagues on *As the World Turns* and thanked them for the tremendous experience I had gotten. I said good-bye to the house and the pretty little church, and packed my bags. Hollywood, here I come!

I'd been in the business for almost ten years. I had been in front of a camera day in and day out. I knew how to memorize a page of dialogue in a snap, take direction and work with other actors. I had tons of video clips. Finding an agent wasn't hard. The work came my way, the way it had back when I lived in New Jersey.

You could see me as somebody's younger sister in a made-for-TV movie, or I was someone else's girlfriend in a feature film. I auditioned for commercials and got sent out for interviews for TV shows. I made a pilot and then another pilot.

But in between jobs I sat in my apartment and wondered why I wasn't having fun auditioning anymore. I remembered how my mom used to sit backstage at the theater during *Annie*, talking with the other moms as she waited for me to finish the show. We laughed about things on the way home, and pretended that the Lincoln Tunnel would take us all the way to Florida. I still talked to Mom and everyone else all the time. Still, you can't pop popcorn and play Monopoly over the telephone.

Allison Smith moved out to LA, too, and I'd call her to have someone familiar to talk to. "You're doing really well, Martha," she said encouragingly.

"I guess so."

But was I? I kept waiting for the one job that would make me happy. That one show, that one movie, that one big part. The next time the phone rings, I told myself, it'll be the thing I've always wanted to do. That's what I was here for. If I could just stick with it long enough. Go to auditions, go to interviews, meet people.

Not far from my apartment was a church with lovely stained-glass windows, a little like the one back in New Jersey. I went there on Sundays, just like at home, but it didn't feel like home. I'd just drive back to my apartment where the phone never seemed to ring often enough and the videos stacked up of the pilots that never went anywhere.

One day my agent called with some disappointing news. A big part I was up for went to somebody else. I couldn't sit in the apartment alone. I needed to talk to someone. Mom and Dad always said you could talk to God when you had to share your troubles. But I'd done my share of talking to God in my bedroom. Now I wanted to talk to another person. I drove down to the church. I went up the steps of the rectory and rang the bell. Soon a white-haired man answered the door. One of the priests.

"Please, I need to talk to someone."

We sat in the back of the hushed, empty sanctuary. The stained-glass windows seemed to slow the light as it filtered through the rich hues. I'd seen this priest on Sundays. We had shaken hands once or twice, but I'm sure he thought I was just another of the many actresses who come and go in Hollywood over the years. Now, though, he acted as though I were the most important person he'd ever met. His eyes almost never left mine.

I told him about the church I'd gone to at home and the school where I'd studied. I talked about my family and the way they would come to all my shows and watch all the things I did on TV. I had such a vivid memory of my sister Fran holding up a sign when I was a finalist for *Annie*. "Go, Martha!" it said, as though I were one of the top scorers on the field hockey team at school.

"You miss your family," he said.

"Not a day goes by that I don't think of them," I admitted.

"It sounds like you really want to go back to New Jersey to be with them."

Tears rolled down my cheeks. My family. Just the word made me cry. That was exactly what I wanted more than anything else. I'd known it all along, of course. Funny that I needed to hear someone else say it. "But what about my career?" I asked. "I had some big dreams . . ."

"God has a way of bringing us what we truly need when we follow our hearts' desires," the priest said.

I didn't need to hear any more. A month later I was back home, living temporarily with Mom and Dad, going to our old church, catching up with my brother and sisters. It was like my life went from black-and-white to color again.

Within a month I met the man who became my husband and the father of my children. At almost the same time I got a call from the head scriptwriter of *As the World Turns*. "Martha," he asked, "would you like to come back on the show?"

I had to explain to him that I didn't come East to look for work. I came here to be closer to home. But since he'd made the offer. . . .Well, I haven't been off the show since. Sure, there are times when the schedule is hectic. I mean, how many traumas can you have even if they are all made-up? But my off-screen life is anything but traumatic. I have all the people I love most close by. It's a beautiful reminder that as wonderful as a job is, it's still just a job. Family? That's forever. Family. There's that word again.

BOB GRIESE

A Father's Story

This story is as much about my youngest son Brian as it is about me. We're both quarterbacks. I played with the NFL's Miami Dolphins in the sixties and seventies, and Brian helped lead the University of Michigan football team to a national championship last year. My playing days are over, but I still outline offensive strategies and dissect defenses most Saturday afternoons in the fall, as ABC-TV's color commentator for college football. I take pride in giving viewers an evenhanded analysis of the game. My broadcast partner, play-by-play man Keith Jackson, provides the exclamations and the emotion, which is fine with me. I'm not a demonstrative person by nature.

That's why I was as surprised as anyone when for a few moments after the Rose Bowl this past New Year's Day (a game I called and Brian played in) I found myself unreservedly showing my deepest feelings in front of a nationwide audience, sharing a side of me that I had pretty much kept away from the public eye—Bob Griese, father.

Raising our three sons had always been the top priority for my wife Judi and me. When she died in 1988 after a long battle with cancer it seemed even more crucial that I be around for them—especially Brian, who was in junior high school.

With his older brothers, Scott and Jeff, away at college, it was often just the two of us at home in Coral Gables, Florida, sitting across from each other at breakfast and supper. We had a lot of support from friends, and our household manager, Isabel Duro, kept things on track. Still, there were tough times when I prayed, *Lord, we really need Your help today.*

I threw myself into Brian's activities, things Judi used to take care of. I drove Brian to school, and made sure he did his homework and kept his grades up.

It was his idea to go out for football, and to play quarterback. I cheered him on at his games. The few times I couldn't make it because of work commitments I sent a family friend in my place. I wanted Brian to have someone waiting for him at the end, just like the other kids.

Looking back, I have to give Brian a lot of credit. At a point in his life when most guys would rather do anything than be with their old man, he stuck by me. If he saw me settling in front of the TV after dinner, he would plop down on the couch and ask, "Hey, Dad, can you go over some film with me? Coach loaned me a tape of last week's game."

"Aren't you going out with your buddies tonight?"

"I can hang out with the guys anytime," he'd reply casually. "Besides, they can't tell me how to pick apart a pass defense."

We spent quite a few evenings together studying videotapes of his games. Only later did I realize he had been doing it for me. He had sensed I needed someone to keep me company, to help me grieve.

Around the time Brian enrolled at the University of Michigan in 1993, I met Shay, a wonderful woman who eventually became my wife. Brian and I talked on the phone every Sunday. He did well academically, but football didn't go so smoothly. Michigan hadn't offered him an athletic scholarship or assured him a place on the team. He had chosen the school for its top-notch education. A walk-on his first year, he didn't play in a single game. Then in 1995, Brian filled in for the injured Scott Dreisbach. That's when ABC execs told me they didn't want me covering my son's games. "We're concerned viewers will think you have a conflict of interest," they said. I wanted to see Brian play, but I could understand why the network gave me other assignments. Since I couldn't be there with my son, once again I made sure someone was waiting for him after each game, usually Shay or my brother Bill just like in high school. He needed the support. With Brian at quarterback, the Wolverines went just 5-4.

One night the following spring he called, sounding more upset than I had ever heard him. "I'm sorry, Dad," Brian said. "I did something really stupid." He had been drinking beer and tried to enter a bar to get a ride from a friend. When the bouncer gave him a hard time, Brian kicked in a window, and got arrested.

"You made a mistake," I said, keeping my emotions in check. I didn't need to tell him how disappointed I was. He knew it. "Now you'll have to work to make up for it."

"I will, Dad," he vowed. Hanging up the phone, I thought, *He's a good kid. He just has a little more growing up to do.* If he had the strength of character to cope with losing his mother, he could handle this.

Brian was suspended from the team he had worked so hard to make. Banned from off-season workouts, he set up his schedule to match the other guys'. If they lifted weights from 2:00 PM to 4:00 PM, he did the same at a different gym. Only school and the community-service requirement the judge had imposed took precedence.

In the fall of 1996 Brian was allowed back on the team. At the same time, ABC decided to let me cover Michigan games again. Even though network execs now believed our father-son relationship might lend a nice human interest angle to the broadcast, I didn't want viewers to think I wasn't being fair when Brian was on the field, or that I was letting my emotions interfere with my job.

The conflict-of-interest issue didn't come up because Dreisbach started at quarterback. As the season wore on, Brian got discouraged. "Look, the best thing you can do is be prepared," I said. "If a spot opens up, you'll be ready." When Dreisbach was injured during the last game of the season, Brian came in and led his team to an upset over highly ranked conference rival Ohio State.

I was thrilled for him, but on the air during the game I went out of my way to downplay our connection. I even referred to him exclusively as "Griese" although I often used the other guys' first names. Later, when I watched a tape of the broadcast, I was surprised to hear myself saying late in the game, "If they want to win, the Buckeyes have to get to the Michigan quarterback!" The QB in question, of course, was my son. I had managed to remain detached.

Brian finished his bachelor's degree in the spring of 1997, and debated whether to return to Michigan in the fall for his last season of football eligibility, wondering if it wasn't time to put the game behind him. He talked with his brothers, and I gave him all the fatherly advice I could. He elected to stay at Michigan. "Even if I don't play much," he said, "I want to help the team get to the Rose Bowl."

He not only played, he won the starting job. "Now that it's my last season, do you think you might loosen up and actually call me Brian?" he asked me the night before their first game, against Colorado. Brian was joking, but I was concerned about his taking what I said—or didn't say—on the air too personally. "You've got a job to do out there and so do I," I told him. "Once I'm in the booth with my headset on, I can't root for you."

"Dad, I think you're more nervous about this game than I am," he replied, laughing.

Brian played great against Colorado, making smart decisions every time he touched the ball. He quarterbacked the Wolverines to a perfect 11-0 record. Keith Jackson and I covered five of those wins. I loved sharing the whole game-day experience with Brian, the way I had when he was in high school. Still, I had an easier time restraining my emotions during broadcasts than letting them out. Besides, Brian knew how I felt.

New Year's Day was different. In the TV booth at the Rose Bowl, I felt more keyed up than usual. Brian was playing in the final game of his college career. The Wolverines had the number one ranking going in, which meant not only the Big Ten/Pac-10 rivalry was at stake, but also what every college player dreams of—the national championship.

The Michigan offense trotted out. I remembered what it felt like to be down on that field, trying to shut out the noise of the one hundred thousand-plus fans and focus on connecting with my receivers. I had played in the Rose Bowl in 1967, when my Purdue team hung on to a one-point victory, yet somehow this was more nerve-racking. *I wish Judi were here to see this,* I thought.

Brian threw an interception on the first possession, and the Washington State Cougars scored to take the lead. But he didn't let it shake his confidence, and I didn't let it break my concentration in the booth. He rifled a perfect fifty-three-yard touchdown pass to receiver Tai Streets to tie the game before halftime. In the second half, Brian threw two more TD passes. Then, on their last possession, he led his team on a long drive, eating up the clock. The Cougars could manage only a field goal in the time remaining.

The final score: Michigan 21, Washington State 16.

High above the field, Keith and I started wrapping up the game for our television audience as the Michigan coaches and players gathered in a sea of maize and blue for the trophy presentation. Then Keith said, "I've got a piece of paper here that says who's been selected the most valuable player of the 1998 Rose Bowl game." He gave me a glance. "Michigan quarterback Brian Griese."

All the emotions I had been holding back the whole game—probably the whole season—came out in a big rush. What Brian had been through and what he had accomplished. I was overcome. "Keith, I've done pretty well up to this point," I managed to tell my broadcast partner, "but you're about to lose me here."

I doubt he or anyone else who knows me ever expected me to get choked up in front of millions of viewers on national television, and I don't think you'll catch me doing it again anytime soon. But I've decided that there's nothing wrong with showing a little emotion when I've been blessed with the opportunity to watch my son play his best in the big game, to see him grow from being a boy to being a man. For this dad, blessings don't get any better than that.

AL ROKER

America's Weatherman

You've probably noticed—if you start your morning watching me, Matt Lauer and Katie Couric on the *Today* show—I don't take up as much of the screen as I used to. Not since I had my stomach stapled. It's a very risky operation that I don't recommend for everyone. But I was willing to take my chances, as much for my family as myself. I want to be around for them as long as I can.

My wife Deborah—who's a correspondent on *20/20*—and I had been married for about a year when we decided to have a child. We already had an adopted daughter, ten-year-old Courtney, from my previous marriage. To me, there is no difference between "natural" and "adopted." My own childhood showed me that when it comes to loving your kids, concepts like that don't apply. I was the oldest of six, and three of my siblings were adopted. Mom and Dad even took in foster children. "There are no limits to how much you can love," Dad always said.

Dad would do anything for us. He'd get up early and leave our house in Queens to go to work as a New York City bus driver. He put in back-to-back shifts and took odd jobs to provide for us. But to him it wasn't work; it was an expression of his love. And the more kids, the more love.

That's why I wanted to have a child with Deborah. But try as we might—for more than a year—she didn't conceive. "This is taking longer than it should," Deborah's ob/gyn, Dr. Janice Marks, told us. "Let's get you both tested."

The problem was me. I was more relieved than anything else. Now we knew for sure what the trouble was. Besides, as a weatherman I'm used to a certain amount of failure.

Dr. Marks recommended we pay a visit to the New York Fertility Institute for a consultation. Deborah hesitated. "Let's try it on our own just one more time," she said. "If it's meant to be, then God will make it happen."

Dr. Marks pinpointed Deborah's window of ovulation. "Knowing when should help," she told us. But it didn't. Every time I saw one of those commercials showing a happy couple with a positive on their home pregnancy test, I wanted to throw something at the TV.

Three weeks later, Deborah surprised me. "Al, I'm late," she said. I scrambled off to the drugstore for a home pregnancy test. Deborah went into the bathroom the next morning while I paced in the hall outside. Finally she opened the door, a smile on her face and test strip in hand. Two pink lines. "Positive?" I asked. She nodded. Was this really happening?

I wouldn't let myself get excited. Not yet. We tried another test. That one came back positive too. Oh man. We're pregnant! We stayed up almost all night talking. What do we do now? Whom do we tell and when? What about Courtney, who had ruled the roost for so long? We decided to wait to give her the news, just in case.

I didn't sleep much that night. I got out of bed around 3:00 AM —a little earlier than usual—gave Deborah a peck on the cheek while she slept, then left for Studio 1A at Rockefeller Center. "You're looking mighty chipper, Al," Katie said. "Really?" I answered nonchalantly. Inside, I was ready to burst. I wanted to tell Katie, Matt, everyone. But I kept quiet and gave the weather report as usual. "Nine months from now," I felt like telling the whole country, "it looks like we're due for a nice, warm baby. And a high probability of an overly sunny dad."

It was good I didn't. A sonogram at two months showed the baby wasn't growing. Its heart rate was way too slow. "I'm sorry," Dr. Marks told us. "I know this is going to hurt, but it doesn't look like the baby will reach term." Deborah miscarried on Labor Day weekend.

"I'd just started to think of myself as a mother," Deborah told me. "And now it's all changed." I squeezed her hand. I knew just what she meant. It wasn't that we weren't parents already. But ever since the day Deborah showed me that test strip, we'd both felt something new at work in our lives. The incredible mystery of God working through us to create a new life. I think we both knew right then and there that there was no turning back.

A few weeks before our second anniversary, Deborah got a checkup from Dr. Marks. She asked about the possibility of trying to get pregnant again. "I see no reason why you couldn't," Dr. Marks told her. "You've healed well, and you're in good health. But you're going to need medical and scientific help."

We went to see Drs. Majid Fateh and Khalid Sultan at the New York Fertility Institute. Dr. Sultan told us about artificial insemination and in vitro fertilization. Then he said, "I'm not going to lie to you. If you choose this road, it is a long one. And difficult. For both of you, but especially for Deborah. There will be a lot of work involved, a lot of discomfort and no guarantees. Are you willing to go through it?"

That night Deborah and I talked it over. "It's your decision," I finally said. "Like the doc told us, you're the one who has to do the real work. But . . ." Deborah took my hand and I knew I didn't have to finish my sentence. We wanted a baby. Come what may, we were going to try.

We opted for in vitro fertilization. It was a success; Deborah got pregnant again.

This time I was afraid to be too happy. The doctors told us how critical the first trimester was. I prayed every day, asking God to keep my wife and our unborn child in his hands.

Twelve weeks later we went into the sonogram room together. I had years of live TV under my belt, and thought I was well past the butterflies-in-the-stomach phase. But I'd never felt so unsettled before. The doctor turned on the monitor and the screen flickered to life. He ran the wand over Deborah's belly. "There," he said. Deborah and I squinted into the black-white-and-gray image on the screen, trying to figure out what the doctor was pointing out. "Those are the arms," the doctor said. Then he ran his finger along two thin shapes near the bottom of the screen. "Those are the legs right there." He flipped a switch and the room filled with sound. A steady, thumping beat. "Good, strong heartbeat. Congratulations!"

In that moment, all my doubts and worries, all my questions about whether or not Deborah and I had done the right thing, completely vanished. Science may have helped us on our path to pregnancy, but it couldn't get us all the way to the end. The only thing that could do that was the power and grace of God. He'd been with us on this journey every step of the way. This was His miracle; the beautiful, glorious, humbling mystery of life.

At 9:17 AM on Tuesday, November 17, 1998, I heard the most wonderful sound: the cries of our newborn daughter, Leila Ruth Roker. A nurse held her up for Deborah to see. My wife started to cry, and so did I. I held my new daughter and looked into her eyes. *Is this how Mom and Dad felt when they held me?* I wondered. I thought back to growing up with my five siblings. They were my brothers and sisters, but to my parents they were much more. Each of us was a miracle.

My little girl wriggled in my arms and all at once I felt warmth surge through me. Love. For Courtney, for Leila and for Deborah. This was the answer to the mystery that had driven Deborah and me to want a child so much. Love without limits, just like God's love for all His children.

ANGELS
ALONG THE WAY

I always wondered if I would make it in show business. Rich
never did. He was always there, through the years, even when
out of sight. He was there in the early days of radio, and he was
there when, as an infantryman, I set up my machine gun on
one of the Normandy beaches and got a piece of shrapnel
in my right leg before I could fire it.

ART CARNEY

BRIAN WILLIAMS

History in the Making

Elmira, New York. Picture a three-bedroom ranch house on West Church Street, just down the block from Our Lady of Lourdes where our family went to Mass every Sunday. Across the street was a convenience store. The house next door was so close we could tell from our kitchen table what they were watching on TV. Not that there was much choice. We only got two stations in Elmira. Today we have the twenty-four-hour news cycle, and hundreds of cable channels. Back then the 6:30 PM national news was with either Huntley and Brinkley or Walter Cronkite.

Now imagine an eight-year-old boy sitting on the living-room floor, his legs crossed, watching a black-and-white TV with the foil-tipped rabbit ears perched on top. He's not the best student in the world, but he's fascinated by the news. He'd never miss a broadcast and he takes in everything said about the war in Vietnam, the space race, the Civil Rights movement, and in his heart he knows he's seeing history in the making.

Night after night, listening to Cronkite's magisterial tone or Huntley and Brinkley's seamless teamwork, he thinks, *That's what I want to do someday*. It's an audacious thought for a boy, especially one who's never been much of anywhere in his life and whom no teacher has ever singled out for public speaking. He keeps his desire inside and nurtures it.

As you've no doubt guessed, I was that boy, and today when I think of that goal, I am astounded that I reached it. There were so many others more gifted or with more advantages. I was the fourth child in a middle-class family in a small upstate town where Dad was in business and Mom stayed home. Sure, I had a goal and a certain drive. But more than that, I had the power of a dream.

My dad is a taciturn Calvin Coolidge-type, a frugal New Englander. A captain in World War II, he'd worked with the Army to help rehabilitate returning soldiers. Back in civilian life, he was in marketing and retailing. Even if he didn't say much, he still gave us kids the feeling that we could do anything we put our minds to. I grew up knowing that the biggest risk you face in life is not risking anything at all.

One day I announced that I was going to write the president to cheer him up. Dad smiled sagely as he watched me scrawl my note at the kitchen table, ornamenting it with a picture of the American flag. I sent it off, imagining President Lyndon Baines Johnson reading my letter in the Oval Office. Soon enough I got a letter back on official presidential stationery. "See, my letter did cheer him up!" I exclaimed. "He wrote right back." Talk about feeling important.

I'm sure Dad noticed what I didn't: The response was a form letter, the signature done by a machine. LBJ himself probably had never read my letter. Still, my parents knew I wanted to believe I was important enough for the president of the United States to read my every word. Not long ago, I wrote to the Johnson Library in Texas and asked if they had my letter. To my amazement, they found it in the archives with a red check in the corner. "Why the red check?" I asked. It was included in the small sampling of letters the president read every night, I was told. My letter, one of thousands. Dad was right.

Soon as I could hold a job, I tried to follow my hardworking father's example. I was willing to do anything—and I did. I sold Christmas trees out of a van. I bused tables at the local pancake house. I worked in the hardware department at Sears. During college in Washington, DC, I interned at the White House, wearing the blue blazer I'd bought with my employee discount at Sears. But money was tight and after the internship ended, I dropped out of school. I was eager to start my career. I still had that burning vision that I never told anyone about. I wouldn't let it go. Working on student newspapers gave me enough experience to know that journalism was indeed what I wanted.

Truth to tell, my launch into broadcasting wasn't auspicious— a job as a clerk-typist with the National Association of Broadcasters, a trade group. I learned to be a pretty good personal assistant, yet I yearned to be reporting the news. When I came back home and watched the local news in the kitchen with Mom and Dad (they'd finally gotten rid of the old black-and-white TV with the rabbit ears), I'd think, *"Yes, I can do that."* Mom and Dad agreed.

One evening in DC, I went to dinner with a man who ran a station in Pittsburg, Kansas. We talked about a million things before I got up the courage to tell him: "I'd like to try my hand at being a broadcaster."

"Come to Pittsburg," he said. "You'll have to pay your own way."

What he offered me was a very basic salary—barely enough to live on even in Kansas—and the chance to work as a reporter. I rented a bright yellow Ryder truck, brought my cocker spaniel Charlie along with me for company and headed for the heartland. A lot of people thought I was crazy. What was I thinking . . . trading a decent job with the chance of advancement for a pipe dream in Kansas? If I really wanted to be a reporter, who would ever see me there? But I knew it was what I had to do. This was the experience I needed. I ate little and slept less. Seven days a week I was writing, reporting, broadcasting. If I made mistakes—and I made plenty—I learned from them and moved on. After thirteen months, I had a stack of videotapes and no new job. But with a sense of accomplishment, Charlie and I headed back to DC.

By fits and starts, my career took off thanks to the brave gut decision of a news director at WTTG, a local station in DC, where I met my wife Jane. We later moved to Philadelphia, where she worked at the local PBS station. Finally, I made it to New York to do the local news at WCBS. Most of the time I was out in the streets, sometimes anchoring the five o'clock or six o'clock news. Then one day out of the blue I got a call from NBC News. "Would you meet with Tom Brokaw?"

We sat at a small alcove at the Sherry-Netherland Hotel, sharing a large bottle of water. And we talked. He wanted me to think of coming to NBC News. At that very first meeting Tom said he was at an age where he was starting to think about a successor. If I came to NBC, I would be considered for that spot.

The halls of network TV are littered with the bodies of men and women who have held out hopes for the next big job—or so they say. But over a twelve-year period, Tom Brokaw was absolutely true to his word. Every step of the way, Tom made sure I was getting the experience I needed. There weren't any big talks. Just a consistent confidence in me and one opportunity after another.

As much as Tom was a role model on the job, he was also an example off duty. I asked him how he handled the formidable pressure of the job. He said that you have to force yourself to get as much from life's relaxing moments as you can. One look at Tom's private side, his wonderful wife Meredith and his terrific and successful children, and you have a living example of how to conduct a life in a public job.

During the invasion of Iraq, I was flying as part of an armada of Chinook helicopters when Iraqis hit the helicopter in front of ours with a rocket-propelled grenade. We were forced down, and then an epic sandstorm blew in. We were stuck on the desert floor for three days. Because it was a secret mission I was unable to tell anyone where I was. Our one satellite phone call went to the NBC News assignment desk to report that we were okay and that an Army platoon had taken up positions around us.

My family was on spring break vacation, and Tom took it upon himself to call my wife and reassure her that everything possible was being done to keep me safe and get me back. That one call cemented Tom's iconic standing in my household. It was leadership by comforting.

In a business known for its egotism and selfishness, Tom was selfless. If I had dropped the baton, it would have been my doing. That the handoff went as smoothly as it did is thanks to Tom.

I often think about that eight-year-old. He never told anyone about his dream, but he never gave up. He had parents who believed in him. And he had the perfect role model in a tireless, selfless colleague. Someday there will be someone who comes along to take the baton from me. The best way to repay those who have helped me is to make sure it is passed smoothly, from one generation to the next.

FRED ROGERS

"I Like You Just the Way You Are"

The rain beat relentlessly against the windshield as we sped down the highway to Mercer, Pennsylvania. Mother sat next to me in the front seat. Since leaving from Pittsburgh nearly an hour ago, we had barely said a word.

It was 1952, and Ding-Dong was dying.

Ding-Dong was my grandfather, Fred Brooks McFeely, my mother's father—and one of my best friends for as long as I could remember. He earned his nickname years before one sunny afternoon when he plunked me down on his sturdy lap to teach me the old nursery rhyme, "Ding Dong Dell." The name stuck.

I was grown up now, two years out of college and working in New York for NBC television. Just yesterday Mother had telephoned me at work with the news of Ding-Dong's illness. Well into his eighties, he'd been in a nursing home for several years. In recent months, however, his condition had worsened. "The doctors say it's just plain old age," Mother had explained to me quietly. "They say he's fading fast." There was a long pause. "Do you think you could come home, Fred? I think we should visit him as soon as possible."

I made plans to fly from New York to Pittsburgh that evening.

In one sense, it was good to get out of the city. Lately it seemed that nothing had been going right. When I first graduated from college and arrived at NBC, I was a starry-eyed idealist—bursting with enthusiasm for the potential I felt that television held not only for entertaining, but for helping people. I was particularly interested in children's programming. But these were the early days of television and there didn't seem to be much interest in such things. So my goals were shifting—and this bothered me. I really didn't know where I was going, or why. My self-confidence had sunk to near-zero. And never had I felt so far away from God.

I'd taken to stopping by St. Patrick's Cathedral on Fifth Avenue for morning prayer before going to work. Mostly, I prayed for guidance. But I was still uncertain and confused . . .

"Fred," my mother interrupted my thoughts as our car continued on the wet highway. "He might not know you."

"What?" I asked.

"Your grandfather," she answered. "He's all mixed-up. He doesn't know what day it is. Sometimes he doesn't even know where he is."

I felt my throat tighten. Poor Ding-Dong.

"But he is happy," Mother went on. "And he loves to watch television."

"He does?"

"Yes, he loves to watch TV—especially *The Kate Smith Hour*. He knows that's one of the shows you work on. And from what I gather, he's forever telling everyone in the home about his grandson in New York City. He's so proud of you, Fred. You're special to him. You always have been, you know."

I nodded silently.

Listening to the rhythmic sound of the windshield wipers, I let my thoughts travel back to childhood . . .

As a youngster, there was nothing I liked better than Sunday afternoons at Ding-Dong's rambling farm in western Pennsylvania.

Surrounded by miles of winding stone walls, the rustic house and red brick barn provided endless hours of fun and discovery for a city kid like myself. I was used to neat-as-a-pin parlors with porcelain figures that seemed to whisper, "Not to be touched!"—to clean, starched shirts and neatly combed hair warning, "Not to be mussed!"—and to the inevitable wagging of an adult's "Don't do that, you might hurt yourself!" finger.

I could still remember vividly one afternoon when I was eight years old. Since my very first visit to the farm, I'd wanted more than anything to be allowed to climb the network of stone walls surrounding the property. My parents would never approve. The walls were old; some stones were missing, others loose and crumbling. Still, my yearning to scramble across those walls the way I'd watched other boys do grew so strong that finally, one spring afternoon, I summoned all my courage and entered the drawing room where the adults had gathered after Sunday dinner.

All were chatting softly, sipping cups of tea and coffee. I cleared my throat. No one seemed to notice me.

"Hey," I said hesitantly.

Everyone noticed me.

"I, uh—I wanna climb the stone walls," I said. "Can I climb the stone walls?"

Instantly a chorus went up from the women in the room.

"Heavens, no!" they cried in dismay. "You'll hurt yourself!"

I wasn't really disappointed. The response was just as I'd expected. But before I could leave the room, I was stopped by Ding-Dong's booming voice.

"Now hold on just a minute," I heard him say. "So the boy wants to climb the stone walls? Then let the boy climb the walls! He has to learn to do things for himself.

"Now scoot on out of here," he said to me with a wink. "And come see me when you get back."

"Yes, sir," I stammered, my heart pounding with excitement.

For the next two and a half hours I climbed those old walls—skinned my knee, tore my pants, and had the time of my life. Later, when I met with Ding-Dong to tell him about my adventures, I never forgot what he said.

"Fred," he grinned, "you made this day a special day, just by being yourself. Always remember, there's just one person in this whole world like you—and I like you just the way you are."

I wondered now if he ever knew how important that day—and his words—had been to me. I wondered if there was any way I could ever repay him . . .

The rain was letting up as we drove in the main drive to the neat clapboard cottage where Ding-Dong stayed. A white-uniformed nurse answered the door. "Mr. McFeely's had a nice day," she said as she let us in. "He's watching TV now. Kate Smith's show is on. It's his favorite program."

"Ding-Dong?" I said, peering into the dimly lit room. He was sitting in a chair next to the bed.

"Ding-Dong?" I hardly recognized him. He was so tiny, so frail and bent. He lifted his head.

"Hello," he said, extending a feeble hand. "Hello, young man. Have a seat." He motioned to a nearby chair.

"Have a seat," he repeated, "and watch this show with me. This is Kate Smith. This is a fine show."

I sat in the chair and watched the program. When the commercial came on, Ding-Dong said, "You know, young man, this television's a mighty great invention. I've got a grandson in New York, and he told me all about it. He's something, that boy. And he's going to do great things in television. Yes, he is."

Ding-Dong was smiling, his blue eyes twinkling ever so faintly.

"Yes," he went on, "I've got quite a grandson. Would you like to meet him?"

It was obvious Ding-Dong didn't recognize me. But that was all right with me. Wherever in time or place Ding-Dong was in his weary old mind, I just wanted to let him be. All I could hear were his own words echoing in my head: *There's just one person in this whole world like you. And I like you just the way you are.*

"That's some grandson you've got," I said. "You know, I believe he is going to try to do good things in television. He sure cares a lot about you. You've helped him understand some of the most important things in life."

Ding-Dong smiled and nodded. He seemed very happy, but he was tired. He asked to be put to bed. The nurse helped him up from his chair. Mother and I tucked him in. We chatted a bit more and then sat quietly until he fell asleep.

On the way home, we were silent. But I felt strangely happy inside—somehow peaceful. Something very special had happened that afternoon. In a very personal way, God had answered my prayers.

I was beginning to understand what it was He wanted me to do with my television career: He wanted me to offer children the same kind of reassurance, encouragement and sense of self-worth that Ding-Dong had given me. I didn't know exactly how or when the right opportunities would arise, but I felt confident now that I would be ready to seize them.

A few weeks later, I received an invitation to leave New York and join a small educational television station in Pittsburgh that was looking for a person to develop new programming. I jumped at the chance. And it was from those small beginnings—hand-built sets, props and puppets—that the themes and characters that now populate *Mister Rogers' Neighborhood* evolved.

That was twenty-six years ago. Today, through the wonder of television, *Mister Rogers' Neighborhood* is visited each day by millions of children throughout America and other lands. There have been changes over the years; characters and special guests to the Neighborhood come and go. But one thing—my message to the children at the close of every show—remains the same.

"There's just one person in the whole world like you," the kids can count on hearing me say. "And people can like you just the way you are."

Ding-Dong, I know, would agree.

MARY DORR

Two Blinks for Yes!

I was at a meeting of entertainment executives in Los Angeles when someone made a comment that would change my life. "For a film to be successful," a movie producer announced, "its story needs to break five of the Ten Commandments every fifteen minutes! That's what audiences want to see."

It's not true! I thought. My husband Gordon and I had been in the business for years. I'd produced thousands of radio and television programs, been national president of American Women in Radio and Television and hosted a long-running radio talk show. My husband and I both knew many successful people in the entertainment industry who had strong spiritual convictions—and had made excellent TV programs and movies reflecting those values.

As I drove home, the producer's words haunted me. And I wondered what I could do to counteract his ideas. Some people might try organizing boycotts or protests over particularly unsavory programs and films. But early in life I'd learned the effectiveness of a more positive approach—the power of well-placed encouragement.

I learned this from a surprising source—my invalid older sister, Vadae Mae.

In 1929, when the stock market crashed, our family lost all our savings. We moved out of our rambling Victorian house and into a small apartment complex near Los Angeles where people paid whatever they could. Mama and I cleaned rooms and collected rents for the landlord while Daddy worked as a bank teller. It was rough going. But life was hardest of all for Vadae Mae.

She was beautiful, with huge dark eyes and coal-black hair like our mother's. She was vivacious, always laughing, and I adored her.

When she was eleven years old, she came home from school dragging her left foot. "I don't know what's wrong," she said. "My foot feels like lead."

In those days, polio wasn't understood the way it is now. None of the doctors knew what to do. Vadae Mae's illness progressed quickly. Before long, her whole left side was paralyzed, and she could barely move the fingers on her right hand. Her vocal chords were paralyzed as well. The only way she could communicate was by blinking—once for no, two times for yes.

Vadae Mae and I shared a tiny, drab bedroom with twin beds. And other than during school hours, the care of Vadae Mae fell to me. She had to be spoon-fed; and I carried her to the bathroom, often in the middle of the night.

You'd think this would be an imposition on an adolescent girl. But in many ways it was a lifesaver for me.

You see, I was a born chatterbox. And while the rest of the family told me to hush, Vadae Mae loved to hear me talk. I told her about everything at school—what anyone said or did or wore that was of interest. After hours of talking, I'd say, "Have you had enough?" and she'd blink once, a fierce no—she wanted more!

I was fourteen and Vadae Mae was seventeen when our father died of a brain tumor. With Mama's faith and hard work, we knew we'd get along, but things were bound to be much harder without Daddy. I tried to think of ways I could do more to help.

Then one day the buzz went around that the California Retailers' Association was looking for a woman to be the radio voice for their consortium of stores. They were holding auditions at the local radio station. Whoever became their spokeswoman would make five dollars a week.

The night before the last day of the auditions, I closed the bedroom door and sat down in front of Vadae Mae.

"Just think, Vadae Mae, five dollars a week!" I whispered. "I hear that hundreds of women have auditioned, some of them real actresses. I'm only a girl. Do you think I should try?"

Two blinks, for yes.

"Do you think I have a chance?"

Two blinks, then two, then two again. Yes, yes, yes!

I went to our dresser, where my meager savings were hidden in a drawer. I carefully counted what I had. I knew my best bet was to look as grown-up and capable as possible. Clutching the coins in my hand, I turned back to my confidante.

"Tomorrow after school, on my way to the auditions, I'm going to Woolworth's—to buy lipstick!"

The next day when I arrived at the radio station, I almost turned around and ran for home. As I signed in, I saw that the other women wore stylish clothes, hats and shoes. I wore a frock made by my mother. But I thought of Vadae Mae at home, praying for me, believing in me. I couldn't disappoint her.

Before long, I was called into the studio. It had a chair, and a microphone hanging from the ceiling. Several men in suits sat behind the plate-glass window of the control room.

"You look very young," said the floor manager as I took my seat under the microphone.

"I'm older than I look," I said with a smile.

The copy they gave me was only a paragraph long. It seemed no problem to read it—after all, I'd read aloud to Vadae Mae from books and *Liberty* magazine and *The Saturday Evening Post* for hours on end. The red light went on, and the engineer pointed at me from the booth and I began.

I did just fine until I got to the word *photographic.*

"Pho-photo-photographic," I said. It was funny I'd stumbled on such a simple word, and I reacted the same way I would have if I'd been reading to Vadae Mae: I laughed.

"Would you like to try again?" asked the engineer.

Again, all went well until—"Photograph-graph-aphic," I sputtered, then collapsed into laughter.

"Once more?" asked the engineer.

This time I sailed through.

Back at home I gleefully reenacted the whole thing for my sister. I didn't know if I'd blown the audition, but even with mistakes, it had been a positive experience.

A couple of days later I got a callback, as did several other women.

After I read again, the producer came over to me. "You've got it," he said. "You have the voice we've been looking for." Then he smiled. "We were also impressed by your self-assurance and sense of humor."

I practically ran home to tell Vadae Mae. She was so excited!

Sadly, she didn't live long after that. But her love and support have stayed with me. Over the years, I've sometimes thought of her as my own encouraging angel, enabling me to help others who needed a bit of bolstering or a word of hope.

Now, as I turned into my driveway, I had an idea: Instead of complaining about shoddy films and shows, why not reward the good ones? Why not create an awards program that would honor worthy media projects and personalities? The more I thought about it, the more excited I got.

I'm involved with the Mother of the Year program, and at the national meeting I asked the gathering of mothers what they thought about my idea. They were all for it. Next I talked to the board of Religion in Media, who said they would sponsor the awards if the entertainment industry would agree to participate.

So I talked to the large movie studios and television networks, all of whom said they would submit programs for awards and attend the banquets. We were off and running!

The first awards were given in 1977, and the turnout of executives, stars and press was bigger than I'd dared to hope. The importance of the awards has grown every year since. At star-studded ceremonies we have rewarded films like *Driving Miss Daisy* and *Aladdin* and TV shows like *Highway to Heaven* and *The Cosby Show*. We've paid tribute to performers such as Gavin MacLeod, the late Michael Landon, and Audrey Meadows.

I can't help but think it all started with Vadae Mae. In a way, the awards are even named after her. They are called the Angel Awards.

Ricardo Montalban

"Lord, Let Me Go Home"

As I hung up the phone on our kitchen wall, I turned to see my wife Georgiana's smiling face. Her eyes were shining with excitement. "You got the part?" she asked.

"Yes," I said slowly—still not quite believing the news myself. The role was in a new Broadway musical, *Jamaica*. It couldn't have happened at a better time.

It was 1957, and with a wife and four small children to support, I badly needed work. Our past few years in Hollywood had been pretty lean; my career had been one of ups and downs. But this, we understood, was the nature of an actor's life—to live from job to job in a state of constant uncertainty. Fortunately, Georgiana and I shared a firm faith in God and in the power of prayer that had never failed to see us through the roughest times. When I needed work, we prayed— with confidence and expecting an answer. That's the way I'd been taught as a youngster.

Still, landing the role in *Jamaica* was more than I'd hoped for. The part was, first of all, challenging; I was the only white actor in an all-black cast and would be playing the part of a Jamaican. The job promised to be steady; advance ticket sales for the show, at Broadway's Imperial Theater, indicated it was going to be a hit. Best of all, the work wouldn't take me away from my family; the contract included our all-expenses-paid move from California to New York.

It seemed too good to be true.

We arrived in New York with great expectations and weren't disappointed. The play opened to good reviews and was booked for a year's run. As a family, we enjoyed the excitement of big city living and new acquaintances. At the theater, deep friendships developed among the *Jamaica* cast and crew. One of my dearest companions was my dresser, Charlie Blackstone.

Charlie was a quiet man, immaculately groomed, with a cheerful nature and quick grin that endeared him to everyone he met. He took his work seriously. From out of nowhere, it seemed, Charlie's efficient hands were always there when I needed them—adjusting a crooked belt buckle, sewing a button, delicately retouching a spot of makeup melted by hot stage lights. Rarely did Charlie speak about himself or his past, and I never asked him any questions; ours was a relationship based on a kind of silent understanding. We just felt comfortable in each other's company and never felt we had to say very much. Charlie loved boxing, and we often spent intermissions watching the fights on television in my dressing room. Saturday nights were special. That's when Charlie and I went to midnight Mass at St. Malachy's, also known as the Actors' Chapel because of its late-hour services and theater-district location on West 49th Street.

I grew to love that old church, with its cozy atmosphere and worn wooden pews. Charlie and I always sat in the same place. It was there it seemed I could best focus my thoughts and get close to God. I often thought how I would miss St. Malachy's when it came time to return to California.

Our year in New York had nearly passed and Georgiana and I were busy planning our trip home when, unexpectedly, I learned that the play was being held over. A new school year was starting, so

Georgiana and the children went on to California without me. I took a temporary apartment with another actor, planning to join my family as soon as the play closed. At first our separation didn't bother me; I didn't expect it to last more than a few weeks.

But as weeks dragged on into months and *Jamaica* kept playing to sell-out audiences, it became apparent that I was stuck in New York indefinitely. I should have been happy for the show's success, but with each passing day I grew more and more miserable with homesickness. My family means everything to me. I missed them terribly. No matter what I tried in order to divert myself—books, television, shopping, museums, shows—nothing held my interest. All I wanted was to be home with my family. Phone calls and letters only made me feel worse; they were poor substitutes for the real thing.

Every day started and ended with the same prayer.

"Lord, let me go home," I'd say. "Let me be with my family soon."

But the show went on. The job that had been a dream come true had turned into a nightmare. With each closing curtain, I felt my throat tighten, my frustration turning into anger. It just didn't seem fair.

Finally, after one Saturday night performance, I thought I would explode. Storming into my dressing room, I slammed the door behind me.

"I am so sick of this," I hissed through clenched teeth. "Sick of it!"

Charlie Blackstone was sitting on a folding chair in the far corner of the room watching television. He looked up at me with troubled eyes, but said nothing. He had been waiting for me to go to Mass.

We walked to St. Malachy's in silence. The midnight sky was inky black, the stars cold and brittle. A bitter wind sounded a mournful cry as it whipped around the old stone church.

Charlie and I entered the chapel and slipped into our pew. The wooden seat was hard. The cement floor was cold on my knees. Whatever charm the church had held for me before was gone. I didn't want to be there. I didn't care who knew.

"Lord," I muttered, "I want to go home. I miss my family. I'm sick of this play. Please . . ." I hesitated. "Please make it end!"

The chapel seemed unusually quiet.

I glanced over at Charlie. His head was bowed and he was smiling, ever so faintly. His voice was low, but I caught the words. What I heard made my heart sink.

Charlie was thanking the Lord for his work—for the very thing I was praying would end. And Charlie, I knew, wasn't the only one. All around the city there were many others—actors, actresses, stagehands, musicians—who needed their jobs and felt the same way.

My face grew hot with shame. I felt torn apart, confused, guilty. I still wanted to go home—but certainly not at the expense of anyone else. For the first time in my life, I didn't know what—or how—to pray.

Charlie, I noticed, had fallen silent. He remained that way for a few moments, then raised his head. His expression was one of absolute peace. With eyes still closed, he began to say the Lord's Prayer.

"Our Father," he began.

His words were soothing. They seemed to whisper in my ear, finding their way into my own thoughts.

"Our Father," I repeated—and stopped.

Here, in these two small words, in this age-old prayer, was the answer to my problem!

Jesus, in teaching us how to pray, had made it clear that we were to speak not only for ourselves, but for all members of His family: not to my Father, but to our Father—not just for me, Ricardo, but for all those around me. This wonderful sense of sharing each others' burdens in prayer was further revealed as I continued . . . "Give us day by day our daily bread. . . . forgive us our sins . . . lead us not into temptation . . . deliver us from evil" (Luke 11:3–4).

In the past, my prayers had always been self-centered. There was a real freedom in thinking of others that I'd never before experienced. It was exhilarating.

Before we left the church, I simply asked the Lord for patience in understanding His will for me for the remainder of my stay in New York City. I didn't have to tell Him how badly I wanted to go home; I'd been telling Him for weeks.

I wish I could say my situation changed—it didn't. The play continued for five more months. But something far more important did happen. I changed. My anger was gone. And, gradually, the stabbing pains of homesickness that had made life intolerable melted away. What remained was a sweet sort of ache that was almost pleasant in the way it served as a constant reminder that there were loved ones at home waiting for me. Besides, I recognized now that I had another family, my theater family, to appreciate and love for however long we were to be together.

It was some time ago that I received word that Charlie Blackstone had passed away. It's been over twenty years since our night together at St. Malachy's. Since then, there have been many more times when I've called upon the Lord for guidance—times of trouble and confusion and despair that we all must endure. But now, thanks to Charlie, it's with the needs of others in mind—as well as my own.

MIKE DOUGLAS

When I Needed Watching

Some boys grow up resenting an outstanding older brother. That isn't the way it was in my family. My older brother Bob was a star in everything he did and he was my hero. He was my special champion and protector. He still is, though that takes some explaining.

There were three of us: Bob, who was five years older than I; my sister Helen, two years older; and I was the baby. We were all scrappy, healthy Irish kids growing up on Chicago's west side during the Depression years, though having no money didn't seem to have much meaning for us then. My father, who worked for the Canadian Pacific railroad, was away from home a lot, which may be one reason why early in the game Bob assigned himself the job of watching over me. I never thought I needed watching over, but he did, and there were times when I was not sorry.

Bob was big and tough and kind and had a wild temper that could work for my advantage or disadvantage. One of my favorite memories is of the day an English bulldog charged at me as I was walking home from school one afternoon. The dog's owner was sitting on his porch and I went up and told him he ought to keep his dog on a chain. The man got so mad that he slapped me. Boy, was it exciting when I told Bob! He did some charging of his own. I can still see him standing on the man's porch, that terrible temper steaming, the man peering out but refusing, wisely, to come out.

There was another time though when some pals and I were out joyriding and we dropped into a honky-tonk. Somebody saw me there and told Bob and the next day Bob got hold of me and shook me and sat me down and told me exactly why I was not to go into such places. And if I ever went again, and he found out, he said, the shaking I had just survived would seem like child's play. The point was well taken.

Bob was directly responsible for the greatest thrill of my childhood. He was seventeen and a basketball star playing with the Question Marks—that's what they called their team—and I was twelve and sitting admiringly on the sidelines during a big tournament. The Question Marks came down to the final minute with a decisive lead when suddenly Bob left the game. He came over to me and shoved me onto the floor in his place. The ball was passed to me, I took aim and scored! Most kids just dream about things like that but Bob had the touch for making them come true.

We were a sports-mad family and athletics was the biggest thing in my life until the afternoon Mom took me downtown to a vaudeville show at the Chicago Theater. That's the day the show business bug bit. By the time I was in my middle teens I was picking up money on local singing dates. Before I was out of my teens I was working on an Oklahoma City radio station, WKY, and it was there in Oklahoma that I met Genevieve and we were married. She was a sophomore in high school and I was nineteen.

The years passed, and though I was only intermittently in Chicago and our lifestyles were utterly different, Bob and I remained close. He married and fathered five children and worked as a tile salesman. He came to be an effective and popular member of his community, as I knew he would, and a strong member of his church. I used to look with respect at the way he conducted his life.

On the other hand, like so many other show business people, I spent the years struggling, hoping, angling for the big break. Eventually it came, but not until I was thirty-five. From nineteen to thirty-five is a lot of years of waiting; that's a lot of food cooked in hotel rooms and a lot of pants pressed by Gen in cramped backstages. It's a lot of maneuvering to keep our twin daughters and Gen and me together as a real family, the way Bob's family was. When the break came, Gen and I had almost decided to give up show business—we had an infant daughter then, Kelly—and Gen and I were both taking real estate courses in a California night school.

Once *The Mike Douglas Show* came into being, however, I worked like the dickens. I drove myself like a machine to make sure that what I had achieved for us did not get away. One reason I didn't trust the meaning of the TV ratings and the publicity and the money coming in was that I seemed to be living on a treadmill. It was exhausting. Life as a TV star wasn't that rich, it wasn't that enjoyable or satisfying, even though in subtle, sneaky ways I began to be pleased by the power that TV success can bring. Yet I was to learn that it can be a deceptive power. I was to learn it suddenly.

In September 1969, we faced one of those crises that most people think happen only to other families. Bob went into MacNeal Memorial Hospital in Berwyn, Illinois, for an operation. The doctors suspected cancer. Mother and Dad were on their way to his bedside when their car was struck by a mail truck. Mother was hurt seriously in the crash and an ambulance rushed her to the very same hospital where Bob lay gravely ill.

And so it was that there in MacNeal Memorial Hospital, Mother on one floor, Bob on another, the family gathered. It became a time for whispering, for deep thoughts and long silences, a time for looking hard at life and at oneself with fresh curiosity.

The word came for certain that Mother would be all right. She was in traction and she was in pain, but she was safe. Bob was not. He was dying.

I paced the halls of the hospital in confusion. I was fully aware that this was my chance, at last, to reverse the roles: This was my opportunity to be Bob's champion and protector. But I was powerless.

During that night I came to terms with some of the subtleties of success and power that I had been grappling with. The very day I had left the show in Philadelphia to fly to Chicago, I honestly had the feeling that I could do something. I could get the best surgeons. I had money and connections . . . .

But I was powerless.

I can't remember how I happened to do it or what made me do it, but somewhere in the middle of those long walks down antiseptic corridors, I began to pray. I knew little about prayer. It had never been like me to rush to churches and light candles; church had always been Bob's department. He had always tried to make me think more seriously about religion, but I had resisted.

My prayer, fumbling thing that it was, was not a begging one. Somehow I just wanted to feel, wanted Bob to feel, the presence of God. I wanted God to know—as if He needed my help—what a fine man Bob was and how grateful I was for him. Strangely, in the midst of approaching death, mine was a prayer of gratitude.

Bob died. As soon as I could after his funeral, I got back to Philadelphia and went to work again. But it wasn't the same kind of work. From the outset I discovered that I had changed. Seeing Bob's wife and kids and feeling once again the texture of his life made me look more closely at my own. I saw the treadmill clearly this time, and in perspective, and I set out to slow the machinery. I found more time, surprisingly lots of time, to be alone with Gen and with the only daughter still at home, our little Kelly.

In learning to accept and enjoy the blessings at hand, no day since then has passed that I have not said my prayers and thanked God for my family and my health and my job. I am new to it and I do not understand the great ramifications of its power, but today I would not live without prayer.

I find it intriguing that ever since I stopped running so hard, ever since Bob died, people have stopped me repeatedly to say, "Mike, you never looked better." I think I have always seemed fairly calm on camera, but it has only been in the past two years that I have discovered that I am calm. Even my golf game has changed. For the better. Are all of these things coincidence? I doubt it.

Before every show there's always a moment or two when I go off into a corner to say a very private prayer. Sometimes then I remember it was Bob, really, who taught me to pray. When this thought comes to me, I smile. You see, he's watching over his little brother still.

JOE BLEEDEN

So You Think You Have a Problem?

Many of us remember the famous sign-off line with which Jimmy Durante always ended his show: "Good night, Mrs. Calabash, wherever you are." As a longtime associate of the comedian who did so much to enliven people's lives, I was one of the few who knew the story behind that line.

But far more important to me was how Jimmy helped me with a personal problem. Early in my career I suffered from an inferiority complex. Unsure, self-conscious, I worried about what others thought of me.

One day early in our relationship (I was his publicist for twenty-nine years), I confessed my problem to Jimmy. It was easy to do, for he was such a thoughtful, considerate man. I knew it arose from his deep spiritual faith. He always wore a chain around his neck bearing Christian symbols, including a cross. And no matter where he was on tour, he made it a point of going to church on Sundays, often taking his whole entourage with him.

So I felt comfortable explaining my problem.

Jimmy smiled, leaned back in his chair and laughed. "So you think you have a problem? How would you like to have a schnoz like mine? When I started out in the business as a kid playing ragtime piano, I never said a word onstage," he continued. "I always felt some cluck would laugh at my nose."

He hesitated. "You've seen my old photos from the early twenties?"

"Sure."

"Ever notice somethin' about them?"

"Yeah," I said, "your head was always tilted down."

"Right," he said, laughing. "I didn't want people to see my nose." He was quiet for a moment. "Oh, I eventually got to horsing around on stage and even doing some singing. But my real breakthrough came in the early 1940s after I got a letter from a young boy."

He pulled a wrinkled, folded paper from his desk and read it: "I've got a big nose, Mr. Durante. Everybody laughs at it. But then I saw you, Mr. Durante, in a movie. And gee! When you kept laughing at your nose, it made me feel good all over. And folks now call me 'Schnoz.'"

Jimmy looked up, his eyes glistening. "You know, a big load fell off me after reading that letter, like some awful curse.

"So, you see, it's not what we think of how we look to others," he continued. "What counts is making the best of your God-given talent in giving yourself to them. In other words, focus on the other guy and you forget yourself.

"When I quit thinking of myself, I performed even better than ever," he went on. "And you know what? My schnoz taught me somethin' important: Never to hurt anybody else. So I never made jokes about someone's large ears, their stutterin', or 'bout folks in Oklahoma not wearing shoes."

"What about Oklahoma?" I asked.

"I did that once," he said, "and an editor wrote in his paper that lots of people in Oklahoma listened to me, and I came into their homes each week like a real friend, and that maybe I would like to know they do wear shoes and are really nice people. Well, that editor set me right and I never did anything like that again."

After our talk I quit worrying about myself, realizing that our only real handicap is the negative thoughts we have about ourselves. I learned to concentrate on the other person, to be interested in what he had to say, find out his likes and dislikes.

It was during one of our talks I asked Jimmy about his famous closing line.

"It just came out of me one night at the end of a radio show," he said. "I repeated it on the following shows and people called, wrote letters. Many said they were the Mrs. Calabash. Listeners loved it, so when I went on to television in the early fifties, it stayed."

"Is it true," I asked, "that it referred to your first wife?"

He smiled poignantly. "More than that. In the early 1920s, Jeanne and I took a vacation. We drove from New York. I don't know where we were at the time, but going west we passed something. It might have been a billboard, a sign, I don't remember. And what we saw became something between us and we used to laugh about it and refer to it as 'calabash.' So help me, I don't recall what it was. But that's the story. Now you know."

I knew Jimmy deeply loved his wife, who died quite young. But I differ with the last words in his sign-off. For I'm sure Jimmy knew with deep certainty where his wife was.

ART CARNEY

The Man Who Spoiled Me for Good

U nder a glass dome on my dresser is a gold pocket watch, not
expensive, but very precious. It belonged to Rich. Whenever I
look at it I see him, and I hear him. And I remember how he filled my
youth with love and wonder and the special magic of hero worship.

His name was Philip Richardson. He was once the mayor of
Woburn, a small Massachusetts city; he was an editor, and gave my
father his first newspaper job. He and Dad became firm and lifelong
friends with an enduring affection for each other. My mother loved
Rich too. Everybody did.

Rich had an unhappy and childless marriage, and when he was
about fifty he was alone. Naturally he came to live with us. My parents wouldn't have it any other way. He quit newspapering and, until
he retired on a pension at sixty-five, worked for the American
Telephone and Telegraph Company (AT&T). Meanwhile, Rich gave
all the love he wasn't able to give elsewhere to the six Carney sons. I
was the youngest, so the relationship between Rich and me was the
longest, and I like to think, the deepest.

My parents were unstinting in their love for us but Rich added a
new dimension to that love. My parents were the security, the authority, the insurance. Rich was the hero, the friend, the reassurance.

Our house was always full of frantic people. Any minor event
could quickly reach the proportions of a major crisis. But Rich had

this wonderful calm that always punctured any crisis. Once, after eating a lot of junk, I got a fierce stomachache. I yelped. My brothers yelped at me to stop yelping. Amid the bedlam my mother and father sternly ordered me to take some milk of magnesia. That was for babies. Stubbornly I yelped back: "No! No! Never!" They appealed to Rich. He silenced the din with his smile, then swallowed a spoonful himself, filled the spoon again, and held it out to me. It was the gesture of an equal to an equal. I took it without a word.

He had a way of leaving anyone, young or old, with his dignity intact.

You were never conscious of his age. He was never older than the person he was talking to. He looked like a medium-sized, gray-haired General MacArthur without the severe face, but with the same meticulous air of distinction. Even when he played marbles with me he never lost that air. We had a crazy rug in our dining room with big colored squares in it and almost every day before dinner we'd play marbles on it. Then he'd go into the living room to read his paper. While he read I'd comb his hair into weird hairdos, pulling it up to points from every part of his head. He'd just go on reading the paper until I asked him to look at the hairdo in the mirror. Rich would get up, look, smile his approval, or frown his disapproval, then return to his paper. And I'd start another weird hair comb.

Rich got me my first ball, my first baseball mitt, my first two-wheeler, and my first dog. He was always at the games when we boys played baseball. He also took me to see the Woolworth Building. But mostly I remember walking with him. Long walks, in a lot of silence and always feeling his love.

It seemed that Rich never had any problems of his own. He did. Plenty. But he never burdened anyone with them. I suspect he eased his problems by being with kids, especially me. Or maybe with painting. He was a good artist. He used oils, charcoal, watercolors or pen. And sometimes on our walks, we'd stop in a nice spot and sit, and we'd both paint or sketch.

Those walks. They were great. Every Friday we'd take a special long walk to Aunt Mabel's, a cousin of my father. Once, on the way there, I thought I smelled gas coming from the ground. I yelled "Gas! Gas!" Rich didn't think I was crazy. Anybody else would have. Not him. He went over, bent down, sniffed very seriously. Sure enough, there was part of an old gas pipe there with a strong gas smell. From then on, every Friday night, when we got to that spot we'd both stop, bend down, sniff, look up knowingly, and walk on happily, sharing our great, dark secret.

Then, coming to the hedges before Aunt Mabel's house, I'd duck behind one, then dash up the steps before Rich would catch me. I don't know if he started that or if I did. But like the gas-smelling it became a regular ritual on the Friday night walks to Aunt Mabel's.

When I got older, much older, near thirteen, the walks got longer, much longer. I mapped them out to pass the house of the girl I was madly in love with at the time. Rich never protested. I knew that he knew, but he never let on.

He was at the heart of my world, really, but once, when I got articulate enough to tell him he was, he said: "I'm not the center of your universe or any universe. God is."

And whenever there was any trouble, big or small, his calm hovered over us, and we'd hear him say: "God and time will take care of it. Just ask, 'Lord Jesus, help me,' and if you really mean it, He will."

At school I spent more time in the principal's office than in my classes because of this irreverent urge I had to mimic my teachers. In one class, off in a corner, there was this bust of Beethoven, very severe-looking, very cold. One day I just couldn't resist: I rushed up, pulled out my handkerchief, and blew Beethoven's nose. The class broke up.

The principal didn't. "Arthur William Matthew Carney," she said, "you will never amount to anything."

I believed her. Rich didn't. Under his auspices I gave my first professional performance. I was nine when one day I got the idea of a one-man show. It was Rich who promptly sat down and wrote twelve invitations in his own beautiful script, mostly to relatives: "You are invited to a special evening of entertainment by Mr. Arthur Carney called 'Art by Art.'" I danced and had funny disguises, doodled on the piano as my father had taught me, and I got by on drums, slide whistle, and flexitone, a kind of musical saw.

I always wondered if I would make it in show business. Sometimes I still wonder. Rich never did. He was always there, through the years, even when out of sight, when I was knocking about the country with Horace Heidt, in nightclubs, in vaudeville, when I couldn't get work of any kind. He was there in the early days of radio, and he was there when, as an infantryman, I set up my machine gun on one of the Normandy beaches and got a piece of shrapnel in my right leg before I could fire it.

And he was there, out of sight, when I drank. I once was able to drink pretty good as a young man. When I got older and had real responsibility, the remorse was worse than the hangover. I told myself I was headed for that endless lost weekend. I tried to quit. It wasn't easy. I could fool a lot of people about it. But when you talk to yourself or to Rich you have to tell the truth. He was gone when I dropped to the depths as a drinker. But at the lowest point I heard him remind me:

"Just ask, 'Lord Jesus, help me', and He will—if you really mean it."

Hearing Rich say that, even when he wasn't there, I learned to mean it.

I try hard not to drink anymore. I don't beat the temptation every time but, whenever I say, "Lord Jesus, help me," and mean it, I win, and the drink loses.

When Rich was seventy he was still playing tennis with me. When he was eighty-one he got a blood clot in his heart, and survived it. But he was never really right after that. For a time he lived with my wife Jean and me, and one night, sitting by his bed, holding his hand, listening to his calm voice, he saw my worried look, and suddenly smiled reassuringly, and asked: "Do you think I'm going to make it?"

"Sure," I said, "you always will."

He died shortly after that. But he made it. He made it here, and elsewhere too.

BROOKE SHIELDS

What Friends Are For

David Strickland was like a brother to me. For three seasons we worked together on the TV show *Suddenly Susan*. My friends tend to be people who are not in the entertainment business. David was different. He was a brilliant but vulnerable actor and an incredibly loyal friend.

Then in 1999 the unthinkable: David committed suicide. I was aware that he was suffering from depression. We'd talked about it. It was as if the emotional vulnerability that made him a great actor destroyed him as a person. I knew he'd been taking medication. We talked about it often. But I always wondered if I could have done more. I kept thinking of things that might have made a difference. But it was only when I faced my own depression a few years later that I truly understood how desperate David must have been, and how hard it is to reach out for help.

Throughout my depression I had the constant support of my husband, Chris Henchy, my family and my friends. There were times I must have seemed impossible to reach. And yet they kept trying and they eventually did reach me.

Here are four crucial things I've learned that you must do to help a friend in trouble:

1. BE THERE

Listening is one of the most powerful things you can do to help someone who is suffering. You don't have to have any answers. A depressed person is trying to fight her way out of a terrible wilderness, and just to be listened to helps her in her quest for a path.

When I came home with my newborn baby, Rowan, I thought what I was experiencing was simple exhaustion. Yet there was an overriding sense of panic that I had never felt before. I wasn't cut out to be a mother, I thought. In the past, if I felt down, I could counteract it with exercise, a good night's sleep or a nice dinner with a friend. But I became convinced that this terrible feeling would never go away.

I called friends and family and cried to them on the phone. I called my stepsister Diana. "Promise me it will get better," I wailed. She begged me to get a baby nurse for a few days so I could sleep. The people in my life were trying to help, but I was in over my head.

Then Rowan's godfather, John, visited. He'd been there for me after David died, and for years before that as a trusted and level-headed adviser. "John," I said quietly to him one day, "I feel like there's no hope. I've fallen down a dark hole and I'll never get out."

John listened to me for a long time. Just listened. Finally he told me that no matter what I was feeling there was always hope. Things would get better. Then, without any judgment whatsoever, he gently insisted that I seek professional help. "When you're not well, Brooke, you go to the doctor," he reminded me.

That was the voice I needed to hear in the dark woods to start to find my way out, back to health.

The most important thing that friends can do is to watch and listen. Watch to see if a loved one is retreating or acting down or moody for a prolonged time. Ask them questions about how they feel, about their state of mind. Listen to their answers. Then reassure them. The best advice you can give is reassurance.

I wanted to hear, over and over again, that this would get better. Maybe that's what David needed to hear too.

2. GIVE THEM INFORMATION

Provide information—even if they're not ready to act on it. Information is a long, strong lifeline. My friend Sherie came over to my apartment one day with a stack of information on postpartum depression that she'd downloaded from the Internet. She told me that everything I had said to her on the phone was repeated practically word for word in this material.

I couldn't imagine that anyone could possibly feel what I was feeling.

I put it near my bedside and said I'd look at it. I didn't say when. In fact, it was a long time before I could bring myself to read it. But when I was ready, I had all that stuff Sherie printed out for me. Seeing what other people had gone through made me feel less like a freak and less alone. There is hope in community.

3. BE HONEST

Honesty is the quality I value most in a friend. Not bluntness, but honesty with compassion. At one of my worst moments I went out to lunch with my friend Stephanie. I'd been taking an antidepressant, but because I felt better I'd stopped taking it without telling my doctor (a foolish and dangerous decision). Now I wasn't doing well.

Stephanie reached across the table and squeezed my hand. "Brooke, you have so much. You can't forget that. I know you're grateful. Let's make a list." She pulled pad and pencil from her bag.

"Write down every blessing in your life." I did as she said. The act of writing made me feel better, but it wasn't enough to feel peace or believe I was going to survive this. Later, walking out to the parking lot, Stephanie made me promise to call my doctor as soon as I got home.

I thought about how David had spiraled out of control. He, too, had gone off his meds without telling his doctor. Why did I think I could make the same bad decision? The answer is that someone in crisis can't always make good choices. The negative thoughts running through my head made sense to me. I not only needed objective advice, I needed medical attention.

4. PRAY

I'm always praying for my friends. Not just when they're in dire straits. I pray for them specifically. I believe that the more specific the prayer the better. So I stay in touch. That way my prayers are focused. Prayer, for me, is about the private quiet plea for help. If I suspect a friend is struggling I'll leave messages on her answering machine, telling her that she's in my thoughts. Can I be a pain? Maybe. Still, I'd rather leave a message for someone every day than let her wonder if I cared or risk letting them feel alone.

My friends know I pray for them. That's important. When I felt there was nothing I could do to help myself, knowing that I was prayed for was often the only thing that stood between me and despair. I made a round of calls. One of the first people I called was my godmother, Lila. All I asked for were her prayers. That might seem like so little, but it felt like so much.

When a friend is in trouble, you need to act. Don't worry about overreacting. It's better than the alternative. Too often we're afraid of intruding or seeming judgmental. But I've been on both sides, and there is nothing of greater earthly help than a friend who is willing to reach out, way out if necessary. Listen, give good information, be honest, pray. That's what friends are for.

Facing
Life's Storms

Whatever your situation in life, you too can step out of that
safe room and proceed with faith minute by minute, hand
over hand, not worrying about what lies ahead or what might
happen, but trusting that God will supply you the energy and
courage to cope with each experience as it arises.

Jim Stovall

MIKE WALLACE

My Darkest Hour

Like most people, I'd had days when I felt blue and it took more of
an effort than usual to get through the things I had to do. But I
always snapped out of it. Before I knew it, I would be corralling
another reluctant interview subject for *60 Minutes* or trying to whip a
crosscourt forehand past my opponent in a tennis match. Relentless
as ever, basically. (And a pain in the neck to my colleagues at CBS
News, who claim that "Mike Wallace is here" are the four most
dreaded words in the English language.)

So my down times invariably passed. Until the fall of 1984, that
is, when I found myself suddenly struck, then overwhelmed, by
something—an emptiness, a helplessness, an emotional and physical
collapse—I'd never experienced before. CBS News was embroiled in
a high-profile lawsuit filed by General William Westmoreland over a
documentary we had made about the Vietnam War, a special report
for which I'd been the chief correspondent.

The case went to trial in early October. Every morning after Mary
and I had breakfast, instead of heading to my office in the mid-
Manhattan CBS News building on West 57th Street, I went downtown to the federal courthouse in Foley Square. As I made my way
into the courtroom, past the phalanx of reporters, I had a feeling their
eyes on me were skeptical. A pretty jarring reversal of roles. Still, that
was nothing compared to having to listen to the other side's lawyers

call into question not only the accuracy of our documentary but also my own professional integrity.

You'd think I'd have just let the allegations roll off my back. After all, they weren't true. Plus, as Mary reminded me, I had nearly fifty years in broadcasting to back up my good name. But day after day, I sat trapped in Room 318 at the courthouse, hearing people I didn't even know attack the work I'd done. Given the way trials proceed, I didn't have a chance to defend myself right then, so the accusations ate at me. Doubts started to haunt me. *Did I do something wrong?* It was as if all my experience in radio and TV news didn't count for anything anymore. *What if I really am dishonest as a reporter? Dishonest as a person?*

I tried to keep going on with life as usual. Whenever court was out of session, I worked on stories for *60 Minutes*, doing research and interviews at night if necessary. But I had a hard time concentrating. Me, the guy who was famous for never giving up on a story, for asking such pointed questions they made everyone from gangsters to movie stars to political leaders sweat.

In November, I had a brief escape from the courtroom. I went to Ethiopia to cover the famine. The tragedy unfolding before my eyes in that drought-ravaged country, the human suffering I witnessed, resharpened my focus. With something approaching my usual vigor, I did a segment for *60 Minutes*. We edited it and got it on the air. *Things are getting back to normal,* I told myself.

But as soon as I returned to the daily grind of the trial, that strange, dark malaise set in again. If anything, it was more pervasive than before, casting a pall over every part of my life the way the chill gray of winter seemed to blanket all of New York City. I didn't have an appetite, no matter what Mary put on the table. I could barely summon up the energy to get out of bed each morning, let alone run after balls hit to the corners of the tennis court. But at night, I would lie awake, restless. Sometimes I'd give up on sleep and switch on the television, looking for something on the late-night shows to get my mind off all my dark thoughts. And even when I could go back to the office and do the work I loved, I felt dead inside.

Maybe the only constant, the only part of my day-to-day life that hadn't changed since the trial began, was what I said before I fell into bed at night. The *Shema*, one of the oldest and most important prayers of the Jewish faith. *"Shema Yisrael Adonai Eloheinu Adonai Echad,"* I would recite each night, as I had every night since I learned those words growing up in Brookline, Massachusetts. "Hear, O Israel, the Lord our God, the Lord is One."

I tried to draw strength from that prayer. And from Mary, who was always at my side, incredibly patient with me and my moods. Still, I'd catch her looking at me, her eyes full of worry. One evening after we came home from the courthouse, she said, "Mike, you need to go see a doctor. Something's wrong."

I denied it. "The pressure of the trial's getting to me," I said. "I'll be myself again once it's over."

Mary insisted on taking me to the doctor. I told him what I'd been experiencing, even swallowed my pride and asked, "What can you do to help me?"

"You don't need help," the doctor said. "You're tough. Everybody knows that. You'll bounce back in no time." He warned me about the damage to my reputation if word got out I was having these emotional difficulties.

Mary was still concerned. "I don't want to be right about this," she told me on our way home, "but I think what you're feeling goes way beyond being under stress. It's taken over your life."

Why is it that the people you love so often know you better than you know yourself? It took a complete physical collapse on the heels of a bout of the flu in December to make me concede I might be in as bad shape as Mary feared. Right before the New Year, I was admitted to the hospital, "suffering from exhaustion," a CBS spokesman announced.

The truth, I was to learn from Dr. Marvin Kaplan, the psychiatrist I started seeing, was something I'd never imagined. My defenses were pretty much broken down by then. When Dr. Kaplan asked me to give him a complete history of my symptoms, I poured out everything to this man who was all but a stranger to me. I told him about the trial; about the doubts that plagued me; about not being able to eat, sleep or enjoy the things I used to. "I just don't see any way out of this," I confessed. "It's like I'm going out of my mind, I feel so low, so . . . hopeless. No, copeless."

"You feel as you do, Mr. Wallace, because you are experiencing clinical depression. Any stressful change in one's life can trigger an episode, and some people are more prone to it than others."

Depression? Wasn't that some sign of emotional weakness?

"Depression is a disease," Dr. Kaplan explained. "A disease that millions suffer from. The good news is that almost all depressed people can get better with treatment." First, he prescribed an antidepressant to relieve my symptoms. "Once it takes effect, it will put a pharmaceutical floor underneath your depression, so that you don't sink any lower." Then psychotherapy to help me gain insight into myself and figure out ways to cope with what was troubling me.

Within a week, I was released from the hospital. I continued my sessions with Dr. Kaplan and went back to work, nowhere near functioning at full capacity, and still too ashamed to tell people in the office what was going on. They must have wondered why Mike wasn't acting like his usual demanding, abrasive self.

I was due to testify at the trial, so while the CBS attorneys prepared me legally, Dr. Kaplan got me ready emotionally. "You believe that if your side loses, it will be the end of your professional life," he observed. "Why don't we talk about how you will go on if you do lose?" A seemingly simple exercise, but it helped me regain some perspective.

Nearly five long months after the trial began, the day before I was to take the witness stand, the other side dropped the lawsuit. Obviously I was hugely relieved, but why didn't I feel well again? "That's not how depression works," Dr. Kaplan told me. "You don't just snap out of a serious illness. You have to stay on the treatment and give it time to work."

I did what he said, and sure enough, within a couple months, I felt better. So much better, in fact, that I disregarded Dr. Kaplan's advice and stopped taking the medication. Less than a week later, I happened to fall playing tennis and busted my left wrist.

And just like that, I was in deep again. As deep as the first time. I'd look out the window at all the people on the streets of New York City. So much energy out there, so much going on, and all I wanted to do was turn my back on it. I didn't care about anything except how miserable I felt and how I might end this pain.

Even so, I was still reluctant to acknowledge that I had what I had. The only ones who knew were Mary, Dr. Kaplan (who put me back on medication), and my son and daughter. And two good friends who were going through the same thing and were much braver than I in sharing their experiences—writer William Styron and humorist Art Buchwald. Arty called me night after night. It was so reassuring to know that what I was feeling was normal for a depressed person, to talk to someone who'd been through it himself and come out the other side.

I continued to take refuge in prayer. When I couldn't sleep at night, I'd turn to the affirmation that had been a mainstay for nearly as long as I could remember. *Shema Yisrael Adonai Eloheinu Adonai Echad.* Those old, familiar words brought me back to my boyhood in Brookline, a town that was simply wonderful to grow up in; back to a place and a time as far away from this oppressive darkness as I could imagine.

Eventually the depression lifted, as it had the first time, and I went back to doing what I loved—reporting stories, playing tennis, going out on the town with Mary. But grateful as I was for the help I'd been given during my darkest days, I still worried that people might think less of me if they knew about my depression, so I kept quiet about it.

Then came the night I was a guest on the late-night TV interview show *Later with Bob Costas.* Bob planned to devote the show to my work, but while I was talking to him about *60 Minutes*, it suddenly occurred to me who might be watching television at one o'clock in the morning. *There are probably a lot of people listening at this moment who can't get to sleep because they're depressed,* I thought. *People who need to know that there's hope.*

That's when I finally went public about my depression. I wanted whoever might be listening and suffering to understand how low I'd sunk and how I was getting better every day with treatment. Help was out there for them too.

Depression, I'd come to see, was a part of me, something I'd always have to watch out for. The difference was, if it hit me again (and it did in 1993), I knew I couldn't retreat into its depths. I had to keep taking my medication and going to therapy, keep talking to people. In a way, that's been the key to my still going strong after eighty-three years. Every time I reach out beyond myself—to my family and friends, to my doctor, to my coworkers and the public to whom we bring the news, to the whole community of people who battle depressive disorders, and to the one I have turned to ever since I was a boy in Brookline—I find the hope that has led me out of the darkness.

DELLA REESE

I Choose to Believe

It came just like a thief in the night. I was taping the *Johnny Carson Tonight Show* at NBC studios in Burbank, California, that October evening in 1979. I had often hosted this show before and felt right at home as I walked out on the stage to sing my second song that night, "Little Boy Lost." The studio audience of some five hundred people who had applauded me so generously quieted down, my accompanist played the first plaintive notes on a bass fiddle. I drew in a deep breath, threw my head back, sang four bars and then I struck a flat note.

The studio and the audience revolved around me, my left knee gave way under my sequined gown, and I crumpled to the floor. Bandleader Doc Severinsen rushed up with a doctor and a nurse who happened to be in the audience. All I could do as they carried me to the ambulance was ask: "Lord, help me. God, help me."

And then everything faded away.

I awoke the next morning to look into the anguished face of my twenty-year-old daughter.

"Where am I, Dumpsey?" I asked.

"In the hospital." She leaned down and kissed me. "Oh, Mommy, I was so worried about you."

"Don't fret, child," I said, trying to smile. "God will take care of me." I glanced at my thirty-year-old adopted son—a psychiatrist— standing next to Dumpsey.

"What's wrong with me, Jim?"

"They believe you have an aneurysm," he said. "But they're going to transfer you to Midway Hospital for tests to find out more about it."

The tests were bad enough, but the grim look on the doctor's face when he came to report was worse.

"You have an aneurysm that has ruptured," he said, explaining that an artery in the right portion of my brain had ballooned and burst. "But we're afraid there may be something else," he added.

After I underwent another series of excruciating explorations, the doctor returned looking even more serious. He told me that two other aneurysms had formed on the left side of my brain, near the optic nerve. In time, with blood surging against the weakened arterial walls, these too would rupture, which could mean the end for me.

"Your only hope now is an operation," he said. "But, I must warn you about it. In operations like this—when the optic nerve is so closely involved—seven percent of the patients have ended up blind." He paused and looked at me seriously. "Or worse."

"What do you mean 'worse'?" I demanded.

He shifted uncomfortably in his chair. "Crippled, or with the loss of mental faculties."

After he left the room, I did a lot of thinking. No matter what he said, I realized I had a choice in the matter.

I remembered what Mama had said about choices when I was about five years old.

Mama and Papa raised us five sisters and a brother in a Detroit slum. But Mama wouldn't allow the outside to touch us inside.

She always made it clear that Jesus Christ was her personal choice. She showed it by living His way every day.

"Pray to Him and expect His help," she told us. "He will not let you down when you need Him."

Her way of life was our best example. Praying and believing were a part of living in our house. There were no set times, just a part of everyday living. And so, early in life, I had made my own choice.

As I grew into my teens and saw the fancy ladies in doorways, the careering police cars, and people nodding on dope, I was so grateful that I had made the right one. For it was my faith in Jesus and His guidance that kept me from that kind of life.

So I continued believing and praying, and I was blessed. The Lord had given me a voice and I had started using it in the church choir at age six. I grew up singing, and for three summers I sang with Mahalia Jackson in her gospel choir. But I thought music was just for fun, and when I entered Wayne University, I planned to major in psychiatry. However, in my freshman year Mama died of a cerebral hemorrhage; there was just not enough money for my schooling—I had to drop out.

So now I was on my own. I did everything from working a switchboard to driving a taxi. But the thing that never left me was my love for singing.

Alone in my cab one night, I switched on the radio. As I listened to some beautiful singing, I knew that was where my heart was. But in those days I also knew that gospel singers hardly earned travel money, and popular singers had to entertain in places like hotels, theaters and nightclubs, which I felt would compromise my religious beliefs.

I got to talking about it with my preacher, the Reverend E. A. Rundless of the New Liberty Baptist Church. He leaned forward in his chair and said, "Della, it's not so much what you do as how you feel inside when you do it. If you feel that you can do a good job for the Lord, why not try?"

I decided to take his advice. If I sang in a club, I'd be sure to include a song about Jesus. It sure wouldn't hurt the audience to hear it.

So I started out at age nineteen in a combination bowling alley and club, and went on from there. I worked a gospel song into each act, and the people seemed to love it. During my one year at college I had organized a gospel group called the Meditation Singers. Ten years later, I was established enough to bring them to Las Vegas to perform with me, and my career continued to blossom.

Now as I lay in the hospital bed, I realized I had another choice: listen to the doom-talking doctor, or call upon my friend Jesus, who promised that anything we ask in His name would be granted.

First thing I did was tell my family to keep that gloomy doctor out of my room. Then, for almost two weeks, while they made further studies and gave me medicine to help keep the blood from breaking through the arteries, I kept repeating over and over: "By the power in the name of Jesus Christ I am healed. By the power in the name of Jesus Christ I am healed."

And I believed that He would heal me. God had already saved me from the streets. He had answered my prayers for music, for everything. I knew He wouldn't let me down now.

Then my right eye began to blur; I would see two Dumpseys standing by my bed. The doctor said it was the aneurysms pressing on my optic nerve. An immediate operation was essential.

In the meantime my good friend, the Reverend Johnnie Coleman, came from Chicago and we prayed together. She laid hands on me and I knew then that all would be taken care of.

But there were only two brain surgeons in the world who could do the complicated surgery, one in Ontario, Canada, and the other in Zurich, Switzerland. Because quick action was needed, I was flown to

Ontario, where I met Dr. Charles Drake. I felt good about him. In his fifties, he was soft-spoken, kindly and, best of all, lighthearted.

We laughed and joked as he examined me. Then, when it was over, he sat down and looked straight into my eyes. "You know, Della. I can't do this surgery all by myself. I will do it with God's help."

I leaned back and relaxed. I was so grateful for this man who did not use eight-syllable words, who knew where his help came from. Within the hour, I was in the operating room where he opened my cranium and began working on the aneurysm.

Dr. Drake had recently designed a new type of surgical clip to protect the optic nerve during neurosurgery on aneurysms. He had sent it to Japan for various modifications and it had been returned to the hospital from Tokyo on the day I arrived. Until now, he had never tried it out.

As Dr. Drake worked on me, he looked at the clip resting on his instrument table and was faced with a choice. Should he use it? His first reaction was: No, it has not been tested yet. But he was overcome with a second thought: *Use it.*

So he obeyed what I believe was God's directive. He used the clip. After five hours of surgery, my shaved scalp was stitched ear to ear and I was returned to my room.

When I awoke, I felt good. Feeling the surgical cap covering my head, I just had to look into a mirror. I had got out of bed to get one when I heard a cry behind me. It was a nurse who had just stepped into the room.

"Oh, Miss Reese," she exclaimed, "you're supposed to stay flat and be elevated by only thirty degrees a day. Otherwise you'll suffer terrible migraine headaches."

"Well, honey," I smiled, "I just don't know about that. And neither does God," I added as I got back in bed.

A second operation to complete the aneurysm repairs followed, and it went well too.

Some people claim that in this life fate rolls over us like some giant steamroller no matter how much we pray. Well, I hate to think of what might have happened if I hadn't prayed, if I hadn't chosen to believe. Would the other aneurysms have held off from bursting? Would Dr. Drake have decided to use his new surgical clip? Would I have healed as miraculously fast as I did?

When I ask myself those questions, I just remember what I learned as a little girl. Jesus makes all the difference. If you pray to Him, and expect His help, you will be given it.

I know. Because I was.

CLIFTON DAVIS

Something to Live For

Perhaps you know me as the Reverend Reuben Gregory on the NBC television series *Amen*. You may even know I am a minister in real life.

But you probably don't know how far away from God I was eight years ago this Christmas. That was when I barricaded myself in my apartment in Hollywood, convinced I had nothing to live for.

It had been only seventeen years since I left home, where I had grown up as a preacher's kid. Being a "P.K." had its advantages and disadvantages. In one way I became very aware of spiritual things, the Gospel, liturgy and hymnology. All became second nature to me.

I was so accustomed to it that I became somewhat insensitive, even hardened, to the biddings of the Holy Spirit. When it came time to be baptized and to accept Christ in my life, I made only a perfunctory commitment. Yes, I had taken all the classes, and I knew what the church and Jesus expected of me, but spiritually I was empty.

When I saw people who called themselves Christians not practicing what they preached, my commitment faded. By the time I went to Oakwood College in Huntsville, Alabama, I had become disillusioned with the church, so I walked away from organized religion.

Impatient, wanting to spread my wings, I left college after a year and in 1963 started working as an engineer with ABC-TV in New York.

When I saw my first Broadway play, I knew that the theater was for me. I wanted to be an actor.

I quit my job to work as an apprentice at St. John Terrel's Music Circus in New Jersey, where I hung lights, made sets and acted in children's plays. My first big break came when I won a role in Broadway's *Hello Dolly* with Pearl Bailey. Soon other parts came, shows that led to my winning awards, even a nomination for Broadway's Tony. Then there was a TV series in Hollywood, *That's My Mama*, and a number of TV movies. It looked as though I had made it. But something inside me said that was not so.

Between jobs I was nervous. When I would land a new part I'd think, *I got it because I'm good,* and I'd glory in it. Then when the show was over, while waiting for the next job, I'd tell myself, *I'm nothing. Nobody loves me.* To cope with my insecurity, I sought the approval of women, traveled around the world and soothed myself with alcohol.

Finally, after one period without work, I told myself, *You're nothing. Get high and don't worry about it.*

By 1979, at the age of thirty-three, lost in a sea of broken relationships, I had succumbed to pressures and become a habitual drug user. Cocaine. I wasn't even aware that it was quietly twisting my senses, subtly turning me paranoid.

Within a year my addiction was destroying me. No director could depend on me anymore. My career went downhill. Having already gone through hundreds of thousands of dollars, I sold my Hollywood Hills home and spent half the money on drugs.

Moreover I was making things more and more difficult for my girlfriend, Ann Taylor. In one of my few lucid moments I realized I was actually a danger to her and sent her home to her mother. But Ann kept phoning me five or six times a day pleading, "Don't snort those drugs, Clifton. Please talk to me instead." I'd slam down the phone. Finally I stopped answering it altogether.

By mid-December 1980 I was drinking a quart of vodka every day and was down to skin and bones. I spent most of my time in my drab apartment. As Christmas approached, a terrible heaviness took over me. I felt there was nothing left for me. With my last thousand dollars, I bought drugs and planned to take an overdose.

While others in my building were hanging wreaths and decorations, I got a hammer and nailed my apartment door shut. I didn't want anyone coming in and stopping me. I scrawled my will on a linen napkin and left it lying on a table.

All through Christmas Day I hunched on my bed, arms locked around my knees, preparing to take that final dose.

Occasionally, faint strains of "Hark, the Herald Angels Sing" and "We Wish You a Merry Christmas" drifted in. The room darkened as night came on. Inside me, the deep hurting became unbearable. I readied myself for the final plunge.

The phone rang. For a while I wasn't even aware of it. But slowly it bore into my consciousness. Something compelled me to pick up the receiver. It was my brother Carlyle. "Clifton?" his voice trembled. I grunted.

"We're all worried about you," he said. "Mama dreamed last night that you were dying."

I started to hang up the phone. He was a pastor and I didn't want to hear any preaching.

"The whole family, with all your brothers and sisters, is here in Jacksonville, North Carolina," he pressed on, "but we are all so worried about you that none of us has opened our presents. Instead, we decided to have an all-night prayer meeting for you."

"Leave me alone, Carlyle," I slurred.

"The Lord has given us the strong impression that we should keep on trying to let you know that God still loves you, that He wants you to live."

"What . . . what does God want with me, anyway?" I groaned. "There's nothing for me. I've seen it all, done it all. Why are you calling?"

"Brother," he continued, "the Lord's got a word for you. It's from the Bible, Daniel 12:3," he said, "and I'm going to read it to you. 'And those who are wise shall shine like the brightness of the firmament; and those who turn many to righteousness, like the stars for ever and ever.'"

He was silent for a moment.

"Clifton," he went on, "God wants you to be a star for Him."

I wasn't sure what this all meant, but something about it touched me.

"Brother . . . will you kneel down and pray with me?"

Steadying myself, I knelt shakily on the floor. The only thing I could say was, "Lord, have mercy on me, a sinner."

Then, breaking down, weeping uncontrollably, I began to pray in moans and groans. Gradually I felt that I was being unburdened of all those terrible years of running away from God. I sensed Jesus standing by me, and I knew without a doubt that He had been standing by me all the time, waiting.

"All right, Lord," I cried, "I surrender to You my life. You do with it what You will. I can't promise You anything because I'm so weak that tomorrow I might get high. But if You take care of me today, I'll try my best to recommit my life to You tomorrow."

As I lay on that cold floor, a gentle hand seemed to touch my head and a warm peace filled me. Sometime during my prayer I had put the phone on its cradle. As I rose to my feet, my head seemed clearer than it had in years. Strange . . . I felt no need for cocaine.

That night, I left the apartment, somehow reached the Los Angeles airport and caught a plane for Jacksonville.

With my family's support I recommitted my life to Christ each day, and each day He was as true as His word. Within two weeks I was completely free of my drug habit. And as I stayed close to Him, doors strangely opened.

Financial help came when it was needed. Guidance too. I went back to college to study for the ministry. Recalling Carlyle's Bible verse, I felt the Lord wanted me to help turn other fallen people like me back "to righteousness."

I worried that cocaine might have diminished my learning capacity, which it can do, but through God's grace, I finished Oakwood College and went on to gain a master-of-divinity degree at Andrews University in Michigan.

More important, Ann Taylor, who had kept praying faithfully for me, had also waited for me. We were married, and today we have a young son and a little daughter, named Noel and Holly to mark the day that was so meaningful to me.

It's the day God showed me that I am something. That I am loved. That I do have something to live for.

We all do—because of Christmas Day.

TOM BOSLEY

Happy Days—and Others

January. Another new year, another ripe chance to begin again. I believe life has given me a pretty good deal. My career has been all that I dreamed back when I was a young, scrambling actor in Manhattan in the fifties. I have a wonderful family, a nice home. But there have been some tough times, times when I despaired that I would ever struggle through another twelve months, when I sensed I was merely going through the dull motions of an empty life.

What do you do then? You stare out your kitchen window wondering if there is any point to anything. You have a hard time imagining that things could ever get better. Yet when life seems bleakest, that's precisely the time I've learned to lean hardest on hope, the very kind of hope that keeps you moving no matter what.

Believe me, hope is something we actors could never get by without. We need it abundantly, especially when we're just starting and the odds are that we won't eke out even a minimal existence in the theater. I arrived in New York City from Chicago, where I'd trained in radio broadcasting after discovering in high school plays that I loved working for an audience. Like most actors, at first I did about everything to make a living but set foot on a stage. I was a bookkeeper for a cigar company and a doorman at Tavern on the Green Restaurant in Central Park. And I was a hatcheck boy at Lindy's, the famous deli with the wisecracking waiters; I got fired there because I returned boxer Joe Louis' tip. I figured he needed the money more than I did, with the IRS after him and all.

Between paychecks I scoured the pages of *Back Stage* for auditions. I badgered my agent to submit my paltry résumé and even got a few small off-off-Broadway parts. I called and recalled the contacts I'd made in the business. And with each rejection, each audition that didn't yield a callback, I clung fast to hope, waiting.

Then came that role. It was unexpected. I thought I'd been called for an understudy audition in the new Broadway musical *Fiorello!* about the celebrated mayor of New York, Fiorello La Guardia. To my utter astonishment, I was chosen to play the lead role of the "Little Flower" himself, a lead role in a big, brassy Broadway extravaganza. It was an actor's dream come true, and like that my career took off! I won a 1960 Tony Award for the part. I got something else out of the play too, something far, far greater.

There was a girl in the chorus, a former Rockette named Jean. She was a willowy, green-eyed beauty who'd replaced another dancer I'd dated for a time. Jean was a constant distraction. Finally I got up the gumption to ask her out. It was not long before my wife-to-be and I were an item, though she never tired of teasing me about my previous love interest. "Tom, you were always in love with the costume," she'd laugh, her green eyes dancing.

For sixteen years I laughed at that joke, though we both knew it had been love at first sight.

Every life has turning points. That show was certainly one for me. Stage and then film offers came. There was interest from television. With Amy, our newborn daughter, Jean and I moved out to Los Angeles, where eventually I landed the role of Howard Cunningham in the series *Happy Days* on ABC. My career was going just as planned.

Then one night I came home from the day's taping to find Jean lying down with a bandage on her head. "Honey, what happened?" I demanded, alarmed.

"Well, I'm not sure," she tried to explain. She'd had a mysterious seizure. The cut on her head was relatively minor, but we were both scared. The next day she had three more seizures. It was terrifying. This was before much of today's medical technology had been perfected, and doctors were baffled by Jean's problems. It took five years before we got the diagnosis we'd dreaded most: an incurable brain tumor.

A hopeless, heartbreaking year followed. Jean lay in the Motion Picture Home in Woodland Hills, California, helpless. She could barely communicate or recognize anyone. She was barely alive. And after a while so was I.

Finally Jean died and with her a part of me also felt it had died. I tried to be a good father to Amy. Never far from my mind, though, was Jean. I'd think about the high-kicking chorus dancer with the irresistible eyes.

Yet I knew I had to go on somehow, so I plunged into my work with a kind of manic drive. The day after Jean was buried, I made breakfast for Amy, sent her off to school and went out to the studio at my usual prompt hour. We were shooting a TV movie called *The Triangle Factory Fire* about a real incident where many women perished in a 1911 factory blaze. I played a widower of one of the workers, and in the scene I was to make breakfast for my little girl while she asked, "Daddy, why did Mommy have to die?"

When I came on the set, the director tugged me quickly aside. "Look, Tom, we can do this scene later. Why don't you take the day off, at least." No, I was there to work. I had to work.

I went on that way, on automatic pilot. Running beneath that hectic pace was a deeper current of despair. It was as if I was going through the motions of living with no hope of ever truly being happy again. There was my work, there was my daughter, but there was no real me.

Then the American Cancer Society asked if I would cochair their education crusade. I said yes, assuming my role would be to raise money. But I was surprised that this time my job was to talk to volunteers who would themselves do the money-raising. Most of them had lost someone to cancer.

For the first time I spoke publicly about Jean's death, talking to others who knew how I felt. Suddenly that was another turning point. I would hear myself saying, "You have to go on, you have to have hope that the pain of loss will eventually recede."

It was advice I should have been following all along, though it was easier said than done. But by saying it, I began to trust in it. Getting involved with the cancer society got me outside myself and my aching grief. I began to do things.

Then about two years after Jean's death an old friend, Bob Cole, who had once hired me as a temporary office-worker in my old New York days, asked me to get involved with a theater project he was starting for handicapped kids. As usual I reached for my checkbook. Bob stopped me. "No, Tom," he smiled, "I mean really involved."

And so I came to sit on the board of directors of The Performing Arts Theatre of the Handicapped, in Los Angeles, along with Ron Howard, Henry Winkler and others Bob conscripted from the acting community. At that first meeting I sat across from a woman named Patricia, a dancer and producer. She was sharp and stunning and very blond and I couldn't keep my eyes off her. Whenever she caught me staring I would blush and look down at my notepad. Eventually I put her on my committee, she put me on hers, and we got acquainted.

By now I'd experimented with dating again and had found it to be as nerve-racking as when I was twenty. Suddenly those long-ago opening nights on Broadway with the critics in the house, pens poised and your future in their finicky hands, seemed like a piece of cake compared to this. I was out of practice; I felt clumsy taking out women I hardly knew. But finally I found the nerve to ask Patricia to dinner. We had a great evening and afterward I took her home and met her children.

Then the night of our first date I suddenly blurted out, "Don't be surprised if we get married!" Patti looked more stunned than pleased, but she laughed in that musical way of hers. Later she assured me that she would never consider marrying a man who didn't get down on his knees and propose. Was that supposed to fend me off somehow? Was she saying a guy my age wasn't capable of getting on his knees? Many dates later I found out where she parked during the day—a garage in the middle of Beverly Hills. At about quitting time I went there. As she wheeled her car from the garage there I was, kneeling in the driveway. Patti hit the brakes and stared wide-eyed and open-mouthed from behind the wheel. Cars began to stack up behind her, horns wailed.

"I'm not moving till you give me an answer," I said stubbornly. More in desperation than passion, I've always suspected, Patti acquiesced.

So here it is January again. Patti and I were married eleven happy years ago, during Christmas week. And as another year begins, I remember the hope that led me from the darkness of my grief. It's been there all along—like the hope described in a favorite line from the poet Emily Dickinson; she said hope "perches in the soul."

I always thought that was the right way to put it, for hope does abide in the soul. It is hope to which we must all hold fast, every year, every day, if we are to go on and meet the challenges God gives us.

WALLY CROWDER

One Take Only

I sat there that day in the driver's seat of the big, shiny black Lincoln Continental, staring out past the end of the pier in San Pedro, California. For a moment I felt butterflies in my stomach again. At the last minute you always feel a little bit of hesitation, a temptation not to go through with it. But I knew I would. In minutes I would be driving that Lincoln at full speed straight ahead off the end of the pier and into the Pacific Ocean. I didn't intend to die or be injured. I'd planned this very carefully—I thought.

I'm a stuntman. And that day I was working on the TV movie *Charlie's Balloon*, doubling as a gangster who, literally, takes a long drive off a short pier.

And even though I thought I'd planned for every eventuality in this stunt, I realized there was always a small chance of an accident. That's why I had been extra careful this time and hired a "safety," another stuntman to ride with me as a passenger, so that if something did go wrong, one of us could help the other out.

Well, I never could have foreseen how I'd need much more than a safety on that stunt.

I'd been in the stunt business only a couple of years when I accepted this job, but by now I was experienced enough not to be worried. I'd been racing stock cars for years, even while I was working full-time as a youth pastor, and the transition to full-time stunt work was not that much of a leap. I was moonlighting as a driver in automobile commercials when I was asked to do my first stunt. The director decided he wanted to use two cars in the commercial instead of one, in a stunt in which the two vehicles would race toward each other and, after hitting a mark, stop on a dime and wind up nose-to-nose. The driving coordinator asked if I thought I could do that.

Piece of cake. The driving coordinator was impressed. And so my career as a stuntman began.

Now, a stuntman isn't some daredevil who spent his childhood picking fights and falling out of trees. He's more of an athlete, a professional whose motto is, Safety first. No piece of film is ever worth an injury, or worse.

That's why we had taken every possible precaution that day in San Pedro, in Los Angeles Harbor, for the *Charlie's Balloon* stunt. The movie's second unit was set up and ready for action. The film crew had been looking forward to the shoot; stunt scenes are always fun and challenging, a break from routine.

Usually in films, you shoot many takes of each scene. But with this scene, since we had only one car, there would be multiple cameras but only one take. It had to be perfect the first time.

Sitting in the car waiting for the cameras to roll, I mentally went over my safety checklist. This pier was fifteen to twenty feet above water, higher than is optimal. You want the car to land flat, so that you have more time to get out before it sinks. The longer the drop from the pier, the more time for the heavier front end of the car to hit first, the engine's weight dragging you down beneath the waves. Cars float for vastly different periods of time, depending on the make and construction. Volkswagens, for example, never sink. You can paddle them from LA to Catalina.

The Lincoln was much heavier than a VW, of course. Ideally I wanted to be out before it sank, but you don't count on the ideal. You prepare for every contingency. Safety divers had already gone down to check the water depth and what was on the ocean floor. They'd found the water dark and murky, and the bottom covered with silt and mud. With any luck I'd never see that.

I'd reinforced the car's windshield with heavy Lexan, an industrial-strength plastic. Normal windshields are made of safety glass; with an impact at forty mph, they're gone. I'd added a metal roll bar across the inside top of the car to keep the roof from caving in should the car flip over and land upside down. And we left the electrically powered windows open.

Inside the car, we'd installed five-point seat belts, the kind racecar drivers wear. They go over the shoulders, across the waist and between your legs. Next to me in the car was bolted an Aqua-Lung, with an extra tank of air, enough for one hour underwater.

Besides the usual film crew, there were two safety divers hidden beneath the pier in case of emergency—for example, if I lost consciousness.

On this particular day, my biggest decision had been to hire the safety to ride in the car with me. For the camera crew this would be a "long shot," filmed from a distance. Since the audience wouldn't be able to see who was in the car, I had the choice of belting a mannequin into the passenger's seat to double for the second gangster. But the drop was so long and a Lincoln is so heavy that I decided it was worth it to split my earnings with a safety.

The cameras started rolling. The director gave us the signal. I stepped on the gas.

The pier blurred past us as we picked up speed. Then we

were airborne, flying between sky and sea on a breezy California afternoon.

But immediately the front end dipped downward. We hit the water at an angle. The impact was intense. The windshield exploded. Shards of glass tore my face. Saltwater rushed in through the jagged, gaping hole in the windshield. My face burned with the scorpionlike sting of saltwater hitting open wounds. The force of the water pinned me back. Within moments we were swallowed by the pitch-blackness of the muddy water.

I fumbled for the catch that would release my seat belt. Across the seat from me, the safety, not confined behind a steering wheel, was able to move much more freely. He unbuckled his seat belt. Then he struggled out of the side window. I last saw him swimming for the surface.

I began to panic. The car was flipping over. I couldn't tell which way was up. Fighting fear, I knew I should stay put and stay in the car till it hit bottom and I could get oriented.

Down I went, rapidly, through forty feet of water. I grabbed for the Aqua-Lung, gasping for air.

The car landed upside down and proceeded to sink into four feet of mire and slime.

I was buried upside down in mud forty feet underwater. Mud clogged my eyes and nose. I couldn't see. I couldn't free myself from the seat belt. Visibility was zero. It could take the divers hours to find me. Blood was rushing to my head. I could lose consciousness. The pro who was trained never to be stuck without a way of escape was helpless.

I was panicking, thinking of my wife and kids, telling myself that I didn't want to die, when out of nowhere, in a clear voice, came the order, "Relax, stupid." Two words spoken in a calm, friendly, commanding voice. *Who spoke them? Could it be God? But does God call people stupid?* Yet the intimacy of the words, the good-natured jibe, almost made me laugh.

That was exactly what was needed to cut through my terror. *Thanks, Lord,* I said in my mind.

He was completely right. I'd been stupid. There was no reason to panic. I'd forgotten: I had air, I was conscious, I had everything I needed to get out of the situation.

I relaxed. The mire eventually settled. Slowly, gingerly, I found the twisted buckle to my seat belt. I undid it. While still upside down, I located the crushed roof and felt around for the open rear window. I wiggled out of it.

Then, like a practical joker, I thought, *Hey, I have an hour of air. I could just wait down here and see how good those safety divers are at finding me.* But of course I couldn't do that. I swam to the surface.

Air has never tasted sweeter than it did that day off the San Pedro pier. I didn't even notice that my face was streaming with blood until I was safely on land.

I have learned a number of things because of that incident. I learned that when driving a car into water, one must add a second duplicate windshield on top of the first—with chicken wire in between. I learned to take down a pink balloon that you can let out of the sunken car to bring the divers straight over to you. And I developed a way to foam the trunk and the backseat so that even if a heavy car goes under, it will bob back up.

But here's the most important lesson I learned: In a stunt, as well as in the tough situations of life, don't panic. That's what the voice was telling me under forty feet of water.

Be quiet. Think things through. It's in the quiet that we can find a way out.

HARRY CONNICK JR.

WITH COLLEEN HUGHES

After Katrina

What a year this has been! Even as little as six months ago, I couldn't have imagined what lay ahead. If I've learned just one thing from this past year—and I've learned a lot—it's that life can change completely in the blink of an eye. Back in August, the last person I thought I'd be on the phone with as contributing editor for *Guideposts* was piano player Harry Connick Jr., a beloved son of the Crescent City. All I cared about and was praying for then was the safety of my own family in and around the Big Easy. You might remember my story in the November 2005 issue of *Guideposts*. Since we prepare the magazine in advance, I told "My Precious City" in the immediate aftershock of Katrina. When we went to press there was so much we still didn't know.

Now some time has passed, and this Christmas, believe it or not, we're going to count our blessings. Mama called me the other day. "Colleen, I don't care what's happened. This will be the best Christmas ever."

I had to swallow a lump in my throat before I replied. "I know what you mean, Mama." She has certainly been on an emotional roller coaster these past months. We had good news and bad news as the waters receded from Katrina, then rose and receded again in the wake of Rita.

Best Christmas ever? I didn't know about that. In the excitement of the holidays, and with the way our culture moves so fast these days, I wondered if the poor people of the Gulf Coast would be forgotten. I could no longer turn on CNN at any time and see pictures of New Orleans with up-to-the-minute reports of what was happening. My new worries extended far beyond my own family's troubles to the entire Gulf Coast region and what we could honestly expect over time. How would we keep the country's attention focused on our crisis when we knew there were other challenges at hand? Had the media moved on before we'd had a chance to address this tragedy with all our collective might? It didn't seem right to be buying Christmas presents when there was so much work to be done, rebuilding neighborhoods and schools, churches and levees. Lives, families and entire communities were still torn asunder.

I knew that Harry Connick Jr. was involved with Habitat for Humanity and dedicated to the long-term effort to rebuild the Gulf Coast. *Guideposts* arranged for me to talk to him. "I'm from Metairie," I said by way of introduction. "We used to see you at church with your daddy sometimes at St. Louis King of France. My brothers went to Jesuit"—Harry's high school too—"and my parents are friendly with your aunt Jessie and uncle John."

"Cool," Harry said. "I used to go with a girl from Metairie." Famous or not, every New Orleanian was connected in one way or another. If you reached back far enough and told enough stories, it would come out that somebody knew somebody that you knew. Probably because people who grew up in New Orleans tended to stay there. Harry and I are unusual in that regard. We'd moved to New York.

"I was up north when I got a call from my dad saying Katrina could be a bad one," Harry said. "He and my stepmom left for higher ground. Hurricane passed. We thought we could breathe easy. A day later I couldn't believe the images I was seeing on TV." Harry did exactly what I wanted to do but couldn't: He went back. Right into the chaos. "These people," he said, "our people, needed help and nobody was coming. Nobody! I took what I had and hoped it would bring attention."

It had worked. Harry took two boat trips into the city, both broadcast on the *Today* show. He passed people wading chest-deep in water, plastic bags of possessions held high above their heads, their whole lives in bags. Some asked for food or water or where to go for rest. "We ferried people from their porches to our SUV, and on to shelter. Some insisted on waiting it out. They didn't want to leave their homes, much less their city. Some of these people had never been out of their neighborhood. The water would go down; they'd just wait."

Some think we move slow down in New Orleans. I say we're patient. You learn to wait things out. Like floods. "Yeah," said Harry, "the water recedes; maybe you have to get new carpets. So what. Hurricanes were just something we got. Remember when we were kids? You grow up with the excitement of them. 'Hey, hurricane's coming. School's closed!' You know something powerful is on the way, but you know it'll pass, and maybe you'll get to splash around in the street, cool off some." Not that you needed a hurricane for street flooding. A good summer rain would put water in New Orleans.

Harry took a boat to the neighborhoods uptown. Everything looked pretty dry around his dad's house and Harry reported to him on his cell phone. "You could actually walk around much of the French Quarter downtown," Harry said. It sits on pretty high ground for New Orleans. But the highest ground in New Orleans, at least in a spiritual sense, is St. Louis Cathedral in Jackson Square. "We passed by Jackson

Square and the cathedral. That's where I got married." The proud symbol of our city, one of the oldest cathedrals in the United States, was miraculously unscathed. Harry walked around back to the courtyard, anxious to check out the marble statue of Jesus, who stood guard among the tall oak and magnolia trees, his arms outstretched over the city. "The courtyard looked like a war zone," Harry said, shocked. "Two huge oaks toppled over. Torn from the ground. Root systems taller than me." The trees lay side by side in a tangle of dirt and broken branches. Chaos. Except for what stood in between: The statue of Jesus, untouched, save for a couple fingers. At the statue's base is an inscription: *J'ai confiance en vous* (I have confidence in you).

"I have faith in my brothers and sisters of New Orleans, Colleen. You can flood the streets, you can burn the buildings, you can leave the city unprotected. But you can't destroy the spirit of the people who live there. This is why we go to church on Sundays. This is what we've been getting ourselves ready for."

I heard what Harry was saying. This was why we practiced our faith, in church on Sundays and all the days in between. Because there would come a time when we'd have to buckle down and use the faith we'd built up. Put it to the test. Draw on it as a resource of strength and reassurance in our desperate time of need.

There are a million things you can do this holiday season and beyond. A ton of good organizations need your help and your dollars. "Me," Harry said, "I'm working with Habitat for Humanity's hurricane recovery effort, 'Operation Home Delivery,' on the Gulf Coast. We need houses to come home to. We need to rebuild our schools, our churches and synagogues, our communities. This is going to take a while and we will have to stay committed for the long haul. It's not a short-term deal."

Like I said, we are patient down in New Orleans. And we will have to be. We will have to ask all who help us to be, to stand by us and support us long after the floodwaters recede. With all of us working together, in faith, we'll make a new beginning for the Crescent City and the entire Gulf Coast. What better time to celebrate a new beginning than Christmas, when a son born to the world meant rebirth for us all? Yep, Harry's right.

This is why we go to church on Sundays.

JIM STOVALL

"Yes, You Can!"

I was at a Colorado Springs convention center in the quiet of late afternoon, preparing to speak at a dinner that night. It seemed that everybody else was off skiing as I stepped onto the deserted patio outside my room. As I took a deep breath of crisp air, I heard a deer rustling for berries in the bushes. I had been told the deer here were tame; maybe I could actually touch one. I moved quietly toward the sound, reaching out. . . .

Suddenly I was plunging downhill, tumbling down a rocky slope some thirty or forty feet until I crash-landed in a heap. I had walked off the edge of the patio. There I lay, cold and wet in the snow. I'm a big guy, but I felt pretty beat up, as well as scared and disoriented.

No, I hadn't noticed how close I was to the edge of the patio, or that there was a steep drop-off.

I'm blind. I can't see a thing.

When I was seventeen, a normal all-American kid in Oklahoma, I went to the doctor for a routine physical. He shone a light into my eyes and sent me off for a battery of tests. The news wasn't good: I had a degenerative eye disease and would progressively lose my sight.

It's a devastating thing for anybody to face, much less a happy-go-lucky teenager. I had never even met a blind person. How did blind people act? What did they do?

As terrible as the news was, it focused my mind in a practical way.

If I wanted to stay independent and make a living, college seemed a necessity. I enrolled at a local university, but it was the early 1980s and there were no facilities or arrangements for handicapped students. I always seemed to be groping around in a gray haze.

During this time, while I still had limited vision, I began volunteering at a school for blind kids. The teachers put me in charge of a four-year-old they thought was particularly difficult to deal with. They didn't have many expectations for this little boy; because of multiple handicaps, they said he would never be able to tie his own shoes or climb stairs. I was determined to prove them wrong.

"You can tie your shoes," I told him. "You can climb stairs." The little boy was just as determined to resist. He said, "No, I can't," and I said, "Yes, you can." We went back and forth like that constantly.

The truth was, I was having trouble saying, "Yes, you can" to my own life. Keeping up with college courses was increasingly hard, and the day came when I decided to call it quits. On my way to the administration building to drop out, I went to the school for blind kids and announced I wouldn't be volunteering anymore either. "It's too tough," I said. "I can't do it."

"Yes, you can!" a little voice piped up beside me. The four-year-old had been listening.

"No, I can't!" I said sharply.

"Yes, you can!"

Then it hit me. I had to keep on trying or admit I had been lying to this kid that the extra effort was worth it. And in that second I knew: It was worth it—for him, and for me.

I resumed college, listening even more attentively as other students read my assignments aloud. One of the sounds that kept me going was the gentle voice of a young woman named Crystal, who read to me patiently week after week. Three and a half years later I graduated. That same week I stood by as the little boy who had said, "No, I can't" climbed three flights of stairs by himself, sat on the top step and tied his shoes.

My dream was to start some kind of business. When I talked this over with my dad, he said, "Come back tomorrow and I'll give you something." Great, I thought, he's probably going to stake me to some money. Instead Dad announced he had arranged for me to have a series of visits with a local man named Lee Braxton. With only a grade-school education, Braxton had become an entrepreneur and made a fortune during the Depression, money he had then used to start and support many charitable and educational organizations. Now he was in his seventies, and I went to his house to listen to his philosophy of life.

One of his favorite biblical passages was, "For God hath not given us the spirit of fear; but of power, and of love, and of a sound mind." Each time, I left his house feeling built up and full of courage. I asked Mr. Braxton how I could ever thank him. He said, "Someday God will give you the opportunity to encourage other people—and you'll pay me back by doing just that."

I was able to start my own investment brokerage and I married Crystal. Then at the age of twenty-nine I lost the remainder of my sight. Any shadings of light that I had previously seen were gone.

I set up a room in my house carefully arranged with everything where I'd always be able to find it. My business was successful, and it was my intention to operate out of this room, where events would be predictable and under my control, more or less forever. I wouldn't fear being awkward or embarrassed or hurt by unknown or unfamiliar situations. I believed that I could spend my entire life here—and for a while I did, mired in deep depression.

But my friends and family helped me work through my blackness. Slowly I started to get back in touch with activities I had enjoyed. I had always loved classic films, and one day I put a Humphrey Bogart movie into the VCR. Even though I couldn't see, I figured I could still follow the plot by listening to the dialogue and sound effects. But about twenty minutes into the film, a character in the movie screamed, there was the squeal of brakes and somebody apparently fled. What was happening?

As the movie went on, I realized there were many other moments when actions or images must have been on the screen explaining or advancing the plot—but I had no idea what they were! Extremely frustrated, I thought: *If the voice of a narrator could be added to describe what was going on, then millions of blind and visually impaired people in the United States could enjoy the movie too.*

It was time to come out of that room. Working with Kathy Harper, a wonderful friend and colleague who is legally blind herself, I started out in 1988 in the basement of a condo in Tulsa. We got permission from the owners of the films to add descriptive narrative to the soundtracks of classics such as *The African Queen* and *It's A Wonderful Life*. Using borrowed equipment, we created a sound studio in a broom closet under my stairs, and I recorded the additional commentary about setting and action.

So far, so good. But now we were technically stumped. I called a Tulsa TV studio and asked for help. "Sure," was the answer. "Our most expert guy will work with you."

I showed up the next day with all our tapes and wires in a cardboard box, explaining that we hoped to splice our newly recorded material onto each movie's soundtrack. "Forget it," the engineer said. "What you're trying to do is impossible."

So I went back to the head of the station and asked him, "You got anybody a little less expert?" Out came a kid, maybe eighteen or nineteen, and I told him what I wanted to do. "Let's try it," he said. He fiddled around in the editing room—and it all came together!

The next step was to try to get our shows on TV. We took a less expert point of view on that one too; after a number of telephone calls, we reached a cable company that agreed to let us air several hours of films on one of their channels. We whipped off letters to "impossible-to-get" celebrities such as Katharine Hepburn, Jack Lemmon and Eddie Albert, asking them to appear on a half-hour show about the films—and they agreed. Every step along the way, it seemed we were too naive to know our dream couldn't work.

Officially launched in 1988, our organization was named the Narrative Television Network. As more and more cable stations picked up our offerings, letters from viewers started pouring in. "For the twenty hours a week that your shows are on," one woman wrote, "you make me forget that I'm blind." It made me all the more committed to continue doing things the "experts" told me were hopeless.

As we added our narrative to more and more movies, channels across the country signed up to carry our programming. In October 1990 I went to New York to pick up an Emmy from the National Academy of Television Arts and Sciences for outstanding contributions to the industry, and other prestigious awards followed. Since I was onscreen a lot as host of many of the programs, offers arrived asking me to be a motivational speaker. That meant really coming out of my safe room, navigating airports and crowded rooms and coping with unfamiliar surroundings.

So there I was in Colorado Springs, scuffed up at the bottom of a slope, freezing cold and bone-tired. Nobody knew where I was, and I wasn't even sure myself. I thought longingly of that room in my house where everything was predictable and safe.

But I also remembered my friend Lee Braxton, and somehow I felt he was saying to me, "Tonight somebody is coming who needs to hear you, and you owe me. God's giving you the opportunity to encourage other people. Get back up this mountain and get ready to give that speech."

I started climbing the hill, hand over hand. Finally I came to the top and felt around till I found a place I could climb back on the patio, then worked my way from door to door—all locked—until I found the one to my room that I had left ajar. I got cleaned up, and gave my speech.

It was a speech I give often, and one of the things I told the audience has become a theme for me: Whatever your situation in life, you too can step out of that safe room and proceed with faith minute by minute, hand over hand, not worrying about what lies ahead or what might happen, but trusting that God will supply you the energy and courage to cope with each experience as it arises.

Yes, there'll be times you will fall off the patio. And you'll feel like shouting, "No, I can't." But I've got news for you: Yes, you can!

ROBBY BENSON

A Comeback Role

I pushed off from ten thousand feet down a ski slope in Park City, Utah, and began my last run of the day. My wife Karla and our two kids were waiting at the bottom for me. It was great to be spending so much time with them. In a month I'd be directing television shows and teaching again. A congenital heart defect had ended my days of being a lead film actor thirteen years earlier, but now my career was more rewarding than ever. Life was sweet.

I settled into a rhythm on my skis. In the distance, I could see a stand of powdery white aspen trees framed by the setting sun. Ever since I was a kid growing up in a New York City apartment overlooking the Hudson River, there'd been few things that soothed my soul like a fantastic view. I inhaled deeply and took in the scene before me. Suddenly that scene got fuzzy. I felt woozy, as if I were going to pass out. It seemed like I might lose control of my skis. *Oh no, this is it,* I thought. *The moment I'd been dreading.*

I made it safely to the bottom. Karla rushed up to greet me. "Wow, you were really flying. What's up, speed racer?"

I just smiled and wrapped my arm around her. I knew exactly what had happened on the mountain, but I didn't want to tell Karla. Not yet. I suspected that the bovine heart valve that had kept me alive since my heart defect was diagnosed in the early eighties had torn. Now I would need another major operation, during which my heart would be stopped. I'd be kept alive only by a heart-lung machine while the valve was replaced, just as the doctors had warned me it would someday need to be.

Funny, I hadn't dreaded the first operation this way. I'd even laughed at the irony—the former teen heartthrob with a bad heart. I was only twenty-eight then, married to Karla for just two years, with a one-year-old daughter, Lyric. A lifelong jock, I'd made my name playing athletic boy-next-door types in movies such as *One on One*, *Running Brave* and *Ice Castles*. Just a year earlier I'd finished the New York City Marathon in less than three hours.

But I started getting so short of breath I couldn't lift my daughter. I was diagnosed as having been born with a bicuspid (two-leaflet) heart valve instead of a normal tricuspid (three-leaflet) valve. My overworked aortic valve had worn away over the years and my heart had swollen to nearly twice its normal size.

"You always say I have the biggest heart of anyone you know," I'd joked to Karla. I guess I was young enough to still think I was invincible. Doctors told me if I got a mechanical replacement valve, I'd need to be on blood thinners for the rest of my life, which meant no more sports because of the risk of internal bleeding. The other option was receiving a valve made from cadaver, pig or cow tissue, but the tissues would eventually calcify and I'd need a new valve about ten years down the line.

I knew my days as a leading man were over. But I couldn't give up being active, playing with my family. I opted for a bovine valve. It was strange enough knowing part of a cow was going to be transplanted inside me. Weirder still was knowing a machine would be pumping oxygen into my blood and my blood through my body for five hours while doctors worked on my lifeless heart.

Two days after the surgery I was running up and down the hospital stairs. Two months later I finished a 10K run. My recovery was so smooth I was shocked to learn that my hospital roommate, a middle-aged man who was having his second aortic-valve-replacement surgery, had died. But not on the operating table. Three weeks after going home, he'd committed suicide. Sure, recovery could be painful and discouraging, but it shocked me that someone would take his own life after just having surgery to save it.

Now I was in that man's shoes—middle-aged and facing my second open-heart surgery. And there was nothing to joke about this time. I couldn't push aside my fear anymore.

Back at sea level in Los Angeles, there was more oxygen than in the mountains, and my symptoms weren't too bad. I took a job directing a sitcom pilot. I had to provide for my family, I rationalized, in case there were complications during surgery and I couldn't work anymore. I'd rebuilt my life once already—trading acting for directing episodes of hit sitcoms like *Friends*, teaching university acting, filmmaking and screenwriting students and doing voice-over work, such as the voice of the Beast in the Disney movie *Beauty and the Beast*. I just didn't know if I would have the energy to start over again. Lying awake beside Karla at night, I'd put my hand over my heart, willing it to beat another day.

As soon as the directing job ended, I confessed to Karla about the blown valve. I don't think she'd ever been more upset with me—or worried. We drove straight to my cardiologist's office.

"You're very lucky to still be alive, Mr. Benson," he told me. "We can't afford to wait any longer. I'll schedule surgery for tomorrow."

I knew I was lucky. After all, my valve had already lasted four years longer than expected. Until now I'd been able to work and play as hard as anyone. Would I be so lucky this time?

Doctors thought my best chance was a new surgery called the Ross Procedure. First they would use my own pulmonary valve to replace my aortic valve. The hope was that it would last longer than a bovine valve. Then they'd replace my pulmonary valve with a cadaver valve. I knew my recovery would be slower this time because I was older, and more painful because of the scar tissue from the first operation. But what really got to me was that this surgery would take twice as long as the first. I kept thinking about that.

Karla's face was the first thing I saw when I woke up. Lyric and our son Zephyr were in my room too. *I made it!* I thought. I was so grateful the doctors had fixed me again. As soon as I was alone, though, a strange cloud descended on me. Shadowy thoughts drifted through my mind: What was the point of all this? I still have to have another surgery one day. And another after that. And each time I'll be weaker. I tried to shake off the thoughts, but they kept coming. *You're weak. You won't be able to support your family. Your life is over.*

I looked out the window at the rugged hills under the cloudless California sky. But even the view couldn't lighten my mood. It was as if the darkness had been transplanted into me along with the new valve.

My family helped keep my spirits up while I recovered. Five weeks after my surgery I took a job directing the first episodes of a new show called *Jesse*, which was slated for the choice time slot following *Friends*. Karla thought it was too soon, yet I went full throttle, confident I would thrive on the pressure. But the dark negative thinking only got worse. I'd never experienced anything like it. I'd always been such a positive, high-energy person. I thought of my old hospital roommate. *Was this how he'd felt?*

One night in my office I sank to my knees, shaking uncontrollably.

It took all my strength to get the phone and call Karla. I was still shaking when she arrived.

"I can't go on like this," I said in a hoarse whisper. "I'm so tired. It's not my heart. It's me. I'm not me anymore."

Karla pulled me close. "Yes, you are," she said. "You're alive and that's all that matters. What would the kids and I do without you? We are so blessed."

I hadn't been feeling blessed. Anything but. Yet here I was with another second chance. All my life I'd been going full speed, just like down that slope in Park City, the beautiful view rushing by. Yet what were the real views in my life? I had my family, my work. And I had my health. Even if it wasn't exactly on my terms. Every minute that passed, my heart was beating, each heartbeat another chance. That was a profound blessing, a gift from God that would see me through this struggle.

I went to my doctor and learned my depression had been triggered by changes in brain chemistry caused by being on the heart-lung machine. That's probably what happened to my old roommate too. But doctors hadn't known about this effect then, so he'd been alone in his suffering. I was lucky—blessed, rather—that help was offered to me. I got counseling and began to believe that even if I couldn't see any light, there was light out there. I used my director's imagination to envision what it would feel like to be well again. And I started taking things one action at a time, as though I were blocking a scene. All I had to do was make one move and then another and another.

Five years later, I am long past the darkness, teaching in North Carolina and producing a play based on a new way of thinking; a truer, deeper way of living and loving moment to moment, heartbeat to heartbeat. And you know something? The view is beautiful.

LISTENING TO YOUR HEART

For five nights the torment lasted . . .

sleeplessness . . . emptiness . . . straining to know . . .

reaching out for something. On the fifth night it happened.

I can't describe it in any other way than to say that

a cloud about me seemed to lift, the answer of faith

formed a pathway to light: He was! He is!

DIANE SAWYER

DIANE SAWYER

Bird on My Shoulder

I was sitting alone in my room at Wellesley College trying to write
on the subject, "Why I Believe in God." After hours of walking in
circles—both mentally and physically—I decided to try out my ideas
on some of the other students in the dorm. A lively argument began.
I sensed in those girls the same confusion that I'd felt so often. Yes,
and the same need for answers.

Perhaps it was different in the adult world. But it seemed to me
in high school—and in college too—that when we young people set
out to find God with our reason, we reached a dead-end every time.
For me, truth was like a parakeet let out of its cage. I chased it around
my room, across the campus, into the chapel itself, but it flew farther
away all the time.

And then when I'd stopped racing after it, perhaps when I was not
even thinking about it, it would come gently and light on my shoulder.

I had one of these inexpressible nudges from something outside
myself the day before the Junior Miss Pageant began in March 1963.
I was driving into Louisville late that afternoon on some last-minute
errands. Suddenly a rabbit was under the wheels of the car—before I
could even begin to use the brakes. I knew I had hit the animal
although there was no impact. I drove on.

Then, inexplicably, I was blinded by tears. An impulse that was
not my own said, "Stop. Go back. Don't leave the rabbit on the road."

"That's silly," my rational self replied. "You just don't stop to pick up a rabbit. Besides, it wasn't my fault."

But the tears blinded me so that I hardly could see ahead. "I won't turn around," I repeated. Everything human in me said, "Drive on."

Yet that something stronger kept insisting. And finally I obeyed. I turned the car around and drove back to the spot where the rabbit had streaked from the underbrush. There it was, lying beside the pavement. It was dead. Gently I picked it up and laid it beneath a bush, well back from the road.

And with that act the tears stopped just as suddenly as they had started.

What was the truth that had touched me so compellingly? Was it a message about the oneness and importance of all God's creation? At a moment when my own plans and affairs loomed very large, hadn't a whisper come to me from the Love that included rabbits—and even the two sparrows that were sold for a farthing?

After the exciting experience in Mobile, there was a lot of travel for the pageant. One Sunday in a large city, my chaperone and I slipped into a church near our hotel. The sanctuary was almost full—not quite. When it came time for the announcements, the pastor solemnly stood up and here is what he said as best as I can remember:

"I have witnessed the disunity resulting from recent attempts of Blacks to worship in a nearby church. In order to avoid what happened down the street, I called a special meeting of the board of directors. We have informed the ushers to tell any of these Black agitators who come and try to attend our worship service, that we haven't room enough for our own members."

That was all. Just a simple announcement. I looked around at the people. Theirs was a routine reaction. Again, I know that the emotion I felt was larger than my own.

I am no crusader. I think I understand some of the complexity of this problem. But suddenly I knew that I could no longer take up this pew space that was so valuable.

The minister was reading some more announcements, but the words that crashed in my ears were different: "Though I speak with the tongues of men and of angels, and have not charity, I am become as sounding brass" (1 Corinthians 13:1). It was that other Voice impelling me to action once again. With my astonished chaperone gathering gloves and pocketbook, I got up and walked from the church—wondering if I ever would be able to explain it to her, or to myself.

Back in the hotel room I tried to describe it. It was as though something more concerned and more dedicated than I had reached down and made a decision for me that I might not have reached by myself. For I often had wrestled in my own mind with this question of integration without reaching a very clear-cut conclusion.

A friend to whom I told this experience said he had no doubt that it was the Holy Spirit. He believes that the Spirit daily tries to reach each one of us with His perfect counsel. "The key," he said, "is our obedience. As long as we obey that subtle prompting, it will come ever clearer and more frequently. But if ever we begin to stop our ears, it will grow faint and then disappear."

That made sense to me, because nine or ten months before there had come a moment when I was sure the Holy Spirit had revealed a new truth to me. It was during a period in my life when I had pulled away from the religious training I'd received as a child.

I think most teenagers go through a time like this, and when adults ask why, the nearest I can come is the word *embarrassment*.

Teenagers are terribly self-conscious. And Jesus represents a kind of simplicity and humility that is not at all attractive if you're primarily concerned with what people think of you.

Furthermore, I'd use the word *vulnerability*. There is something about Christ's life of sacrifice and service that made Him totally vulnerable to people. Whether we admitted it or not, young people pulled away from situations where we could be hurt. And so we pulled away from identifying with Christ who was hurt.

I hadn't realized how far it had gone in my own case until one of the boys in high school said some things that bothered me. He, too, was reared in a Christian home, yet he had become a doubter.

"I could step on a Bible right now and not feel a thing," he said. Then he scoffed at church ritual and the idea of a divine Christ.

I tried to talk to him, but inside I was more upset than I showed. What bothered me was not as much his attitude as mine. For I'd realized suddenly as he talked that I could not counter his disbelief with a really strong faith of my own.

That night I could not sleep. A feeling of despair surrounded me. Why must I be so confused? It was nearly 4:00 AM before I dropped off to sleep.

The next night it was the same . . . a great feeling of depression . . . inability to sleep. I was tortured by questions about Christ. Was He a myth? Was He God? Did He really perform those miracles? My thoughts seemed to start off in one direction and end up back at the starting point. There the big question was always waiting: Was Jesus Who He said He was?

I've wondered since then why I did not turn to my parents for answers when I needed them so badly. Mother and Dad are the kind of Christians who live their faith and had tried to teach my sister and me to live it too. Perhaps that was just the trouble. What faith I had was given to me, with no effort on my part. Perhaps it was time to earn a faith of my own.

For five nights the torment lasted . . . sleeplessness . . . emptiness . . . straining to know . . . reaching out for something. On the fifth night it happened. I can't describe it in any other way than to say that a cloud about me seemed to lift, the answer of faith formed a pathway to light: He was! He is!

I got up and began to read the New Testament. I had read the entire Bible through twice before, but never like this. Once I'd read it as a lover of literature, once for its history. Now I read as a seeker. Words leapt at me from the page, thrilling and true. I read on and on, excited, with a feeling of great joy.

When I arose the next morning—to the same breakfast of eggs, the familiar school routine—the feeling of elation and belief was still there. But I had no idea as to how to share it or use it.

There have been other whispers from God, not as loud nor as clear as that night's revelation, but enough to keep me remembering that He seeks us even more fervently than we seek Him. Sometimes in my search for truth I feel as if I'm climbing a ladder up the side of the Empire State Building. At the one hundredth floor there is great vision and wisdom for the climber. Right now I'm up to the fifth floor and sometimes when I look up and see the distance to go, my heart sinks.

Then a bird lights on my shoulder and I remember that it's really not like this at all. It's not a long climb that we must accomplish alone. The distance was overcome when Truth came down to our level. Now He stands outside each separate heart, and we must only be ready to fling wide the door when we hear His gentle knock.

KRISTIN CHENOWETH

Listening

Y ou've got to have a lot of things go right for you to make it on Broadway. Not just the obvious, like a strong voice and the ability to bring a character to life. You also have to find the right characters to play. And you need a thick skin because this is a competitive business. Great roles, I've been fortunate to have. But I'm still struggling to develop that thick skin.

I've always been sensitive. Too sensitive, my mom might argue. I can't help taking to heart what people say about me. Back home in Broken Arrow, Oklahoma, that wasn't a problem. I loved to sing and dance, and folks encouraged me, even when I got it into my head that I wanted to be in show business. In my high school yearbook, classmates sent me off with, "Become the famous singer you hope to be."

The New York theater world is just a little tougher. Don't get me wrong. I've been blessed with my share of praise, and I'm grateful. But all it takes sometimes is one critical remark to cut me to the bone. Like the comment I heard—well, overheard—in the ladies' room of a Broadway theater one day after auditioning for a new show. Two women came in.

"I mean, she can sing—I'll give her that," I heard one of the women say. I recognized her voice right away, an established Broadway star. "But funny? Come on! How hard is it to play a cartoon character? I don't get all the hoopla!"

They're talking about me, I realized. I'd just won a Tony Award for my role as Sally Brown in *You're a Good Man, Charlie Brown*. Sure, the part was based on a comic strip character, but I'd put all of myself into playing it.

One of the biggest names in the business, and she thinks I'm overrated. What if she's right? I wondered. *What if all the hoopla really is for nothing?*

That's when a little voice inside me said, *You're better than that, Kristin. Don't doubt yourself.* The voice I'd listened to—listened for—ever since my very first performance.

I was seven years old and playing a bunny rabbit in *The Nutcracker* at the Tulsa Ballet Theatre. (They wrote in parts for all the little kids.) Opening night I took my spot beside the Sugar Plum Fairy. I watched girls dressed in beautiful gossamer gowns dance and twirl across the stage with vines in their hands. As the last dancer finished I noticed something lying on the stage. A vine.

Someone must have dropped it, I thought. You're not supposed to have anything on the floor during a ballet. Someone might trip on it.

The Sugar Plum Fairy was staring at the vine too. How could we get it off the stage without stopping the show?

Go, Kristin, said a voice deep inside me. *Hop to it.* So I did. I hopped over to the vine, put it in my mouth and hopped back to my spot. The audience erupted. I was one proud rabbit.

When the curtain went down, the artistic director exclaimed, "What a smart little bunny you are! How did you know to do that?"

I shrugged. I didn't know then whose voice it was. But in the years to come I would hear it and depend on it time and again.

In 1993, for example. I'd just completed a master's degree in opera performance at Oklahoma City University and won a scholarship to The Academy of Vocal Arts in Philadelphia. *The Lord was laying out a pretty clear path for me,* I thought. Then I came to New York City to help my best friend move into his apartment.

On a whim I flipped through the audition listings in *Back Stage*. One jumped out at me. "The Marx Brothers' musical *Animal Crackers*, singers and dancers needed."

I want you to try. What have you got to lose? There was that voice again. The voice that had never failed me.

That's why I walked into the Paper Mill Playhouse for the audition. All the other girls had headshots, résumés, an air of confidence. And I had no idea what I was doing! The only thing that kept me from walking out was that inner voice. *Just have fun with it, Kristin. Show them what you've got.*

I sang and I danced. I read the scene they gave me. I was in my element, enjoying the moment. I never expected one of the producers to ask, "Who's your agent?"

"Agent? I was just doing this for fun," I tried to explain. "My dad, I guess. I mean—I don't really have an agent."

Right then and there they offered me a part. A lead. Arabella. I told them I'd have to think about it.

I called home as soon as I got back to my friend's apartment.

"Mom, you'll never guess what happened," I said excitedly. "I got a part, a real part in a musical!"

"But what about your scholarship?" Mom said. "The academy only takes five people a year. Are you sure you want to walk away from that?"

"Mom, I'm supposed to be Arabella. I just know it," I said. "I was sent to that audition for a reason."

Mom and Dad gave me their blessing. After all, they had raised me to trust that guiding voice. Faith and church were at the center of our family, and we always sought God's blessing on whatever we undertook.

I called the academy director and explained my situation. "I'm sorry, but I'm giving up my spot."

She didn't say a word at first. Then she let me have it.

"You are making the biggest mistake of your life," she said. "Once you wake up and realize what you've done, the door is going to be shut. Don't even think about trying to come back here."

She slammed down the receiver. I felt sick, listening to the loud, empty dial tone. Her words really hurt.

I'm glad I trusted my inner voice, though, and took the role of Arabella. It led to other parts. Two jobs came up at once; a lead in *Annie Get Your Gun* and a minor role in *You're a Good Man, Charlie Brown*.

The director of *Charlie Brown* called me. "Kristin, I want to expand a role just for you," he said. "I can't tell you about it until I get Charles Schulz's approval, but please take it on faith, it's perfect for you."

Take it on faith. For a month I prayed about the decision, listened for that voice. Everyone from my friends in the business to my grandmother back home in Oklahoma thought that I should choose *Annie Get Your Gun*, a tried-and-true show.

But I was drawn to the role of Sally Brown, Charlie's little sister. The dialogue and the characters were simple, yet honest and genuine. The entire play was about being happy with who you are—something I believed in.

Almost as deeply as I believed in the inner voice pointing me to Sally. It was the right role for me, a role that earned me the Tony Award.

The day after the Tonys I was on a high. A high that came crashing down with one phone call.

"I really hate to tell you this, Kristin, but the show is closing," the producer said. "We're just not making expenses."

I was devastated. Doubts about my decision came seeping into my brain. If I'd listened to everyone else, I'd still have a job. I hung up the phone. *You just won a Tony,* I told myself. *Move on.*

I tried. I went to an audition. Only to wind up in the ladies' room afterward, overhearing that catty comment about all the hoopla over my performance. It hurt.

But I knew what I had to do. I couldn't give in to doubt. I had to stand up for the show and the role I put all my faith in. I had to stand up for myself. *Lord, please help me handle this with class.*

I pushed the stall door open and walked up to the row of sinks. I stood right next to the Broadway star. Silence. I washed my hands and headed for the exit. I turned around and looked back at the pair.

"I don't get all the hoopla, either," I said with a wink and walked out of the ladies' room, head held high.

And really, that's the truth. What does all the hoopla matter in comparison to that inner voice, that voice deep in our hearts that always keeps us true to ourselves, that never fails us. It is the voice I listen to—and for—each and every day.

MELISSA SUE ANDERSON

Now I See

"Barney!" I yelled irritably at my dog, giving him a firm push with my hand. "Get out of the way."

He regarded me with soulful eyes, then dashed off to more peaceful quarters in our house.

It was Saturday, 5:00 AM, and the Hollywood sky outside my bedroom window was still pitch-black. I was hurrying with last-minute packing for an out-of-town weekend promotional trip for *Little House on the Prairie*. I disliked packing. And I was tired of these trips, too, with their nonstop schedules of interviews, luncheons, autograph and photo sessions. It seemed I never got to see my friends anymore. All I ever did was work.

"Missy!" yelled my mom. "Time to go!"

"Okay," I muttered, struggling to zip my bulging carry-all. Slinging the bag over my shoulder, I glanced around to make sure I hadn't forgotten anything. My blow dryer was still lying on the vanity.

"Darn." I let the bag drop to the floor, and walked across the room to pick up the missing item.

"Missy!" Mom was standing in the doorway. "What are you doing? If you don't hurry up, we'll miss the plane!"

Dryer in hand, I glared at her.

The hurt look that crossed her face made me feel terrible, but I just couldn't bring myself to apologize.

"I'll meet you in the car," said Mom quietly. She turned and left the room.

Stuffing the dryer in the bag, I felt my throat tighten with frustration and anger.

Lately, nothing had been going right. Gossip magazines were printing silly stories about me and anyone they could think of. And because of my age—fifteen—I'd been turned down for a really good TV movie role in favor of an older actress who was legally allowed to work beyond an eight-hour day. Then, there were always these trips.

But these, I knew, were just surface annoyances. Deep down inside, what was really bothering me was the drastic change being written into my television role as Mary Ingalls, the oldest daughter on *Little House on the Prairie*. In a special two-part program, the last two shows of our fourth season, Mary was going to go blind. But that wasn't all. For as long as the series lasted, she was to remain blind. Shooting was scheduled to begin in a few weeks, and I was dreading it.

It wasn't the script that had me worried; I had read it, and it was good. (Mary would eventually learn to cope with her affliction and go on to meet her lifelong goal of becoming a teacher.) What I wondered was: *What will happen after the first show?* I mean, what more could Mary do than be a sort of silent, sad background character? After all, the girl was blind.

Over the weekend, I couldn't stop thinking about the matter— and the more I thought about it, the more my resentment and bitterness grew. Acting is what I love more than anything else. I just didn't understand how, in the long run, this turn of events could help my career.

By the time I returned home on Sunday evening, it was clear there was only one thing for me to do: Through research and study, I would prepare for the role professionally. I would do my best to accurately portray a blind person down to the most minute detail. I would be perfect.

With this in mind, I picked up the phone and made an appointment to visit the Foundation for the Junior Blind in downtown Los Angeles.

The following Saturday was a beautiful day—sunny and warm—but I was a bundle of discontent as Mom drove me to the Foundation. All my friends were at the beach, shopping, having fun—while I would be spending the morning in a dull institutional classroom.

I was greeted warmly by one of the Foundation teachers. I explained that I was interested in technical information only: that is, how to sit, stand, walk, eat like a blind person. So the instructor kept her approach straightforward, matter-of-fact.

"When you sit," she said, "take time to reach out and make sure the chair is there. Then, sit on your hand. It's a small thing, but it's something every newly blinded person does."

"Good," I said, "that's just the kind of detail I'm looking for. Viewers will know I've done my research."

Giving me a rather odd glance, the instructor continued. "When you stand," she said, "brace yourself before attempting any forward movement. You will shuffle at first. Later on in the program, when you've learned to use a cane, you will walk with confidence."

"Great," I said glumly, again feeling stirrings of resentment for the change in Mary Ingalls' role. What future could there possibly be for a helpless, stumbling heroine whose great accomplishment was "walking with confidence"?

"Any questions so far?" asked the instructor, interrupting my thoughts. Her eyes searched mine, as though expecting something.

"No," I said.

She went on to explain such things as how to pour liquid from a pitcher into a glass without spilling: By placing my index finger inside the glass, I could feel when it was nearly full.

"One more thing," she said, when nearly an hour had passed and I was about to leave. "There's something else I'd like you to do when you go home. I want you to close your eyes—no need to use a blindfold—just close your eyes, and take four steps forward."

"Is that all?" I asked.

"Yes," she answered. "It should give you a small idea of what it's like to be without sight. I think you might be surprised at how it feels."

It seemed rather silly to me, but I promised to try it. Thanking the instructor for her time and help, I left.

That afternoon I was home alone with Barney. Mom had gone shopping. The southern California sun was streaming in through our living room windows making patterns on the thick brown carpet. The room was bathed in golden brightness. Sunlight danced on the brass and crystal fixtures, burnished the wooden coffee table to a rich walnut. I kicked off my sandals and knelt to the floor to play with Barney. We roughhoused for a while until, exhausted, we both flopped flat on our backs. Looking up at the ceiling, the air seemed to sparkle with suspended particles of glittering dust. It was such an everyday thing—but so pretty.

My thoughts returned to the morning's visit to the Foundation for the Junior Blind. It seemed remote—so far away. I remembered the instructor's request.

Why not? I thought, standing up and brushing my hands on the back of my jeans. It was a simple enough request. Facing the window, I shut my eyes. An explosion of colors, swirling and brilliant, took me by surprise. I was "seeing" the light from the window.

Casually, I took a step, and then another—but on the third step I froze. I felt as though I were about to fall off a cliff! The room seemed to have dropped away from me; I was alone and facing nothingness—with nothing for support.

Incredulous, I sank to the floor and opened my eyes. The room returned, reassuringly warm and cheerful, bathed in color and light.

I was limp—overwhelmed by the experience. How I had under-estimated the enormity of blindness and, at the same time, the pow-erful accomplishment of any person who has faced and overcome such a handicap! Talk about blind—if anyone was blind, it had been me. I felt sick with shame for my hard heart. The instructor at the Foundation had read my lack of compassion like a book. I would have to return and speak with her again. There was much to talk about, much to learn.

Suddenly, the things that had seemed so troublesome to me—the gossip magazines, the lost roles, the inconvenience of out-of-town trips—were reduced to trivia in light of the overwhelming sense of gratitude I felt for the blessings in my life. Not only was I thankful for my sight, but for my family, friends, career, and—especially—my abil-ity now to bring to the role of Mary Ingalls the courage, confidence and strength that rightly belonged to her. Any fears or doubts I had about Mary's potential as a vital, involved character had dissolved.

"Thank You, Lord," I whispered, "for all You've given me. Help me always to focus not on the dark side of life's little problems—but on the bright side of Your wonderful blessings!"

Barney came over and nuzzled me under the elbow. I held him tightly. We had been sitting like that for nearly ten minutes when Mom came home.

"Missy?" she said, wondering what I was doing sitting in the middle of the living room floor. Curious, she came over and sat down next to me.

"You all right?" she asked.

"Yes," I answered—and before I knew it, I was blurting out all that had happened, all I'd been thinking about. I apologized for the many times I'd been so snappy and disagreeable for no good reason. Then we hugged each other real tight. I guess Mom and I got a little choked up—until Barney's attempts to get into the act set us off giggling. It was a very special moment.

JOE PINNER

You Are Special

It was my forty-ninth birthday—April 18, 1984—and I had just finished the *Carolina Today* talk show and the noon weather report on WIS-TV in beautiful Columbia, South Carolina, I'd forecast a glorious spring day, hoping I'd be right! Lunch was next—and an afternoon retreat to my office, where I'd prepare for the taping of the show I loved most, my children's program, *Mr. Knozit*. But as I left the production area, someone called my name.

Mr. Pinner?

I turned and saw two uniformed security officers. They were from a nearby company, one of Columbia's largest concerns. Their expressions were grim.

"Mr. Pinner . . . ," one said.

"Call me Joe," I said.

"Sir," he continued, "would you come with us, please? We'll explain later. It's urgent."

"Sure," I grinned. I had a hunch about what they were up to. "Are you guys certain you don't want to read me my rights first?" I joked as we headed for the door.

"We've got to hurry," said the second officer, holding open the door and nodding me through. *Somebody,* I thought, *has gone to a lot of trouble for a birthday surprise.*

I was accustomed to folks playing all kinds of good-natured

pranks on me. As I looked at the two young men who were escorting me, I wondered if either of them had ever been on the Knozit show. It wasn't impossible. For more than twenty years I'd entertained and, I hoped, helped educate the children of South Carolina. I'd shown cartoons, announced birthdays, interviewed guests, given safety and health tips, and got to know the children who came down to WIS-TV to be on the show, tens of thousands of them through the years. I loved that part of my job best, the chance to touch the lives of these youngsters.

It took only a few minutes by foot to reach our destination. We entered a modern office building across the street from the company's headquarters. Odd place for a surprise party, I mused. I was whisked through the lobby and into an elevator.

The doors hissed shut and we rose to the fourteenth floor. I braced myself for the inevitable chorus of "Surprise!" that would greet me when the doors opened.

But there was no chorus of cheers, no laughter or party horns. Instead, the office was filled with cigarette smoke and men in dark suits looking very concerned. An architectural blueprint was rolled open across one of the desks. Then I saw the walkie-talkies and the police revolvers.

"Joe Pinner," said a tall man walking quickly toward me. He was obviously in charge and introduced himself as a police captain. "We've got a problem," he said, motioning me over to one of the desks. "There is a man, a former employee named Irwin Beck (name has been changed), and he's holding a hostage at the company's headquarters across the street. We've tried reasoning with him over the phone. He wants to talk to you."

The hostage-taker's name meant nothing to me.

"He's seen you on television. He trusts you," continued the captain. "And he knows your voice. He knows we're not tricking him with a policeman or a company official."

Of course. My voice. But what could I possibly say to help someone like this? I wasn't a psychologist or a priest. I was just a guy who did the weather and hosted a children's show.

"Has he hurt anyone?" I asked.

"Not yet," replied the captain.

The room was full of police detectives. There were also representatives from the company, including the president, in whose office Beck was holed up with the hostage. They all turned toward me.

"What do you think I should say?" I asked finally.

"Just keep him calm while we get our men in position around the building."

I picked up the receiver. My palms were so moist that I could hardly get a grip on it. The captain dialed the number.

"Yes?" a voice answered quickly.

"This is Joe Pinner."

"Thank you, Mr. Pinner," said Beck politely. "I don't mean to bother you."

His voice sounded strangely calm. Too calm.

"Call me Joe."

"I know I can trust you, Joe."

Beck, who had lost his job due to his erratic work habits and behavior, proceeded to spin a rambling tale of his grievances, imagined and otherwise, against his former employer, of his troubles with his divorce, his family, his neighbors. With each new complaint, the knot in my stomach tightened. Many of his problems were the same that the rest of us faced every day. He didn't sound demented or vicious. Yet something deep inside this man had snapped. He had lost his grip on reality.

As I talked, I kept thinking of the young man, a clerical worker, whom Beck was holding at gunpoint.

I had never been part of such a desperate situation. The captain indicated he wanted to put Beck's lawyer on the phone. I told Beck I hoped to talk with him some more later, and said good-bye.

I looked at the police captain. "I just don't think he has it in him to hurt anyone," I offered.

"I know," he replied. "I'm more afraid of what he might do to himself."

The afternoon dragged by, and an exchange of hostages was negotiated. Beck's lawyer took the young man's place. Everyone pleaded with Beck to surrender. A group of police officers concealed themselves directly outside the office, should Beck venture out. Around dinnertime he released his attorney. My offer to talk with Beck face-to-face was quickly dismissed by the police, who feared for my safety.

"All we can do now is wait," the captain remarked.

Afternoon slipped into evening. Finally the phone rang. The captain answered it.

"Yeah?" There was a pause. The captain winced and heaved a sigh. "Okay. Thanks." He replaced the phone slowly and looked at me. "He did it. It's over."

I sat stunned. *No! It couldn't end like this! Not suicide!* A terrible chill went through me. Suddenly I was very tired. I just wanted to go home and be alone.

For only the second time in my career at WIS, I missed my nightly news broadcast. I drove straight to my house. I just couldn't believe what had happened. Yes, something had snapped deep inside

Irwin Beck. But even so, how could anyone love life so little and hate himself so much that he would put a gun to his head? Why? If nothing else, had he no idea how much his Creator loved him? It tore me up to see a person so despondent that all sense of self-worth vanished. It was wrong.

And I hadn't been able to help him. I knew it hadn't been my fault, but still I couldn't keep from being a little depressed about how ineffectual I'd been.

That night, and in the days that followed, I brooded over the suicide. Even some of the pleasure went out of doing the Knozit show as I began to wonder just how much good I was actually doing those young people. *Mr. Knozit* is meant for fun, but underneath it all there is a serious intent. And one of the things I had been trying to get across to these youngsters was this very matter of self-worth—self-esteem; I wanted the kids to see how important their lives were in God's plan. In this I'd been deeply influenced by a school superintendent in nearby Sumter County, Billy Mitchell. Dr. Mitchell had come on *Carolina Today* and told of his belief that low self-esteem was a root of many of today's ills, and said he was doing something about it in his school system. "Drugs, dropouts, vandalism, all have their origin in the lack of pride young people have in themselves," he said.

"Research shows that while eighty percent of the kids entering our schools have a positive self-image, only about five percent still have it when they graduate." Somewhere along the line, kids get an earful of no, don't and can't. But self-esteem can be taught and nurtured, insisted Mitchell, and it's up to all of us to pitch in—parents, teachers, even TV hosts. On the Knozit program, I adopted some of Mitchell's principles, putting up placards with motivational slogans Mitchell calls "attitude boosters," inviting on guests with you-can-do-it stories, and just quietly pointing out to kids how important they are.

But now I wondered how much good all this was doing. And just when I was feeling most discouraged, I happened to go to the opening of a new shopping mall in Columbia. There, a young man approached me. "Joe Pinner," he said, holding out his hand. "You don't know me, but you've made quite a difference in my life." I looked at him quizzically. "I'm a real fan of *Mr. Knozit.* Watched you often while I was in prison."

Prison? This well-mannered, well-dressed fellow didn't look like my idea of a criminal.

"At first when I was in jail," he continued, "I made fun of all that corny junk you gave out about thinking positive thoughts and stuff. But gradually it began to make sense. When I went in, I thought I didn't have it in me to make anything of my life. Now things are going pretty good, and I just wanted to shake your hand and say thanks."

"W-well, thank you," I stammered.

"You know," he continued, "guys in prison sometimes cop a real cocky attitude. But I'll tell you something: Most of those guys don't like themselves much at all. Probably haven't since they were kids."

And with that he walked away quickly. I was touched, deeply touched.

There it was again: self-esteem. *If the Knozit show had had such an impact on a man behind bars,* I thought, *imagine what it might do for impressionable kids.*

Suddenly my own self-esteem soared. I hadn't been much help to Irwin Beck. I realized now there was nothing I could have done for him. His self-esteem had long been crippled. But maybe some of the things we were doing on the Knozit show were making a difference.

Now when I do a Knozit show, I look at the kids and marvel, marvel at the miracle each and every one of them is, a precious miracle of life. And I tell them. I start each show by saying, "You're special and I like you." Corny junk, right? But I believe it.

I think of God as a positive God, a "yes God" rather than a "no God." I think He says yes to all of us. His love for us allows us to love ourselves. Adults, I believe, have to pass on that love to the children of the world, the way our Father passes His love to us.

We can do no less. That's the one thing *Mr. Knozit* knows for sure.

JANE WYMAN

A Case of Shyness

How annoyed I get today when I hear someone teased for being shy! "Come on!" they shout, dragging him into a crowded room. "Don't be shy!" As though not being shy were a matter of willpower. Or, "You're just shy!" as though that were the most minor of problems.

Shyness is not a small problem: It can cripple the whole personality. It crippled mine, for many years.

As a child my only solution to the problem of shyness was to hide, to make myself as small and insignificant as possible. All through grade school I was a well-mannered little shadow who never spoke above a whisper. In ballet class I haunted the corners of the room, hoping the dancing master would not see me.

The very thought of performing in front of someone made me wilt with fear, quite literally.

The saddest part of it was that I idolized Dad Prinz, the dancing master. He was the most understanding man I had ever met and I longed to tell him so. I never did.

Then my parents left St. Joseph, Missouri, and moved to Los Angeles. And now a new and more threatening dimension had been added to life outside the big city high school walls. Dating. It seemed to me that on some prearranged signal, every boy and girl in school paired off.

Every girl, that is, except me. I don't know whether I could have had dates or not; it simply never occurred to me to try. Hadn't I been told many times that I was not pretty? I lugged home piles of books every night and disappeared into them.

And then the Depression came. In California it seemed to hit older people like my father especially hard. Overnight I was thrust from my safe little book-world into the world of job hunting.

In all that vast, bewildering city, I knew only one person who might give me a job: LeRoy Prinz, the famous Hollywood dance coach, Dad Prinz' son. He gave me a tryout and discovered I had a sense of rhythm. "As long as you've got that," he said, "I can teach you the rest."

Under LeRoy Prinz' coaching I began to get chorus parts in the movies, those lavish, glittery, extravagant movies we loved in the hungry thirties.

It was work when the family badly needed the money, but for a girl who had grown up in terror of being looked at, it was also agony.

Then I made a discovery: A good shield for shyness is a bold exterior. Did my heart turn over when the man with the megaphone bellowed out my name? Were all the other dancers prettier? Never mind. I covered up by becoming the cockiest of all, by talking the loudest, laughing the longest, and wearing the curliest, most blatantly false eyelashes in Hollywood.

And then one day a fellow chorus girl gave me a piece of advice:

"Jane, you'd improve your looks about a thousand percent if you'd peel off those trimmings and wash your face."

I was crushed. I wept. I hated her. But the next day, feeling completely bold, I showed up on the set without my disguise. We hadn't been rehearsing half an hour before a comparative stranger stopped and stared at me.

"Gee, Jane," he said. "You look great."

For me it was the heavens parting. Could he have meant that I looked great? It was the first hint I had that I could be myself without the sky falling in.

But the insight went only skin deep. I shed the eyelashes, but I wasn't about ready to shed the tough, smart little shell. I had begun to get a few minor acting parts and they were just the kind you would expect. I was the brash blonde girl reporter rushing into the newspaper office to shout, "Stop the presses!"

Then one day on the set someone else said something that shone another bit of light through the defense I'd set up.

"When I first came out to Hollywood," he said, "I discovered there are two kinds of people here. There are the 'closed people,' the careful ones who don't take risks and don't get hurt. And there are the 'open people,' the ones who give life all they've got. They make mistakes, they get hurt, but they also get back a lot of joy."

I recognized myself right there as one of the closed people and my bright personality as the shell for a clam. I began to want very much to open the shell. I began to loathe the brassy blonde I played in the movies. Suddenly I longed to play real people, to move the hearts of real people. Today I would call this quality of deep yearning, "prayer," and what happened next, a small miracle. Then, I only knew that no sooner had I set my heart on changing than I was offered two roles about unmistakably real people: first in *Lost Weekend* and then in *The Yearling*.

I worked on those parts as I'd never worked before, sat up nights with my lines, studied them for hidden meanings over my meals. When those films were finished, the studio decided I was ready for the role of the deaf-mute in *Johnny Belinda*. With that part came the

Academy Award, and surely, I thought, surely now I will stop hiding. Surely I will feel some kind of self-esteem and confidence.

But the months passed, my Oscar collected dust on a shelf, and I made a dismal discovery. External achievements change nothing: inside I was the same tormentingly shy person I always had been. My real self still was hiding in the shadows, sending someone else out front to greet the world. It was an exhausting way to live.

Then, ten years ago, I went to England to do a picture for the Royal Academy. It was a lonely time: I knew no one outside the cast and I did a lot of walking, and thinking. During my solitary rambles I found myself wandering into Westminster Abbey, first as a sightseer—then over and over again to try to grasp something I felt there. Something that felt like approval. Like acceptance. Like love.

I tried to dismiss the experience. It was, I rationalized, only the reaction of a homesick woman in a foreign land. I almost had convinced myself when I met the man who at last threw a searchlight on the girl in the shadows. I was back in Hollywood and he was a kindly old priest with a manner so gentle, so uncritical, that suddenly I found myself talking to him about things I'd never told anyone. I found myself telling him about the little girl who was too shy to speak above a whisper, about my lifelong struggle with the same feelings. "I thought if I only could succeed at something, then I wouldn't be shy. But I have had success, of a kind, and I feel just the same."

"Of course you do." The priest smiled at me. "Shyness isn't a matter of doing well, or not doing well. It isn't a matter of whether you're handsome or plain."

Over his cluttered desk, he looked at me. "Shyness, Miss Wyman, is a little matter of self-centeredness."

I blinked. The words were harsh but he said them so mildly, that I resisted a familiar impulse to flee into a protective shell.

"That's all," he continued cheerfully. "Just a little tendency to think of the whole world as terribly interested in oneself. You know, the feeling that every eye in the room is focused on one—whereas actually most of the other people there are pretty much involved with their own problems.

"Now fortunately," he went on as he rummaged for something in the maelstrom on his desk, "the Bible gives us some very specific instructions for dealing with self-centeredness." He located his Bible, found the passage he wanted, and handed it to me.

I looked at the Bible passage. It was the Ten Commandments.

"The first four," he said, "deal with our relationship to God. They get our attention out where it belongs: on Him and His majesty. And the last six tell us how we ought to conduct ourselves toward other people. They keep our attention out there, away from ourselves and onto our neighbors."

I looked down at the Commandments again. I had read them a hundred times, of course, but something in the old priest's voice filled them with an unspeakable promise.

It was the first of many interviews with this priest who became my spiritual mentor. And I have never forgotten what he told me the first time we met, about the cause of shyness, and its cure. Not that I have succeeded in following all the Commandments in all their fullness, but the act of trying to has worked a big change in my life.

For when I looked away from myself I discovered a whole world full of other people. Fascinating people, people with woes and joys I had never imagined. I didn't have much time left to worry about the impression I was making, once I really began seeing them.

But best of all, out there, I am finding God. Not much of Him, yet. At first it was just a shadow, a glimmering. But getting to know Him better, listening for Him, contemplating Him, loving Him, is a twenty-four-hour-a-day assignment. Shy? I just haven't got time.

HUGH DOWNS

The Cynic in My Past

One morning on our *Today* show we reported on a group of teenagers whose demonstrations had shocked their community. In the faces of the young people pictured on the screen I saw a total rebellion against authority.

"That could have been me twenty-five years ago," I said to myself.

It started me thinking back to the age of fourteen when the change within me occurred. Up until then I had accepted without question the patterns my parents had set. Then slowly I began to see things through a haze of contempt and rebellion. Perhaps it was partly because I stood first in my class and took great pride in my pseudointellect and glib tongue. Success, I concluded, was all that mattered.

As captain of my own ship, I decided that I needed help from no one. Sensitivity to need and concern for others were, to me, signs of weakness or guilt. I had a theory for everything.

Since a great percentage of those in my home town of Lima, Ohio, were churchgoing people, I divided them into two neat groups: the ones who used church once a week as a cleansing ritual, and the others who attended church with the thought, "I want to be on the winning side in case there is something to all this."

So I argued that all churches should be abolished because they stood in the way of faith. I theorized that a man can worship God as he sees fit—where and when he chooses. And if he doesn't choose to, that is his privilege too. (I didn't choose to, by the way.) My name for this theory was "Reverse Piety." It sounded very smart to me.

But as a working philosophy of life it was to prove more and more unsatisfactory. Actually I should have known better. My father was a Methodist, my mother a Baptist, but in a spirit of early ecumenicity they became Episcopalians when they were married. Time after time they showed their concern for others.

For a while, my father and a partner ran an auto accessory store. When they went into the red, the partner declared himself bankrupt. My father and mother decided that there was a moral as well as a material obligation involved. My father took a job and over the years paid back every penny he owed.

I resented it since it meant there was no money for me to continue college. I had to quit after the first year. My bitterness increased when I applied for twenty-six jobs in a row and didn't get one.

Then one day I stopped at the radio station in Lima with the halfhearted hope that there might be some kind of job open. They gave me an audition—and to my surprise I was hired as an announcer. The pay was seven dollars and fifty cents a week.

There was hardly any direction to go but up. I was married and a father when one of those experiences occurred which, in retrospect, you can call a turning point. The radio station where I worked had to cut costs. My job was in danger. Thinking that my boss was looking for a good excuse to let me go, I built up a real dislike of him.

Then one day he called me into his office. To my surprise his manner was kindly. He was concerned about me. And he worked out a plan for me to stay on the job.

Something happened inside me at that point to chip away at the crust of cynicism I had built up around myself. I thanked him for his thoughtfulness, then said impulsively, "You do this for me when all the time I have been hating you because I didn't think you wanted me here?"

My boss said calmly, "Why don't you try to get outside of yourself, Hugh? If you do, you'll tap a source of spiritual and physical energy that will make you feel inexhaustible."

I chewed that thought long and hard. The words were certainly not new, but now they had meaning.

For a time I had been examining other faiths, from Judaism to Buddhism and Islam. Each has much to offer. Inevitably I came back to a reexamination of Christianity. While pondering questions of faith and systems of philosophy, I was moving from radio to television, from Ohio to Chicago and then to New York. The years passed. I worked with *Kukla, Fran and Ollie*, with Sid Caesar, Jack Paar and the *Today* show.

As success came I followed the pursuits I liked: astronomy, boating, flying, celestial navigation, music. They can satisfy body and mind, but they leave the spirit unfulfilled. Yet, answers to my quest for faith were coming and piece by piece, like putting together a mosaic, the picture was taking form.

An actor contributed to it. I don't even know his name. But he was in a very successful play and he was asked how life could possibly remain fresh after giving the same performance, day after day, seven hundred times.

"The audience hasn't seen the play seven hundred times," he said. "It's a new play for them every night. If I thought only of myself I'd be stale by the tenth performance. But every night I think of the audience instead of myself and they renew and refresh me."

Last year I sailed across the Pacific in a small boat. It was immensely satisfying to navigate that distance, even though I had a fall during the voyage that injured my spine. Back home, doctors said it required surgery. I was taken to the hospital in a wheelchair. The operation was a success and I walked out without any help. Yet the experience added something to me. First, the ordeal was neither fearsome nor intolerable though from the outside it seemed so. Second, there was always someone along the corridors whose troubles and pain were worse than your own. Cheering them was not depressing or morbid, but just the opposite. You got outside yourself.

At one time I served on the Citizens' Advisory Committee of the New York State Mental Health Association. That committee was scheduled to make one of their regular visits to patients. I would have ducked going, if I could. I couldn't. In our car pool the driver of our auto was a rabbi whose sense of compassion interested me.

At the hospital we walked through the clean, neat rooms. Two very disturbed boys caught our attention. One was thirteen, the second, perhaps two years older. The older one said very little. The younger one said nothing at all. As the rabbi talked with them I asked a nurse, "What hope is there for these boys?" She shrugged her shoulders. "Very little," she said.

As we were leaving, I looked over my shoulder and saw the younger boy sitting on an oak bench, all alone, staring into nothingness, the picture of endless despair.

"That boy," I said to the rabbi, "looks very much like my own son. I can't help it, but I'm glad—" I was starting to express thankfulness for the fact that my son was normal.

"I know how you feel," he interrupted. "That boy is my son."

It was days before I got over the shock of that experience. The picture of the rabbi not only ministering to his own son, and to all the afflicted in that institution, but also moving to save me embarrassment is still vivid before my eyes. For in his agony he had learned to lose himself in his concern for others.

This was what my parents were trying to tell me as they scrimped and sacrificed to pay off a debt that was moral, not legal. It was what my boss at the radio station was saying to me when I was twenty-two; and it was what the actor meant when he talked about playing one role seven hundred times.

Different people were getting the message to me, but it took a long time before I really heard and embraced as the heart of my faith the words Christ uttered to His disciples: ". . . he that loseth his life for My sake shall find it" (Matthew 10:39).

KEEPING THE FAITH

"What does it profit a man if he gain the whole world but lose his own soul?" Actors are often faced with this dilemma because they do in a sense "gain the whole world" when success comes to them, but in the process they risk losing their own souls, their own hard core of personal values, as perhaps no other group does. That's why I repeat those words to myself just about every day of my life.

DICK VAN DYKE

Paula Deen

Simple Blessings

Loneliness? Y'all might not think that's a problem for someone like me, but you'd be surprised. I might seem happy as a lark on my Food Network series, *Paula's Home Cooking* (and I am). Down here at the restaurant I run, I seem to know half the world that walks in for some good Southern cookin'. They are friends. They kept me in business when I hardly had a cent. But you can be the life of the party, with everybody knowing your name, and still feel the ache of loneliness. I guess it happens to all of us at one time or another. In my case, the solution to my loneliness was the most incredible answer to prayer I ever got.

It really hit me a couple years back right in the middle of one of the most exciting periods of my life. Things had finally taken off. The restaurant was filled night after night, my two cookbooks were doing well and I was hard at work on a new one. I was launching my own TV show and I'd even let myself splurge and buy a sleek twenty-seven-foot motorboat, although I didn't know much about piloting it. I had my own dream house looking out over the sky-blue water and the green palm-drenched islands on the horizon. I could watch the dolphins play. But when I was home with just my two shih tzus, Sam and Otis, I didn't enjoy it. I tell you, all that success just left me feeling lonesome.

Pray, Paula, pray, I thought. I know about prayer. Prayer has been as big a part of my life as food. You can pray anytime, even when you cook. You can hold a person's name in your head as you stir a sauce or chop a tomato or flip a piece of chicken in a frying pan. You can ask for God's help while you sift, salt and season. Prayer is what got me through the death of my parents when I was only nineteen. Prayer was about all I had when my marriage failed, leaving me with two boys to take care of. So why couldn't I pray now?

Day after day, I'd sit in front of my computer, working on the book. I felt so isolated. I'd look out at that boat bobbing at the dock and just shake my head. What had I been thinking?

I searched for the right words to pray. I knew I had plenty to be thankful for. After years of struggle I could surely count my blessings. I could thank God for my boys, Jamie and Bobby, who had helped me in my business from the day I started out with the little catering company, which I called "The Bag Lady," run out of my kitchen. The boys ran all over town delivering my meals. They were my busboys, hosts and waiters. Their girlfriends helped too. Bless me, how they helped!

But when I closed my eyes, I would also think of all the people who were gone. My mother and my daddy. My uncle George. My grandmother, who really taught me all the principles of good Southern cookin'. It's a hand-me-down art. She started out with a little hotdog stand in Hapeville, Georgia, and her cookin' did so well she moved up to country steak and creamed potatoes. The staples of Southern food are butter, sugar, salt, pepper, hot sauce, vinegar, ham hocks and, to put it bluntly . . . fat! It's comfort food. Pretty easy to love. The dishes don't require split-second timing and they don't fail. And your kids don't have to acquire a taste for it, 'cause we just heap good food on a plate and start eating.

Maybe what I needed was somebody I could cook for, all on my own. I had a vision of my life as a big pie, with ninety-five percent of that going toward work and five percent left for family. Something was out of whack. Sure, I needed to get out and meet people. But how was I going to do that? I wasn't going to drop in at some bar. And though I love going to church, I couldn't be away from the restaurant most Sundays. It was our biggest day. My one day off, Monday, I had to use for writing the book. Catch-up day, I called it. But putting down one recipe after another made me all the more lonesome. No amount of hard work could cover up for that. I just had to let it go. Unlike a good recipe, my life wasn't perfect. Fact was, it was a mess! And now it was time to hand it over to the Lord—the whole thing— and let Him deal with it.

One day I shut down the computer and put my head on my desk. I needed to say a prayer. But what? What did I want? Suddenly the words came: Lord, I need a neighbor. I had no idea what that meant. The words were no fancier than the old jeans and T-shirt I was wearing. Just, I need a neighbor. With that I went to work.

I'd been working for half an hour when my shih tzus came running up to me, barking. They wanted to go out.

"Hold on, boys," I said to Sam and Otis. "Give me another fifteen minutes. I want to finish this recipe."

Nothing doing. They weren't taking no for an answer. "Okay, okay," I said. I put on an old hat to hide my undone hair. Outside it was hotter than a June bride. "As long as we don't run into anyone we know."

I opened the door and they made their jailbreak. Except they shot off in the opposite direction than they usually go. I turned right and those rascals went left and dashed away on their short, shaggy legs.

"Sam! Otis! Get back here!" It was not a day to run anywhere.

They darted around the low wall at the end of our row of town houses and I shimmied around after them. They went straight to a man leaning on a fence and talking on his cell phone. He looked kinda shaggy, like Ernest Hemingway with a beard that was out of control. And he didn't look like he wanted to meet anybody.

"I'm sorry about my dogs," I said.

He closed up his cell phone and looked at me. "Oh, no bother."

I introduced myself and he said he knew of me because of my cookbooks, and that made me even more embarrassed because of my old T-shirt and jeans.

"Nice to meet you. I guess we're neighbors. We should get together sometime." He said it so soft I thought he was just being polite.

"Sure, sometime," I replied quickly. I was anxious to get Otis and Sam back home so I could get back to my work. My life was as out of control as this guy's beard. Today was catch-up day. I didn't have time for small talk. I waved good-bye, thinking that was that.

Two weeks later, I was at home working and my Sam and Otis came barking crazily at me again. I was in my crummy stay-at-home-to-write clothes, naturally, and my hair was in wet-mop mode. I put on the hat, headed out the door and turned right. They darted left. Again! Tore straight to the fence and there was that man with the beard, leaning there, like he'd never moved.

All right, Paula, you've already had a conversation with that guy. You can't just wave and walk on, I thought. Sam and Otis were doing their business and I didn't want to talk about writing cookbooks or running a restaurant. I looked over to the water and saw my boat sitting there.

"You know anything about boats?" I said to him, figuring he didn't know anything more than I did.

"A bit," he chuckled. Here's the kicker: Turned out he was a docking pilot. His family had been working on the waters in Savannah, Georgia, for generations. I guess that made him a real neighbor. "I'm Michael," he said.

"Well, Michael," I said, "I just got this twenty-seven-foot Blackfin and all I know how to do is sit on it. Think you could show me the ropes?"

He took me out the next day. We cruised out to Wassaw Sound and then he turned back and brought me into the most beautiful sunset I'd ever seen. The boat was jumping on the waves, really bouncy, just the way I like boat-riding, and Michael was the kindest, most considerate man I could ever imagine. He had real substance and I'm not talking about just the facial hair, though it would be something I would have to get used to. "How about if I cook for you?" I asked him.

"That'll work," he chuckled again. So it was the beginning of a romance that led to a great marriage and a friendship that has brought a heaping slice of care and love to the mess of a pie that had been my life.

I still run around like crazy some days, cookin' at the restaurant, writing books, doing my TV show, seeing my boys. But I'm constantly reminded that all of these blessings don't mean a thing without acknowledging that they have come to me from a loving God who has looked out for me from day one. . . . Who even tells me what to pray for when I can't figure it out for myself.

It's sort of like Southern cookin'. You mix up all these different ingredients, and you do everything like you've been taught or you've seen your mama or grandmother do. You say a prayer that whoever is going to eat it will like it. And then it turns out better than you ever expected it would. It's grace, pure and simple, that makes all those things work together. And when grace pours into your life, there's no room left to be lonely.

LISA WHELCHEL

Acting on Faith

When I first came to Hollywood from Fort Worth, Texas, I was twelve years old and had a running role as a Mouseketeer in Walt Disney's *The New Mickey Mouse Club*, a revival of the original. From that I got other parts.

One of them, *The Magician of Lublin*, made when I was fourteen, was filmed in Europe. To my distress it received an R rating. As the daughter of the main character in the film, I had no scenes that I was ashamed of, yet I determined that from then on I would take a stronger stand for Christ and would either act in decent films or none at all.

And that's the way it's been. Two years ago I was offered a role in a TV-movie about a college girl who has an affair—with a married professor. I turned it down.

A short time later I ran into a friend. "How's the TV-movie coming along, Lisa?" she asked. "What a break for you!"

"I won't be doing it," I replied. "I turned it down as soon as I read the script."

My friend seemed surprised. "Well gee, Lisa, you couldn't have given it much thought . . ."

"Thought?" I replied. "Hey, I didn't have to think about it. I didn't even have to pray about it!"

Surprise was replaced by a look of blank puzzlement.

"You know," I said, "Shakespeare wrote in one of his comedies—

I think it was *Measure for Measure*—'Virtue is bold, and goodness never fearful' (Act III, Scene 1). I like to keep those words in mind."

I really enjoy being an actress. Playing the part of Blair ("the snob you love to hate") on TV's *The Facts of Life* was good clean fun. But if the day should come when I can no longer accept the kinds of roles I'm offered in Hollywood, I'll simply have to go on to other things.

I've learned that being a Christian means not just talking about your commitment to Christ, it means acting on it. Commitment gives you the courage to do what you know is right, even when everybody else is pressuring you to go along with questionable things. That holds true if you're a mechanic, a mother, a bank clerk, a student—or an actor. And you don't need to waste time doing a lot of hemming and hawing about it either. After all, "Virtue is bold, and goodness never fearful."

BARBARA WALTERS

My Search for Heaven

When I left *20/20* I signed up to do four or five specials a year. I didn't want to just focus on show-business personalities or big newsmakers. I was looking for subjects with broader interests, ideas and concepts that were important to people on the deepest personal level. I read that eighty-three percent of Americans believe in heaven. Wow, I thought, that would make a very interesting show. To think that in a country as diverse as ours, eighty-three percent share this one powerful belief. I wanted to know more.

We spent a year on the project and I must say I learned a breathtaking amount of information. We spoke to people from many different religious backgrounds, everyone from Ted Haggard, president of the National Association of Evangelicals, to Maria Shriver, a Catholic, who's written a book about discussing heaven with your children. I learned about the Muslim view of heaven, which is surprisingly earthly—luxurious banquets—and the Buddhists' view that there are various stages of heaven. What almost every religion has in common is the need to feel that life doesn't end here. There is something beyond. Something better and beautiful.

Growing up, I had very little religious education. Our family was Jewish, but not particularly observant. And yet, in the public schools of Brookline, Massachusetts, I sang Christmas carols, which I still love (my favorite is "O Holy Night," although I can't reach the high notes), and I knew the Lord's Prayer: "Thy kingdom come, thy will be done on earth as it is in heaven . . ." All these years later, those words have meaning to me. And, yes, I still pray. Especially on airplanes. And I'm on airplanes a lot.

But what about heaven? Father Theodore McCarrick, the cardinal from Washington, DC, told me, "This life is not what we're made for. We're made for heaven. We're made for the future."

"Do you mean that all these years on earth are only to get to the next place?"

"Absolutely," he said.

Speaking for the Jewish faith, Rabbi Neil Gillman stated: "I'd think that the purpose of life is to live a decent life. You do it for its own sake, not to get a reward."

One of the most fascinating glimpses of heaven came from a woman who'd had a near-death experience. Deb Foster, a forty-two-year-old Californian, was clinically dead for four minutes. But she was somewhere else, somewhere utterly incredible and as real as any place she'd ever known. "I was on a staircase that went as high up into the sky as you can imagine. The sky was the most incredible color of blue. There were dogs and cats going up and down the staircase and they were gleeful. There was this light above, which I could look toward. I was in this place of incredible peace."

She brought up a very pressing issue for us pet owners (I can't imagine heaven without my dog Cha Cha!): Are there pets in heaven? Anthony DeStefano, author of *A Travel Guide to Heaven*, was clear on that point. "Why not?" he said. "God can do anything He wants."

No matter what religion, people want to know that there is more to life than what's here on earth. That they will be reunited with their loved ones and that any suffering they've had here on earth is over. It is a place of peace and understanding that will last for all eternity, of union with God. That's what heaven is for. That's the promise of faith.

Dick Van Dyke

What I Live By

The other day I was talking with a teenager who goes to the church where I'm an elder. "How often do you read your Bible?" I asked him.

"Frankly, Mr. Van Dyke," he said, giving me kind of a funny look, "I never read it." Then he continued, "Oh, I should, I suppose, but to tell you the truth the Bible scares me."

"Scares you?" I echoed. "What do you mean?"

"Well," he said, "it's written in that old-fashioned way. And it's all about old men in long white beards. And it's so negative. Thou shalt not do this, thou shalt not do that. No, the Bible may be a great book and all that, but nobody reads it. Nobody my age, anyway."

Now I don't know whether this pessimistic statement is right or not, but I do know this: A lot of people—old as well as young—never open a Bible because they let their preconceptions scare them off.

Take the objections my young friend had: The writing is old-fashioned, he said. Well, I suppose that's true, if you're talking about the King James Version. After all, it was written more than three hundred years ago. But the Bible has been translated many times before and since. J. B. Phillips' rendering of the New Testament is one of my personal favorites: It's as contemporary in style as a current best seller.

And his idea that the Bible is full of bearded old men: Think about that one for a moment. How old was David when he went out against Goliath armed with nothing but a sling? Fourteen? Fifteen? How old was Samson when he astonished his countrymen with feats of strength? Seventeen? Eighteen? The New Testament too: remember the young men who wanted Jesus to heal their sick friend? When they found themselves blocked by a crowd, they climbed up on the roof, broke a hole in the ceiling and lowered their friend's bed with a rope. Who but teenagers would have thought of that?

And as for the notion that the Bible is full of negatives, that's mostly nonsense too. The Bible is a handbook for living. And so it does contain rules—rules hammered out over the centuries on the anvil of human experience.

There's tragedy, sure, and violence and all the great clashing human emotions: courage and cowardice, greed and selflessness, hatred, jealousy, pride, anger . . . all the ingredients that go into any great love story or great action story. And out of these ingredients the men who wrote the Bible drew conclusions about what works and what doesn't work in human affairs. That's why the Bible, far from being something to run from, is a book to live by.

Anyone who does try to live by the Bible sooner or later comes across a text that seems designed especially for him. For me it's that tremendous question in Matthew: "What does it profit a man if he gain the whole world but lose his own soul?" (Matthew 16:26). Actors are often faced with this dilemma because they do in a sense "gain the whole world" when success comes to them, but in the process they risk losing their own souls, their own hard core of personal values, as perhaps no other group does. That's why I repeat those words to myself just about every day of my life.

But it's not enough to find a relevant quote, latch onto that and let the rest go. I believe the whole Bible is important to each of us, and that from its daily reading a certain priceless and otherwise unobtainable something enters our lives. If I had to say what it is in my case, I think I'd say that Bible-reading gives me a sense of God working in history, gradually unfolding a plan for His most complex creation—mankind. And, of course, as I read I try to measure myself against the outlines of that plan and see where I fit.

This is an amazing thing at all times, but especially when problems come our way. I'm thinking of some times in my life, for instance, when I was broke and jobless. Like the day I arrived in New York City in a beat-up station wagon with a wife, two small kids, no job and exactly four dollars in my pocket. Or the time when a supper club act that a friend and I worked up laid such an egg that the management not only threw us out without pay but even towed our car out of their parking lot to make sure we left.

I don't mean that on these occasions I rushed home and read the Bible furiously. But I do mean that my familiarity with God's word and my acceptance of His plan for my life kept me from ever really hitting the panic button. In other words, I believe that in reading the Bible a kind of invisible ingredient had seeped into my life—and will seep into anybody's—which makes the rough spots less bumpy. Perhaps it's a sense of proportion, of the smallness of our own little disappointments, of being part of a picture so big that we can never see more than a fraction of it.

Whatever it is, it's something I would like to share with the anxious, fear-ridden people of our age, and especially the young ones. To my friend who was "scared" of the Bible, I make three suggestions.

The first: Get your own Bible. One you can take on trips and leave on your bedside table. One you can mark up if you feel like it, underlining passages that speak to you, making notes in the margins.

The second: Make an effort to discard all your preconceptions and stereotyped ideas about the Bible before you open it. This includes all your hazy childhood recollections, all your stained-glass oversimplifications, all your dim resentful memories of droning preachers. Just try to wipe the slate clean and start fresh, as if you had just dropped in from Mars and found a book you had never seen or heard of before. If you can do this, the Bible will have tremendous impact for you.

And the third: Find a friend, or friends, who will make this voyage of exploration with you. I find it helps to have someone with whom to compare notes, someone who will throw the ball back. Eventually I hope this young man will want to join our church Bible class where, with a trained teacher, we go deeper than any of us could alone. But at first I think it's more fun and meaningful just to experiment and compare reactions with a friend.

The Bible scary? On the contrary. The Bible takes the scare out of living and puts purpose, joy and faith in its place.

SALLY-ANN ROBERTS

Quiet Time

I have to get up before dawn to anchor an early morning news show in New Orleans. The show airs at 6:00 AM and I need to arrive at the studio by 4:30 AM to get ready. Even before that, though, I do my own preparation at home. Quiet time, I call it. No one else is up. The house is still. I close my eyes and listen.

It hasn't always been that way. Quiet time is something I stumbled into in my midthirties, at a moment a few years ago when I needed God in a way I had never needed him before. The first inkling of it came when I was visiting my maternal grandmother at her apartment in Akron, Ohio. I was a young mother and Grandma Sally was well into her eighties.

That day, before lunch, I walked into the living room to see Grandma Sally sitting on the couch, her eyes shut. As I stood there wondering if I should disturb her, she opened her eyes. Looking serene and rested, she smiled and said, "Let me fix you a sandwich."

The daughter of a clergyman, Grandma Sally was a woman of great spiritual strength. Her own faith was considerably tested during the Depression, when my grandfather lost his business, and she supported the family by cleaning houses. My mother remembers times when their electricity, water and gas were shut off and the family gathered around a kerosene lamp at night for light and warmth.

For years Grandma Sally remained active in the church her father had started. She taught Sunday school and gave Bible lessons to the neighborhood kids, luring them in with fresh-baked cookies. The pastor of the church had attended those sessions when he was a boy. He told me my grandmother bought him a new pair of shoes when she noticed the scuffed hand-me-downs he wore. There was always an element of practicality to her religion.

So what could she possibly be doing sitting on the sofa in the silence of the living room? I didn't know. And because it seemed like such a private thing I didn't feel right asking.

The kind of prayer that was familiar to me was when you spoke aloud to God. You said everything that was on your mind and asked for his help. That's the way Mom and Dad had prayed when I was a kid.

Dad was an officer in the Air Force, so we had to move a lot. To Arizona, to Iowa, to Alabama. After we had the station wagon loaded up for those trips, we gathered in a circle, holding hands. Then Dad prayed, "Please be with us, Lord, as we travel. Take us safely to our destination. Help us settle in at the new base."

The hardest time came when Dad was assigned to a base in Canada for a year, and Mom and we kids stayed in Akron. Everyone was solemn as we watched Dad pack his duffel bag. Mom tried to cover her sorrow by bustling around the kitchen. I stood at the screen door and watched my thirteen-year-old brother Butch play one last game of catch with Dad before he left. Suddenly Butch dropped the ball and put the mitt to his face, bursting into tears.

That day when we were gathered in the family circle, Mom said the prayer. "Dear Lord," she prayed, "bring Larry back safely to us." At the end of the year's tour of duty he came back safe and sound, our prayers answered. Much later, after I had kids of my own, I realized

Mom must have said countless prayers when she was alone at night that difficult year.

It was only when my career suddenly hit a huge pothole in the early 1990s that I discovered a greater depth of prayer. Back then I was the anchor of a morning show called *Early Edition*, on WWL-TV in New Orleans. In the space of a dozen years I had gone from being a cub reporter on the city-hall beat to being an education reporter to doing some investigative work. And then anchoring my own show.

I was doing well. My boss and mentor at the station, Joe Duke, the news director, made that clear. What also became clear was that the station was undergoing financial challenges. Joe had intimated that our show might be in trouble. Then one morning, he asked me to come into his office.

There was no hint of his usual genial smile. "We're going to have to cancel *Early Edition*," he said. "We have to make cutbacks. I'm sorry."

"I understand," I said, nodding. But I was trying desperately not to cry. If *Early Edition* was no more, it seemed likely that my employment would be terminated too. I left the office and drove home. I went up to the bedroom, pulled the drapes and closed the door. Only then did I start crying.

How was I going to find another job I loved as much? How would we survive financially? My husband Willie had just started his own business and we were dependent on my salary. Finally I got down on my knees and prayed. "Dear Lord, what are we going to do? I'll never find another job as good as this one . . . "

After a while I was spent. I couldn't say another word. And that's when I did something I had never done while praying. I closed my eyes and listened. In the silence of the late morning, I listened to the Lord. I didn't hear any specific words, but it was as though God said to me, *I am here. You have nothing to fear.* An extraordinary peace came over me.

Whatever that feeling was, I couldn't live without it. For the next few weeks I made sure I had some time to myself every day. I got up early to pray. First to tell God what was on my mind. Sometimes I wrote the words, as in a letter. But then came the most important part. I closed my eyes—usually for about half an hour—and listened. Invariably I came away feeling refreshed.

The next time Joe Duke called me into his office I was sure he would be giving me a pink slip. I knew that no matter what happened I could depend on God to be with me. But as I listened to Joe talk, I realized he was asking me to anchor another show.

"I thought you were going to fire me," I finally admitted.

"Fire you?" he said. "I'm giving you a promotion!"

Six months later, my grandmother died. I went to Akron for the funeral and afterward helped Mom clean out Grandma Sally's apartment. That's when I discovered a priceless treasure trove she had left behind: journals she had kept for decades.

Sometimes she had written only a few words: "Went to Sally-Ann and Willie's for dinner" or "Fixed lunch for Lucimarian." But page after page my gaze was drawn to the same phrase. Whatever else Grandma Sally did, every day she made this notation: "Had Quiet Time."

"What was Quiet Time?" I asked.

"That's when your grandmother sat quietly to be with the Lord," Mom said.

Of course. I thought of the day I had seen Grandma sitting in the living room with her eyes closed, the most peaceful expression on her face.

"She couldn't get through a day without it," Mom said.

"I know," I said. Because now, neither can I. Every morning, I start my day by reading a few passages of Scripture, then sitting quietly. And listening.

CHERYL LADD

Look Up

Two things I take very seriously in life. My golf game and my relationship with God. Neither one is simple.

I took up golf after playing Kris Munroe in *Charlie's Angels*. Those were heady years. Pictures of the Angels were everywhere—magazine covers, posters, even lunch boxes, which I'm told you can still get on eBay. I couldn't go to the supermarket without being asked to sign an autograph. But behind the scenes my marriage was falling apart.

The year *Charlie's Angels* ended I remarried. My husband, Brian Russell, and I discovered golf and rediscovered church together. In 1990 we moved to the Santa Barbara area, full of beautiful golf courses, emerald swards in the soft dusty hills. Golf became a way to escape the pressures of life. Thanks to Brian's coaching I brought my game up to a seventeen handicap. I even made the rounds of celebrity tournaments.

We also made the rounds of churches until we found one that felt right, a Presbyterian church with a minister who helped us work on our spiritual lives in the same methodical way Brian helped me with my golf swing. I read the Bible cover to cover, every word. Passages came alive, and whole books, like Job and Psalms, spoke vividly to me. I trusted God as never before.

All this concentration on my faith even taught me something about my golf game. You do the hard work—your swing, your putting, your short game—and it pays off. Not just in the expected, prayed-for way, but sometimes in the most extraordinary ways.

A little example. Brian and I were playing golf with our friend, tennis champ Jimmy Connors. The weather was perfect. My game was so-so. We were on the ninth hole, a par three. I used a five iron. I stared down the fairway at the pin, 145 yards away. Then I closed my eyes and pictured how I would swing and how the ball would fly. Just hit the green, I told myself. That's your goal.

I said a quick prayer, opened my eyes and then swung. I watched the ball fly through the air, past the trees, headed right for the green. Good shot. I bent to pick up my tee.

"Cheryl, look up!" Jimmy yelled. I lifted my head. The ball bounced on the green, once, twice, rolled and then disappeared as if the green had swallowed it.

"A hole in one!" Brian shouted.

I looked at the guys in wonder. "Thanks," I said. "If you hadn't said anything, I would have missed that." It was a magical moment, the culmination of a lot of hard work. But it also seemed unearned—like grace.

So that's what I've learned to do in golf and, I guess, in life. Work hard and hit the greens. And don't forget to look up. You never know what you might miss.

JUDGE JOSEPH A. WAPNER

From a Judge's Study

As presiding judge on television's *The People's Court*, where real people bring real cases, my judgments are based on twenty years' experience on the bench of the superior and municipal courts of California.

But in a sense, many of my decisions—of every judge's decisions—go back more than three thousand years to the children of Israel wandering in the desert after their exodus from Egyptian bondage.

I'd never fully realized this until our men's Bible study group at my synagogue, Valley Beth Shalom, explored the Book of Leviticus. The third book of the Torah, or Pentateuch, opens with the ringing Hebrew word *Vayyikra* ("And He called") and records the words God spoke through Moses when God gave the Jewish people His instructions for worship and behavior.

Shortly, the Jews were to launch a unique nation, the first in history to be guided by the Word of God. In these few brief pages lies the seed of modern western law.

Chapter 19 of Leviticus especially, with its simple, nobly expressed rules of moral behavior, lets us glimpse embryonic versions of many of our own American laws. Read, for instance, verse 13: "The wages of him that is hired shall not abide with thee all night until the morning." In other words, pay promptly for work performed—a rule we see reflected in today's Fair Employment codes.

Today's concern for the handicapped is prefigured in verse 14: "Thou shalt not curse the deaf nor put a stumblingblock before the blind."

And as a judge, I take special note of verse 15: "Ye shall do no unrighteousness in judgment; thou shalt not respect the person of the poor nor honor the person of the mighty; but in righteousness shalt thou judge thy neighbor."

This evenhanded system of justice was not the rule in the rest of the ancient world. Indeed, for most of human history, a person accused of a crime could hardly expect to be tried before an impartial judge who was versed in a region's own laws. The judge might be a policeman or a priest. He might be an imperial prefect sent from Rome to try a Greek merchant or an Egyptian farmer. He might be a priest of one religion trying someone of another religion. The judge might simply be a friend of the king, trying a case according to his own interests or his temper or how he felt after lunch.

A historic example is the thirteenth century's King John of England, who was so cruel and oppressive that his noblemen rose in angry revolt. On a whim, John might accuse a nobleman of treason, order a magistrate to find him guilty, and seize the hapless victim's land—and perhaps his head. In a treaty with King John—the famous Magna Carta of AD 1215—the nobles gained several crucial rights, including protection from such arbitrary "trials." The nobles wrote into the Magna Carta a law of trial-by-jury. Never again were they to be tried for a serious crime except by a jury of their peers.

Taken for granted in America and Great Britain, trial by jury, one of the strongest safeguards against government's arbitrary authority, remains a rare privilege in much of the rest of the world. But where, long before the Magna Carta, did it gain its first, rough expression? That's right, in Leviticus. To be precise, and as cited above, in chapter 19, verse 15: "In righteousness shalt thou judge thy neighbour."

And where do our laws against slander originate? In chapter 19, verse 16: "Thou shalt not go up and down as a talebearer among thy people."

Or our laws against unfair interest? Read chapter 25, verse 37: "Thou shalt not give him thy money upon usury." This not only reflects our rules against unfair moneylending, but is also a forerunner of the Hebrew Free Loan Societies that operate through synagogues all over the United States, extending interest-free loans to needy individuals.

One of the most offbeat memories from my career relates to Leviticus 19:11, which reads in part, "neither deal falsely, neither lie one to another."

When I was a judge of the Municipal Court of Los Angeles, I was obliged on my very first day to judge a defendant's claims literally with my own eyes. The man, whom I'll call Mr. Tobin, was charged with speeding on Olympic Boulevard, where the limit was thirty-five miles per hour. The policeman said he had followed Mr. Tobin's 1949 Cadillac and clocked it at sixty.

"Your Honor," pleaded Mr. Tobin, "my car is broken. It won't go over thirty-five!"

The policeman laughed out loud.

"All right," I told Mr. Tobin. "If you'll wait until I finish my other cases, I'll ride in your car myself. If it won't go over thirty-five, you win."

Later, during our lunch break, my bailiff got behind the wheel with Mr. Tobin and me as passengers.

No matter how hard the bailiff pressed down on the accelerator, that car wouldn't go over thirty-five. The transmission was broken.

I returned to court, banged my gavel lightly and ruled, "Not guilty."

That case taught me an invaluable lesson: Like the great Solomon, look for the truth with your own eyes and ears and good sense. Don't trust others when your own common sense tells you something's wrong.

But of all God's commands in Leviticus, I feel that the most important is Leviticus 19:18, which says, "Thou shalt love thy neighbor as thyself."

Jesus repeated this again and again. As did the famous thirteenth-century scholar of Gerona, Rabbi Nahmanides: "One should place no limitations upon the love for the neighbor, but instead a person should love to do an abundance of good for his fellow being as he does for himself."

I think often of this commandment as I look out on this golden land of ours. I see the links between families, friends and neighbors dissolving. Silly quarrels that shouldn't last five minutes get into state courts. Neighbors arguing over a spare parking space have to get a judge to settle the matter; children need a court to patch up arguments with their parents. Men, women and children are alone. Without the healing power of love, we are becoming a nation of lonely people.

Neither the law nor a thousand judges can retie the bonds between people. Each person will have to start doing that himself. And I know a good place to start—with Leviticus 19:18: *Love thy neighbor as thyself.*

MIKE EMRICK

On Air

There I was in the TV booth at Madison Square Garden minutes before hockey legend Wayne Gretzky's final game, about to face my biggest challenge. You would think that after twenty-six seasons doing play-by-play for hockey games, I would be used to speaking on camera. Ordinarily I am. But today my broadcast partner would be down on the ice emceeing the pregame ceremony.

I was all on my own. I would have to open the game by myself live before several million people who would be watching this historic event on national television. I had to fill fifty long seconds of airtime before the ceremony began; to me, that seemed like an eternity. I've never done a game of this magnitude before. What will I say?

I went over the lineups and player bios. Did I have every detail down? I flipped open my hockey notebook for a final check. There on the first page was a prayer by Dr. Norman Vincent Peale that I had copied down long ago.

Lord, sometimes our problems are too hard to handle. But You will let us know what to do and how to do it. Let us be troubled no more.

The lights came up for the ceremony. A hush fell over the crowd. I took my spot in front of the camera. "You're on," the director said.

I took a deep breath and began, "Hi, everyone. I'm Mike Emrick." Suddenly the words flowed effortlessly. "If you're a hockey fan, just bring your best memories of Wayne Gretzky. If you're not, we'll tell you he's the most productive hockey player ever and he's a better person than a player. . . ."

Later I was nominated for a Sports Emmy for play-by-play. The first sequence on the tape the network submitted to the nominating committee? You guessed it. Those fifty seconds before the puck dropped for Wayne Gretzky's last game when my words felt truly inspired.

CAL THOMAS

Putting Myself on Record

O ne of the cardinal rules I was taught while growing up was that there are two things one should never discuss in public—religion and politics.

While I tended to abide for a long time with the first caution against what my father sometimes referred to as "wearing one's religion on one's sleeve," I soon departed from the second and became an avid debater of my political viewpoint.

Still, as much as politics fascinated me, growing up as I did in the Washington, DC area, and beginning a career in journalism with NBC News at the ripe old age of eighteen, there was always a reluctance to talk about religion, about God, with anyone else.

Mostly this was because I had little to say. Sure, I went to church occasionally, but the only serious consideration I ever gave the Bible was when my grandfather told me he would give me a silver dollar if I memorized the 23rd Psalm. I was ten years old at the time and it seemed like a good deal. The silver dollar is long gone, but the memorized Psalm remains with me to this day. Which says something about the value of money, inflation and where real value lies!

It was nearly thirty years after my paid encounter with Psalm 23 and about ten years after I made a personal commitment of my life to Jesus Christ that I was confronted with perhaps the biggest challenge to sharing my faith that I have ever had.

I remember my initial effort to tell people what I thought about God and the Bible. I would sometimes break out in a cold sweat. It was far easier to discuss my favorite football team or a good place to eat. Perhaps that was because I knew more about football and good food than I did about God.

I had begun writing some newspaper columns in the fall of 1983, never really expecting the papers to publish them. To my astonishment, the *New York Times* published the first column I ever wrote. *The Washington Post* followed by publishing two of them, and then *USA Today* called. Soon I was appearing in that national newspaper; then the *Los Angeles Times* accepted one of my pieces, and I began to think that something important was going on!

As I prayed about what message God was trying to send me (He so often worked in the midst of unexpected circumstances in my life), I asked Him to show me whether this is something that He wanted me to continue to do.

I wrote all of the top newspaper syndicates in the country, enclosing samples of my recently published columns and asking to be carried by one of these prestigious companies. Each of them sent me a rejection notice. "We have too many already," said one. "You write well, but we can't add anyone else at this time," said another.

It was then that I wrote Tom Johnson, publisher of the *Los Angeles Times*, one of the nation's biggest newspapers. I had met Tom while he was a White House Fellow during Lyndon Johnson's Administration in the mid-1960s and I was with NBC News. I remembered him as a kind, decent, talented man.

He agreed with me that there was a lack of good conservative commentary with sometimes a spiritual touch in most newspapers today, and he offered to set up an appointment for me with two executives from the *Los Angeles Times* Syndicate. He told me, "If you can sell your column idea to them, we'll take you on."

In March 1984, I flew to Los Angeles for the meeting. I remember praying that morning, "Lord, You have given me all the skills that I possess, but it will take a major miracle for them to give me a syndicated newspaper column. So I am asking You to deliver it into my hands and I promise that if You do, I will use every opportunity to give You the credit for it."

Later, at a luncheon meeting in the executive dining room of the mammoth *Los Angeles Times* newspaper complex, I sat between the two people who would decide whether I would be allowed to write a column for one of the country's top syndicates. The *Los Angeles Times* Syndicate publishes Art Buchwald, Joseph Kraft and former White House Press Secretary Jody Powell, among others, so I was aspiring to be in top company.

For one hour the two executives told me all the reasons why they couldn't possibly take me on. There were already too many columnists, they said. It would cost too much to add a new one. I answered each argument as best I could. After one hour of this, one of them turned to me and, without any advance warning, said, "You're a Christian, aren't you?"

"Yes, I am," I replied a little nervously, wondering where this would lead.

"Tell me about it," he said, taking another bite of his food.

I nearly choked. In a flash, all of those childhood memories came rushing back. The advice from parents and friends not to talk about religion and politics, but especially religion.

Were they leading me into a trap? If I was honest about my religious feelings, would they use that as an excuse not to take my column, because they might think it would be "too religious"?

Just at that point, a remarkable peace came over me, and I decided to tell them what Jesus Christ meant to me. I spoke without fear or trembling for about ten minutes on how Christ had transformed my life in the middle of a personal battle to reach the top of the ladder at NBC as a network TV correspondent and how empty it seemed after I nearly made it.

Immediately upon finishing this mini "testimony" I had never expected to give (or thought I had the nerve to give), one of the two executives turned to the other and said, "I just thought of something. Isn't so-and-so leaving us in April?"

"Why, yes," said the other decision maker. "I had completely for gotten about it."

The first executive turned to me and asked, "Can you begin writing two columns per week starting April 17?"

I was shocked. This was the miracle I had asked for as dramatic for me as the parting of the Red Sea must have been for Moses. I mumbled something incoherent about how I would be honored, thrilled, etc., and walked, weak-kneed, into the street.

Later a verse of Scripture would remind me what had happened that day. It is the one where Jesus Christ tells us that if we confess Him before men, He will confess us before His Father in heaven, but if we are ashamed of Him before men, He will be ashamed of us before His Father in heaven.

I could almost hear God saying that day, "Let's see if this fellow Thomas has learned anything. Let's see if he is ashamed of Us. If he is not, then We will give him the desire of his heart, this newspaper column, but if he is ashamed of Us, he won't get it."

I thought of the Prophet Abraham and his willingness to sacrifice Isaac, his son, who had been promised to him by God in his old age. When God saw that Abraham would not even withhold his son from Him, He was convinced of Abraham's love for God and worked great and mighty miracles and delivered marvelous blessings to Abraham's life.

In a much smaller way, this is what happened to me. I believe that because I spoke up about my faith, even when something I wanted very much could easily have been denied me, God intervened and allowed me to have it.

I can't say there aren't times when I still get a little nervous in certain circumstances, with certain people, when I talk about God, but He has given me a new boldness and a new awareness that if I will only open my mouth and tell people about Him, then He will give me the words to say.

FOLLOWING
YOUR DREAMS

*For four months, I worked at Amtrak by day and did
stand-up at night. Since I was the new comic on the block,
I didn't go on until everybody else was done—usually at four
in the morning, when there were only two people left to hear
me. Then I had to be at work by seven. I was so desperate for
sleep that I'd take an early lunch, sit at my desk and prop
a book open, and fall fast asleep with my head in my hands.*

LARRY MILLER

★ 241 ★

DAVID MICHEL

Happy Landing

Late one night, my wife and I were talking about the problems I was having getting a project off the ground. "Maybe you should think about doing something else, David," she said. "Like getting your old job back. You've given this your best shot."

On our dining room table I saw the box for a video called *Jay Jay's First Flight*. "But I was so sure this was what God wanted for me," I said. "That I'd finally found what I was meant to do." I'd taken the risk, and I'd failed. Maybe my wife was right. Was there any choice but to throw in the towel for my family's sake and for my own?

I thought back to when my idea first took root. I'd been on yet another business trip, that time on a flight from Dallas to St. Louis. My job as a physician recruiter for a health-care consulting firm took me all over the country. Some people are excited by travel. I used to be too, but it had become routine. Usually I'd spend my time on the plane preparing for meetings, but instead I found myself thinking of my two-year-old son John. Bedtime for him soon. And I'd miss it again.

My own dad had always been there for me. He'd tuck me in at night, then tell me a story. I usually insisted on my favorite. "Well, David," he'd start, "One time the U.S. government asked Daddy if he would be willing to get on a rocket and go to the moon. I said, 'Sure.' I got in this rocket that was taller than the church house, and blasted off. It took two days and two nights to get there, then I just turned around and came back." I knew Dad was making it all up, but I didn't care. His wild tales fueled my imagination, and sometimes I'd make up my own stories.

I tried to keep up the same storytelling tradition with my son whenever I tucked him in. "Tell me a story, Daddy," he'd say. "About airplanes." John was fascinated by planes, and since I'd spent so much time on them, it was easy for me to make up stories about flying. The star of those crazy stories became a little plane named Jay Jay. He got into all kinds of adventures, and once in a while a bit of trouble. But he always learned something in the process: Tell the truth, be kind, follow rules and other lessons in faith and fair play. The smile on John's face when I spun one of my yarns made all my travel worthwhile.

It's not that I didn't like my job. I did like it, and I was good at it too. I'd won the Marketer of the Year award as a rookie employee. Since then I'd gotten a big office, an impressive title and a good salary. *Is this it?* I wondered. Something inside me told me it wasn't. The discontent nagging at me was familiar.

All my adult life I'd sensed there was something I was meant to do, something I hadn't quite found. Back in high school I'd attended a youth gathering that was a time of singing, Bible study and prayer. That's when I first felt it, a mysterious certainty that God had something big in store for me. But I had no idea what.

I shared the experience with my girlfriend Deborah. "How do you know?" she asked. I couldn't find the words to explain. I just knew that God had a plan for me. My job was to find out what it was.

Deborah and I got married in 1984. After many false starts, I graduated with a degree in chemistry from Southern Methodist

University. I kept praying for direction, but all I would get back was the sense that there was something out there I was meant to find.

Finally I landed the job with the recruiting firm. At first the travel was exciting. Then it became a chore. I hated being away from my family.

I wish I were tucking in my son right now, I thought as my flight soared toward St. Louis. I wanted him to grow up and remember the stories I'd told him, just like I'd never forgotten the stories my dad told me. *I shouldn't be doing this,* I thought, buckling my seat belt for landing. *I should be telling stories about Jay Jay the Jet Plane.*

Something clicked inside, as clearly as the buckle on my seat belt. Yes, David. That's what you are meant to do.

Tell stories? Ideas shot through my head as if a movie had started running: a town populated by talking planes, maybe a helicopter too. They'd get into all sorts of adventures, and there'd always be a good, strong lesson at the end. It would make a great TV show, especially with all the bad stuff on the tube these days.

"We need to talk," I told Deborah after I got home. I explained what I had in mind, sketching the whole thing out on a yellow legal pad.

"David, it's a great idea."

"I'd have to leave my job," I said. Working such demanding hours wouldn't leave me any time to pursue my idea.

"Are you sure about this?" she asked.

I told her I was. "Everything will work out. You'll see."

Deep down I couldn't help having my doubts though. Surely my idea was the big thing God had in mind for me. *It's what you're meant to do,* I reminded myself when I took the first huge step. My boss looked at me in disbelief when I quit. Especially when I told him why.

"A TV show for kids?" he asked.

I nodded. He predicted I'd come crawling back for my job soon enough.

I took out all my savings, and a loan, then contracted with a Dallas production company. I found someone to make a set, and a writer to work on the script. He and I came up with a Norman Rockwell kind of place named Tarrytown. Jay Jay the Jet Plane lived there with Herky the Helicopter, Snuffy the Skywriter, Big Jake the Prop Plane and a bunch of others.

In two and a half months we finished *Jay Jay's First Flight*, a half-hour video. In the story Jay Jay takes off one day without a flight plan. He gets into danger and almost crashes. But he makes it home okay, and learns the importance of knowing where you're going before you head out.

It was a lesson I could have heeded. Regardless of how ordained I felt the project was, I honestly had no idea what I was doing. A full-page ad in a national parenting magazine cost just about every penny I had left. It resulted in about two hundred orders for the video, nowhere near enough to cover the expense. I borrowed more money and made a TV commercial. It was an even bigger flop. We got fewer than fifty orders.

What on earth are you doing? I wondered. *You've got a family to provide for and you're nearly broke.*

That's when Deborah suggested that maybe I go back to my "real" job and make *Jay Jay* a side project. "Lord," I prayed after we got done talking, "I thought this was what you wanted. Show me what to do!"

At that moment John ran into the room, his arms spread out like wings. "Vrooooom!" He was pretending to be Jay Jay. He was only three, but he'd already memorized lines from the video, and he was swooping around acting out the story. He was the reason I'd done this in the first place.

Okay, God, I thought, *I'll give it one more shot. I'll just trust You completely.* I got the help of a professional. I borrowed the last bit of money I could and found a savvy production partner, who made a sixty-second commercial that was broadcast on the Cartoon Network and Nickelodeon. More than one hundred thousand orders came in.

That enabled us to make two more videos, and they sold well too. Our success was noticed by Bruce Johnson, who used to work for Hanna-Barbera. He was interested in launching a new kids' show, and *Jay Jay* was just the kind of thing he had in mind. With his help, *Jay Jay* was picked up for broadcast on The Learning Channel. It ran there for a year and a half, and then it moved to PBS.

The show's audience is mostly preschoolers. John, who's eleven years old now, doesn't admit to his friends that he still watches. But he's usually eager to explain how *Jay Jay* got off the ground. After all, how many successful TV shows started out as impromptu bedtime stories? And a certain feeling that there was a plan out there just waiting to be followed.

BOB ALLMAN

I Don't Need Eyes to Be a Sportscaster

I've discovered that one can be handicapped and still do practically everything he has his heart set on—as long as he has faith in God, knows how to pray and devotes his talents to the welfare of others.

My sports scripts are written in Braille. For eyes at sporting events I use my old college chum and fellow scriptwriter, Bob Paul. The rest of the job involves the acquiring of a complete knowledge of all sports so that an image is always present in my mind. I ask questions constantly.

Sometimes I've been in tight situations. On one dramatic sports broadcast a page of my script slipped from my hand and fell to the floor. The announcer picked it up, but did not know how to hand it to me with its strange dots and perforations in Braille. Still I had enough knowledge of my subject.

Recently I "watched" a number of wrestling matches at Yale University. When queried as to why I called one young man outstanding, I could speak authoritatively since I had felt his arms and legs. This, combined with how the young man talked and acted, created the picture in my mind.

I got a very special kick out of one incident that happened to me recently. In a subway a blind person brushed against me and asked me to help him toward an upstairs trolley. I did it happily, never letting on that I, too, had no sight.

As a lawyer, I have also had some interesting experiences. During one case I made a particularly stirring speech for my client, and won the case. Later I discovered that I had my back to the jury during the whole plea!

Anyone with a handicap or a limitation can lick it if he will consider everything in life as an adventure. God intended for every one of us to be useful.

KEN WALES

A Dream Called Christy

I first dreamed of bringing Catherine Marshall's novel *Christy* to the screen nearly twenty years ago. At the time there was no way I could have imagined how long and how difficult a struggle it would be.

I was a young film producer in 1976 when I saw a poster announcing an appearance by Catherine Marshall at the Pasadena Civic Auditorium. Her book *A Man Called Peter* had been a successful motion picture. As a minister's son, I was quite moved by it. It struck me that *Christy*, based on her mother's experiences as a young, struggling schoolteacher in 1912 amid the grinding poverty of the Great Smoky Mountains, would also be a natural for the screen. I knew MGM owned the rights to the book. Why hadn't the movie been made? I called a friend at MGM and asked.

"It's dead," he told me. "Buried in the basement with a lot of other old properties."

"I want to see about the rights," I pressed.

"Forget it, Ken."

It was an old Hollywood story. After *Christy* had been bought and put into development in 1969, a new studio head had taken over. He cleaned house, shelving a lot of scripts and bringing in his own projects. But studios don't easily give up production rights, even to properties they have no interest in producing. They use them as business write-offs. That was what had happened to *Christy*.

Next I called Catherine Marshall's editor. "Catherine's been upset about this for a long time," he explained. "She has tried to buy back the rights but the studio just ignores her." He suggested I call Catherine directly at her farm in Lincoln, Virginia.

When Catherine came to the phone, she was understanding, but not very encouraging. She explained that she had made the mistake of selling the rights with no time limit stipulated in the contract. MGM owned *Christy* in perpetuity.

"I had such hopes for it," she sighed.

There was a long pause. "Well," I said finally, trying to muster some optimism, "maybe there is some way."

"Ken, maybe God has a way," Catherine replied quietly. But in that simple remark I sensed a deep and powerful conviction—the passion of Catherine Marshall's faith that had drawn millions of people to her writing. And I knew that it would be faith that we would have to rely on.

A few weeks later I went to hear Catherine speak. Afterward I visited with her and her husband, Len LeSourd. We discussed *Christy* and before I left I promised that I wouldn't give up.

There was still one key person at MGM who might be able to help—Frank Davis, a senior vice-president. He'd been executive producer on *The Greatest Story Ever Told* and also served on the vestry of St. Matthew's Episcopal Church in Pacific Palisades, which I occasionally visited. Frank was sympathetic but felt I was up against a stone wall. "I wish I could be more encouraging."

One summer I traveled to Evergreen Farm to meet the true-life heroine who inspired *Christy*—Catherine's mother, Leonora Wood. Even at eighty-four, Leonora retained a remarkable beauty. Her blue eyes still radiated the spirit that had led a young girl to leave her comfortable Asheville, North Carolina, home to teach mountain children in the wild, raw Smokies.

I returned to California even more determined to bring *Christy* to the screen. Early in 1983 I got a call from Len LeSourd. Catherine had died. When Leonora Wood died a few years later, it seemed that my dream died too.

One Sunday in 1986 I drove over to St. Matthew's. I hadn't been there in a long time. But that morning an insistent urge wouldn't let go. The next day I got a call from my old friend Frank Davis. "Nice to see you in church yesterday," Frank said. We chatted a bit and then he asked me, "By the way, are you still interested in *Christy?*"

"I certainly am," I said.

Frank explained that media mogul Ted Turner was buying MGM. "Now is the time to act, Ken. It may be your last chance."

After Frank hung up I stared at the phone for a long time, almost afraid to hope. Then I made the call.

A few days later MGM laid out the terms that would allow me to hold a production option on *Christy*. I would have to come up with a great deal of option money every year while I looked for a studio to produce the film. I was willing to take the risk.

I turned down other projects to pursue *Christy*. As time passed, the expenses stretched my finances. I mortgaged my house. But when investors in the project left after the 1987 stock market crash, I found myself without backing.

Early in 1993, seventeen years after I met Catherine Marshall, the president of CBS Entertainment inquired about *Christy* as a television series. He was very interested. But I wasn't.

I was a film producer. I had envisioned *Christy* on the big screen, where the Smoky Mountains could be captured in all their majesty.

But the more I prayed about it, it seemed that God was telling me that letting the story unfold in a television series would give us a better chance to explore the characters and their lives by bringing them into the homes of millions of people every week.

Still I resisted. Then my wife Susan reminded me of Catherine's article about the Prayer of Relinquishment. "Remember how it goes?"

I'd memorized a passage from it years ago: "Our relinquishment must be the real thing," Catherine had written, "because this giving up of self-will is the hardest thing we human beings are ever called on to do."

Was my self-will preventing me from relinquishing my insistence that *Christy* be a movie? I recalled what Catherine had said: "Ken, maybe God has a way." I knew that I had to place my dream into God's hands.

Last September we started filming *Christy* for CBS in the Tennessee Smokies, where Leonora Wood had taught some eighty years ago. We worked under looming mountains wrapped in a blue haze. And as I followed the leaf-strewn path into Cutter Gap, where Christy's old mission stood, I was reminded that if we trust in God and persevere with faith and prayer, dreams can come true.

Joe Barbera

The Solution Is Here Somewhere

Bill Hanna and I had worked as cartoonists at MGM for twenty years when we were let go. We'd produced an Academy Award-winning series of shorts starring a cat-and-mouse duo, Tom and Jerry. We had a good reputation and secure positions, but by the 1950s the movie studios were facing tough competition from the television industry. Animated shorts seemed too expensive to make. One day in 1957 Bill and I were out on the streets.

What were we supposed to do? I loved my profession, working with my God-given gifts, and wasn't about to give up. Bill wasn't either, so we joined our last names together with a hyphen and hung out our shingle. I drew and he was the mechanical wizard, a perfect combination. We figured we'd produce cartoons for television. There was one minor problem. TV couldn't afford us either.

We were horrified when we saw our first budget. Our sole client couldn't pay more than a tenth of what we were used to spending. "The solution is here somewhere," I said to myself. But what was it?

I did the storyboards at home, and my twelve-year-old daughter Jayne colored in the drawings. We worked night and day, making progress. Still, neither Bill nor I could guess how to create a five-minute cartoon that normally took, say, twenty-eight thousand drawings with a budget for only five thousand. "The solution is here," I said to myself again. "I just haven't seen it yet."

Bill and I looked at the problem from every possible angle. Then we remembered "pencil reels," sample preview reels we'd pioneered at MGM to show our bosses what we had in mind.

In a pencil reel we didn't sketch each millisecond of Tom and Jerry's motion. If Jerry was running, for instance, I'd do just two drawings for the pencil reel, one with the left foot in front, one with the feet reversed. Bill would expose the two on film so the legs looked crisscrossed, like scissors, and that image gave the impression of running. *Is this the solution?* I wondered.

We tried it, and surprisingly enough, it looked great! Quick, explosive, with the kind of action we liked. Our characters moved in a realistic blur of "limited animation," a concept that eventually revolutionized the industry, making a whole lineup of Saturday-morning entertainment for children affordable.

What did I learn from the experience? When hope is hard to find, when I'm stymied by a problem, I think: *The solution is here. I just haven't seen it yet!*

LARRY MILLER

Will the Real Larry Miller Please Stand Up?

When I graduated from Amherst College in 1975, I had no idea what to do with my life. Now, I know this isn't uncommon, but at the time it seemed everyone else was on the fast track to success. So while most of my friends headed for jobs or to graduate school, I moved back to Valley Stream, New York, to live with my parents.

It's odd moving back home after you're grown up. My parents were great about it. They never nagged me, but I could tell they were hoping I'd get on with things. While I was growing up, they wanted me to become a doctor. My dad would say, "If you're a professional, a doctor, people will respect you. Even before they meet you, they'll respect you."

"Which people?" I'd counter. "And why should they respect you for your job? They should respect you for you."

My folks took it pretty well when I majored in music instead of prelaw or premed. Now here I was, puttering around, playing drums or cello in local clubs and doing some house painting. But while I felt aimless in the job arena, there was a subtle change taking place in my relationship with God.

My parents are devout Jews. In fact, they "keep kosher," using one set of dishes for dairy and another for meat. My father begins and ends each day with the *Shema*, daily prayers, and my mother lights the Sabbath candles every Friday night.

Growing up, I took comfort in these rituals, and in going to temple every week. In college, while I never turned my back on my faith, there were "more pressing" issues—schoolwork, friends and girls. I still went to temple on High Holy Days, but that was it.

Now that I was older, my parents' rituals began to have new meaning for me. I could see it was not enough to pray just because I was "religious." Prayer had to be talking, really talking, to God. I discovered that although I had been religious my whole life, nothing had changed. But when I sought to know God, things couldn't stay the same.

As I prayed and pondered what to do with my life, and how to get people—and my parents and God—to respect me, I remembered a story told by a rabbi named Rashi, who lived in the twelfth century. He said, "When I meet God, I'm not afraid He's going to say, 'Rashi, why weren't you Abraham?' or, 'Why weren't you Moses?' I'm afraid He's going to say, 'Rashi, why weren't you Rashi?'"

I didn't want God to say "Larry, why weren't you Larry?" But how did I go about finding out how God intended for me to be Larry?

Well, if you look in the Scriptures, Moses and Abraham weren't born knowing everything either. They followed God and took things one step at a time. My conversation with myself went something like this:

"Okay, Larry, what do you want to do? Where do your talents lie?"

"I think I want to write or act."

"Then what's the next step?"

"Move to New York. Get a job. Get an apartment."

So one summer day in 1977 I got on a train headed for New York City. While most people move to New York planning to hit the big time, it seldom works out that way. I found myself living in a bustling place with four roommates. Nor was I exactly "on Broadway": I was working in Pennsylvania Station as a railway reservations clerk for Amtrak.

This could have seemed depressing. Instead, it seemed very funny. Day to day there were few crises at Penn Station that didn't have a germ of humor in them. It's amazing how a slight shift in perspective will take someone from being very upset to having a good laugh. I also enjoyed keeping people in the office in good humor, often by just recounting daily experiences. My acting career wasn't getting off the ground, but I was undoubtedly the star clerk at Amtrak.

"Gee, Larry, you're a riot," people would say. "A regular comedian."

Maybe I'd heard this often enough that thoughts were already brewing when I had dinner with a coworker and her friend Maureen. It was Maureen who said, "Well, have you thought of being a comedian? Instead of just cheering up people at the office, you should cheer up people for a living." Maureen was working in a new comedy club called the Comic Strip. She said if I came by the club she would introduce me around.

Later that week I went over. I was fascinated by what I saw. It was amazing. People got up on that stage, and with nothing except their minds, their hearts and a microphone they knit a roomful of people together through laughter. Still, the comedians I admired were those who, like Bill Cosby, spoke from their own experiences.

By the end of the first evening, I went up to the fellow in charge and said, "How do you get started doing this?"

The first night that I was given five minutes of my own on stage, I was nervous. And justifiably so. The stage seemed tiny and the room was suddenly cavernous and dark. My name was called, the people clapped, I bounded up the steps and started to tell jokes. No one laughed. I was awful. In the lingo of comedians, I died out there.

But the odd thing was, it was exhilarating. Coming off that stage, anyone in his right mind would have headed for the nearest exit and investigated how to change his name. But instead of being embarrassed, I was fascinated. Fascinated how come some comedians got the audience to respond and I didn't? What should I do differently?

Although I couldn't have put it into words at the time, when God finally asks, "Why weren't you Larry?" I now suspected that this was it. This was the Larry I was supposed to be.

My parents came to see me, and it couldn't have been easy for them. After all of their patience and paying for my education and standing by me through thick and thin, their son was going to be a stand-up comedian?

Yes. I'm afraid the answer was yes.

That was the beginning. For four months, I worked at Amtrak by day and did stand-up at night. Of course, since I was the new comic on the block, I didn't get to go on until everybody else was done—usually at four in the morning, when there were only two people left to hear me. Then I had to be at work by seven. I was so desperate for sleep that I'd take an early lunch, sit at my desk and prop a book open, and fall fast asleep with my head in my hands.

I went on stage again and again, and I began to get it, to get the audience to respond, to communicate with them, to be vulnerable, to offer them my heart. Since that first amateur night ten years ago at the Comic Strip, I've been on the *Tonight Show* and on *Late Night with David Letterman*. I've even opened for Frank Sinatra's show in Las Vegas.

And you know something? When I started, I thought that the

good I was doing was to let people laugh at the end of a long day. But a comedian can't be funny without sharing something of himself and his worldview—and his faith. He can reassure people. He can say, "You're all right. So you circle the phone eleven times before you get up the nerve to call a girl. So do I. It's the human condition."

And he can explore what's really important in life. Look at fads, for instance; they are awfully silly. Are you thinking for yourself? Are you acting on the courage of your convictions? Do you take TV commercials at face value without realizing how blatantly silly they are?

Most importantly, he can ask, "Where do you seek your respect? Is it from 'cool' people? Or is it from God?" He gave us the Ten Commandments, you know, not the Ten Helpful Hints.

And you know what? I think my parents respect me. Maybe even more than if I'd become a doctor. Because if God gives you a talent and you discover it, you don't have the option of burying it.

God isn't going to say to you, "Why weren't you Jonas Salk?" Or even, "Why weren't you Larry Miller?" He's going to say, "Why weren't you you?"

And you know, "you" is the best thing God could ever ask you to be.

HENRY G. SANDERS

Tough Choices

E ver wonder how actors get those parts you see them playing on a TV series? Well, strange as it might sound, I got my role on *Doctor Quinn, Medicine Woman* because I turned it down. And saying no wasn't easy.

For more than twenty years I'd studied, auditioned and acted in every show that would have me—and more often than not, those parts were small. Throughout it all, my wife Naila and our two children encouraged me. I longed to give my family a good, regular income—and spend more time with them. But in the meantime, I had to take what roles I could get, wherever they might be.

That's why, when in the spring of 1992 I was offered a good part at the Alabama Shakespeare Theater, I kissed Naila and the kids goodbye and headed for Lafayette, Alabama, for five weeks. The play was *Miss Ever's Boys* and it was a chance to present a thought-provoking drama to an appreciative regional audience.

The play was interesting and I settled in to concentrate on my part. And then one day as rehearsal broke, I was told I had a call. I went backstage and picked up the phone.

"Henry? It's Beth in Los Angeles."

Beth Sullivan and I were longtime friends as well as professional colleagues. Beth develops ideas for television series, and I'd had parts on some of her shows.

Beth sounded excited. "I'm working on a new TV drama," she said, "and there's a part you'd be perfect for. The pilot will establish the character as a regular."

A feeling of anticipation was building in me too. The job sounded like the kind of break I'd been hoping for.

"We'll be shooting the pilot next week," she said. "I know you're under contract in Alabama, but the theater is dark on Monday, right? I've arranged to film all your scenes in Los Angeles on Monday, starting early in the morning. You can fly to LA, tape the TV pilot, and fly back without missing any performances."

It's true, Monday is traditionally the day when the theater is dark. "Terrific!" I said. "I'll be there."

"I have a good feeling about this," Beth said. "I'll bet you anything the pilot is picked up as a series."

A huge grin spread across my face. If I landed a role on a good dramatic series, I could stay home in LA with my family, do interesting work, and bring in a steady paycheck.

I nearly floated over to the theater office to tell the managers so I could start making my travel plans.

They were enthusiastic as I described the opportunity. "That's great, Henry," the director said. "Which Monday did you say you'll be gone?"

"In a week," I said. "The Monday before the play opens. I'll fly out to LA on Sunday and be back here in plenty of time for Tuesday night."

A look of concern passed over the director's face. "You realize there's a paid preview here at eight o'clock that Sunday night?"

No, I hadn't realized.

"If you can work it out, go ahead," the director said. Okay, so I'd leave for California the moment the curtain came down on Sunday night. I immediately began calling to check on airline tickets. But I discovered there were no flights leaving after 10:30 that night. There wasn't even anything to New York, where I could connect with a red-eye.

I hurried back to the office. "There's no way I can do the preview here Sunday night," I said. "Could you possibly cancel that performance? Change the time? Get someone to do my part?"

"I'm really sorry," the theater manager said. "People have already bought their tickets; we're nearly sold out. And you don't have an understudy who's able to go on."

Some actors in this dilemma might decide that a network TV series was much more important than a repertory play in a regional theater and would simply walk out. But I'd accepted this part in good faith. I'd signed the contract, made a commitment. People were counting on me.

As I sat in my hotel room, I thought about who I was, what I believed in. I'd been raised in a single-parent home by a mother who had a strong faith, and I remembered what the Bible said: "Let your yes be yes and your no be no" (James 5:12).

I had given the Alabama Shakespeare Theater my yes. It would have to stand.

With a heavy heart I called Beth Sullivan's office back in California. I told them I wouldn't be coming.

It took me two whole days to get my concentration back, to give one hundred percent to *Miss Ever's Boys*. But I did, and the show was well received.

Soon after that, I wrote Beth a letter thanking her for the offer. I explained that it was friends like her who had given me jobs over the years—and that when I make a commitment to any job, I honor that commitment. I said I hoped she understood why I had to turn down her show. In a few days I got a letter back. "Henry, we've been friends a long time," she wrote. "Of course I understand." She told me I had "a refreshing attitude."

A month later, Naila and I attended a friend's open house in Santa Monica. "Henry!" It was Beth, coming over to greet us. "Remember that TV pilot I wanted you to do?"

How could I forget it? I hoped Beth couldn't see my disappointment. But she kept talking, clearly thrilled. "The network's picking up the show!" she said. "It's going to go to series."

"I'm really glad, Beth," I said.

"Still interested in that role?" she said. "It's yours if you want it."

As I stared in disbelief, Beth gave me one of those I-know-you-all-too-well looks. "Henry," she said. "If this show is going into a long run, I need a good actor I can count on. And that's you."

The show is both an exciting adventure story and the saga of different people trying to get along in a changing world. My part is that of an independent village blacksmith in the old West: Robert E is an ex-slave carving out a place for himself and his family on the frontier.

Doctor Quinn, Medicine Woman has been a popular show for the past two seasons. Families all over the country enjoy viewing it together. Our "family" of cast and crew watched it together too. That first year we gathered at Beth's house every Saturday night with our wives and husbands and children to see "our" show on TV—and the job I got because I had to turn it down.

CLIFF ROBERTSON

Johnny and Charly and Me

Back in 1960, a role that I played in the television drama, *The Two Worlds of Charly Gordon*, began an unusual chain of events that has affected my life to this day.

The script was based on Daniel Keyes' short story—and, later, novel—*Flowers for Algernon*, the fictional story of Charly Gordon, a mentally retarded man who undergoes brain surgery and blossoms into a genius only to learn that he is doomed to slip back into his former retarded state. To prepare for the part of Charly I wanted to learn firsthand about mentally challenged people, to try if possible to put myself into their shoes. Actually I wasn't very eager about the prospect. I'd always thought of the mentally challenged as rather scary people to be around. They made me feel uneasy.

A friend directed me to what is called a "sheltered workshop" in lower Manhattan, one of a number of centers where mentally challenged adults like Charly Gordon perform useful work for pay. Carefully supervised, the workers usually do simple, repetitive tasks such as assembling shopping bags, filling containers, stamping envelopes.

"You'll be surprised how well they do," said my friend.

Even so, on my first visit to the workshop, I was a very skeptical and wary man. I went into a big workroom where several dozen men and women were sitting at their stations, some of them folding boxes, some simply staring into space. There was a certain amount of muffled giggling, a shuffling of feet, and the strange slurring sound people make when they cannot form their words. I watched for a while, chatting with the supervisor, all the time feeling odd and out of place myself.

However, I began to learn from my friend that there are many different types of mental retardation. There are those people suffering from Down syndrome, caused by a genetic disorder, others whose problems stem from a disease affecting them prenatally, and some who are brain damaged at birth. Their IQs vary in a fairly broad range.

Pointing across the room, my friend added, "Now that man in the corner is one of our brighter workers." For some time I had been noticing this man stuffing envelopes with furious energy. He was about my size and age, and there was something about his clear blue eyes that I liked. I decided to take the plunge.

"Would you introduce us?" I asked the supervisor.

And that's how Johnny Doherty came into my life.

"This is Mr. Robertson, Johnny," said the supervisor. For a moment Johnny Doherty didn't see my outstretched hand. Then, when he did, he grabbed for it vigorously.

"Oh . . . uh . . . uh . . . glad to know you, Mr. Robinson."

"Just call me Cliff," I said.

"Okay, Mr. Robinson."

I smiled.

The two of us began to talk. Johnny's speech was somewhat slurred and he often strained at his words, giving undue emphasis to some, skipping over others. To my surprise, we actually carried on a conversation. Johnny told me about the room he lived in on Staten

Island, that he kept it clean and neat all by himself, that he loved Sundays when his cousin took him for drives in Central Park and visits to the zoo. He loved the seals.

At closing time, I asked Johnny if I could walk with him to the subway. I could tell that this pleased him. As we picked our way along the broken sidewalks, he proudly told me about the job he had recently been given. His cousin had found him work as a messenger.

"I know . . . I can do it . . . Mr. Robinson," he said. "Lots of people . . . tol' my cousin he was crazy, but Jack . . . he's my cousin . . . he knows I can do it."

"And so do I," I said, and when I left Johnny at his subway station, I told him that I'd like to come see him again.

"When?" he shot at me, pinning me down.

"Sometime when I can accompany you on your job."

Johnny smiled, and thrust out his hand, "Good-bye, Mr. Robinson."

The strange thing about it was that I was looking forward to seeing him again.

Shortly after that, I started joining Johnny on his rounds from time to time. He liked working. He liked the adventure of subways and buses, and he was proud and careful of his responsibility for getting letters and packages delivered safely and speedily. On our first day together we hadn't been out on the street very long when Johnny stopped and began puzzling over the envelope in his hand. He was confused by the address. "Here, let me help you," I said. But he shook his head. We went to the address on the envelope, but Johnny was correct, it was wrong.

Again I offered to help, but again Johnny declined. "This is my job, Mr. Robinson," he said earnestly, "and I got to get it done right."

His second try was an office up a long flight of stairs where the receptionist looked at the envelope and impatiently thrust it back at him. Once more Johnny furrowed his brow and examined the envelope closely. "Maybe the person who wrote this meant two-six-nine instead of two-five-nine," he said. I watched him, admiring his doggedness in seeing his job through. I thought of the many so-called "normal" people who, by now, would have given up. But not Johnny Doherty.

On the third try, he successfully delivered the letter. It was two-six-nine.

Johnny didn't like people staring at him. It bothered him. Sometimes, if we were riding on a bus and somebody began looking at him as if he were a freak, Johnny would suddenly get up and move to another seat. But what people said about him in his hearing was another story. One afternoon I waited in the background while Johnny placed a package on the counter of a small office on Bleecker Street. "Hey, now," said a girl behind the counter as she looked up from filing her nails, "here comes the dummy again."

"Sh-h-h . . . ," said another girl.

"Him? He doesn't know from nothin' . . . he's one of those, what you call . . . ?"

I couldn't believe what I was hearing.

As time passed I was to find that even beyond people saying cruel and thoughtless things, there were those who pointed and laughed and even played tricks on him.

But more and more I discovered how guileless and open Johnny and other mentally challenged people were. They were endowed with a purity of heart that made me wonder if this was what was meant in medieval days when people like them were referred to as "children of

God." Surely Johnny and the others I had come to know were blessed with some rare innocence, some personal security that most of us lack. I began to wonder if the truly handicapped are not those "normal" people afflicted with greed, trickery, rancor.

Johnny was pleased with the idea that I was an actor preparing for a television drama and that he was somehow a part of it. When the show went into production, I took him to the studio with me one morning and positioned him safely behind one of the cameras. I asked him to stay there where he'd be out of the way. Several hours later we broke for lunch, and I was at the door of the cafeteria before I realized that Johnny hadn't come with us. I rushed back and found him in the darkened studio dutifully standing behind the camera.

The Two Worlds of Charly Gordon was well received and I was happy about that, but the most important reward for me was my new appreciation for these gallant human beings who yearned to be useful but who were often feared or misunderstood. The TV play about Charly Gordon was a touching drama that helped people understand the mentally challenged. *Wouldn't it be wonderful,* I began to think, *if its message could reach millions of people around the world through a full-fledged movie production?*

Soon I did something that surprised even me. I secured the film rights for the story. Now I was a committed man. I began contacting film people in New York and California, but it didn't take long to find out that nothing I could say or do had the slightest effect in convincing a producer that *Charly Gordon* was a sound investment.

One day in 1967, after seven long years of trying, I went to see still another Hollywood producer. He leaned back in his leather chair, staring at me across a gleaming mahogany desk. "You want to make a film about a retarded man?" He shrugged. "Sweetheart," he said, drawing on a cigar and spewing out a blue cloud of smoke, "it'll never make a nickel."

"Why?" I said, though I anticipated his answer from experience.

He waved his cigar, swung his chair around and flipped through some files.

"Here," he grunted, "listen to this." Pulling a file, he reeled off the financial losses of a film dealing with mental retardation made years before. I started once again to explain that it all depends upon the recipe, the blending of talent, script and direction, and then I just stopped. At last I'd had it. I was ready to give up.

That night I drove south to the house I owned in La Jolla, the little Pacific Coast town where I'd grown up. My mother had died when I was two years old and I was raised by my Grandmother Willingham. How I wished that my grandmother—I'd always called her Willin'ham—were alive now. She was the one I always took my problems to. She would have understood Johnny Doherty and why I wanted to make a picture about Charly Gordon.

When I turned out the light that night I lay in bed listening to the crashing of the surf on the beach nearby. *That producer is right,* I thought. No one wants to invest in a money-loser. For a long time I tossed and turned. Sleep wouldn't come. Outside, the waves went on pounding the shore, rhythmically, steadily. Lying there wide awake, I found myself thinking about my boyhood days. I thought of an afternoon when I was building a sand castle. I could hear Willin'ham tell me that the sand in my shovel had once been solid rock: "Like those cliffs back there," she'd said, "but the waves pounded at them until the rock crumbled into tiny pieces of sand. It's persistence that did it, son."

And then, as she often did, Willin'ham told me a story that Jesus had told first. "Late one night a man had an unexpected guest but didn't have any food for him. So he knocked on a neighbor's door. The neighbor stuck his head out of a second-story window and said, 'Go away! It's too late for me to get up, and my family is all asleep.'

"But do you know what he did, Clifford?" I shook my head. "He kept knocking and knocking until finally that man took pity on him and came down with the food he needed. So as God told us, if we keep asking, keep on looking, we'll keep on finding . . ."

I lay in bed, gazing at the glimmer of reflected light wavering on the ceiling.

Persistence.

It had been seven years, but I could see my old friend Johnny Doherty relentlessly pursuing the correct address on a mislabeled envelope. I could see his steadfast stance behind the camera as he waited for me. Persistence . . . the attribute that had helped see him through a life that otherwise might have been tragic. If Johnny could persevere, then so could I. *Besides,* I thought, *what would he say if I told him I was giving up on the movie?* I'd promised him that he and I would see the very first screening of it alone, just the two of us.

I turned over and went to sleep, knowing what I had to do.

The very next man I saw was Selig Seligman, of Selmur Productions, a top-ranking producer. When I left, he kept a copy of my story and a tape of the television show, and a week later he called me in. Heavy drapes shielded the intense Hollywood sun. Selig sat at his desk, thoughtfully examining his folded hands, then he turned to me. "Cliff, I may be crazy, but I'm going to take a chance. Anybody who has stayed with a project as long and as determinedly as you have probably has something."

Charly was made on a very low budget; few people wanted to invest in it. It was finished in the fall of 1968, but Johnny Doherty was not there to see its first private screening. A week before we were to see it together, he was out riding in the car with his cousin. There was a crash. Johnny was killed.

I went to the premiere knowing that *Charly* wouldn't have happened without him. It was still another of this gentle, loving, mentally challenged man's achievements in a world of limited opportunity.

A lot of good things came out of that picture. I've heard it said by many mental health professionals that it has helped people everywhere look at the mentally challenged with compassion instead of apprehension. Needless to say, I derived much personal satisfaction from the film, but especially from two telephone calls. One call came from that cigar-smoking producer.

"Sweetheart," his voice rasped on the phone. "Let's you and me do a sequel. There's more money to be made."

I declined politely. *Charly* was very special to me; I didn't want to exploit him.

And the other call came from Selig Seligman. "Cliff," he said, and it sounded as though he were close to crying, "I've got a son in college who confessed last night that he'd never thought too much of the pictures I made. He thought I was just doing them for the money. But when he came home from *Charly* last night, he put his arms around me and kissed me." Then Selig hung up.

I stood holding the phone to my ear. Was it the broken line or could I faintly hear something in the background like, "I'm glad . . . uh . . . you kept tryin', Mr. Robinson."

CLAYTON PRINCE

With All My Might

It was a hectic evening in the Manhattan telemarketing center where I sold magazine subscriptions over the phone. After having my ear burned by an angry "prospect" whose dinner I had interrupted, I slumped back in my chair. Though my dream was to be an actor, this was the way I made my living at the time. I didn't blame prospects for being upset, and in truth there were always some folks who seemed happy to hear about our special offer of the *Weekly Reader*.

So I plugged away: "Good evening, Mr. Brown, would you like an opportunity to save . . ."

During the day I haunted television studios and casting agencies. I had wanted to be an actor since I was a tyke in Philadelphia watching *The Wizard of Oz* on television. I had recorded its sound track on my cassette tape player so that I could study the way those actors handled their lines. And I watched *To Sir, with Love* so many times that I had just about memorized Sidney Poitier's part.

Mother, a high-school teacher, felt my future was in education. Even so, she didn't object when in seventh grade I joined the Children's Repertory Company and then went on to the High School for the Creative and Performing Arts. At sixteen I began traveling to New York City to audition for commercials, plays, anything that came up. But no one ever called me back. By my senior year Mom got tired of giving me money for train and bus fare.

"Son, don't you think you've pushed this acting thing far enough?" she asked.

"No, Mom," I answered. "I've got a feeling that it's what God has planned for me to do."

"Well, in the meantime," she said, "don't forget that Bible verse, 'Whatever your hand finds to do, do it with all your might'" (Ecclesiastes 9:10).

She was referring to my studies—and I didn't neglect them. In fact, that verse, which I knew quite well from Sunday school at Mount Calvary Baptist Church, motivated me in just about everything I did. To earn fare for my New York trips, I set up a fruit stand in front of a Philadelphia discount food store that sold only canned and boxed goods. I would go to the wholesale market, buy a box of apples for thirty dollars, then hawk the fresh fruit to people coming out of the store. Not only did I make enough for bus fare, but I also earned spending money. And I learned how to spark people's emotions with the right words and tone of voice.

I went to Temple University (to please Mom), but after a year I moved to New York, where the acting jobs were. Except there weren't any for me, it seemed. At first, with hardly any money, I lived in a tenement house with no heat but plenty of rats and roaches.

But my job selling subscriptions began to pay off, as I kept on trying with all my might. Soon I was making 150 dollars a week, saving two-thirds of it so I could move into a better place.

Then came my first break: a Burger King commercial. The producer wanted somebody to do a Michael Jackson impression. To do it right I went out and had my hair curled. It took some time in a hair salon and was expensive.

It was all for naught. When I showed up at the studio the client had changed his mind—no Michael Jackson, no job for me. However, because I had put so much into the part, the producer was impressed. He gave me a role in a new commercial—wearing a cap.

A few other commercials came along, but it was obvious after two lean years in New York that I had to keep on selling those subscriptions. I realized I wasn't going to be a Sidney Poitier. I would just be myself, Clayton Prince, and whatever God had in store for me, so be it. And because of the commercials I made, I was able to get an agent. So I kept on selling the *Weekly Reader* and going to auditions, giving both pursuits my best.

Then I was called to audition to play Denise Huxtable's boyfriend on *The Cosby Show.* My big chance! The role called for someone wearing glasses. I had to borrow a friend's pair. I shoved them into my pocket and jumped on the subway. When I got off, I discovered someone had picked my pocket. Those glasses cost one hundred dollars. I was so shaken I auditioned poorly and didn't get the part.

A year later my agent called to say I was up for another part on *The Cosby Show,* a wisecracking suitor of Denise Huxtable. It looked like it would be a recurring role. I was picked up by limousine, along with the casting director and his associate. It was a long ride through heavy traffic, and to lighten things up I began cracking jokes and making humorous references to scenes on the street. Soon everyone was folded over laughing.

However, when I got out of the car and faced that studio, fear of failing hit me. I gave the worst audition of my life. Even so, I took the script home and carefully studied it, going over and over it, just to prove to myself, I guess, that I could have done a good job. Finally, letting it drop to the floor I lay back on the couch (which doubled as my bed), staring at the ceiling. "From the way things look, God," I said, "I'll be selling the *Weekly Reader* for the rest of my life."

In the morning my phone rang. It was my agent. "Clayton, the *Cosby* people want to see you again."

"Again?"

"Yeah, the casting director said you were quite funny in the car. He told the others you must have been nervous and asked them to see you again."

"Thank You, God!" I said as I jumped into my trousers. This time, believing that God had arranged the turn of events, and that He was with me, I didn't feel nervous at all. Moreover, I knew that part so well from having read it so many times, the audition was a cinch. I got the part.

Unfortunately, they told me, the role was for just one episode. But by now I had learned that even the smallest thing given us to do was important. So I went all out on that part.

After the show was televised, my agent called. "Clayton, we're getting calls about you. Better get ready to give up that telephone job."

"What?" I gasped.

"Well, it just so happened that the episode you appeared in broke records in the Nielsen rating."

I knew my brief stint didn't have anything to do with the show's rating. But I also knew I didn't hurt it either. My dream was finally coming true—because I had kept on trying—with all my might.

FINDING YOUR
TRUE CALLING

*The words shot out like blazing arrows into the
darkened theater. They must have hit their mark;
the performance earned good reviews. From that night on,
I knew I was destined to be an actor.*

ED ASNER

MARTHA WILLIAMSON

TV Is Touched by an Angel

O f all the television series I have produced in the past twelve years, none has affected me more than the one that came to my attention in the spring of 1994.

That's when CBS asked me if I would be executive producer of a new show called *Touched by an Angel*. "We'll send you a tape of the pilot," said my contact.

When the tape arrived, I slipped it into my VCR and sat on the living room floor to watch. The show was about angels, and I had barely viewed half before I decided against it. In fact, it upset me. It wasn't true to what I knew about angels. From studying the Bible I knew angels were God's messengers who could do nothing but His will.

But the pilot I saw portrayed angels as recycled dead people with power over life and death. They didn't treat one another with respect, and the show gave the audience the option of believing in them. I felt anyone wanting to see a show about angels would expect to see heavenly beings who were enthusiastic about their work, did it with joy and integrity, and loved their Boss.

I turned off my VCR and, without really taking time to pray about it, went to the phone and told CBS I couldn't work on the show.

A week later I had lunch with Andy Hill, president of CBS Productions. We met at a restaurant in Hollywood, and as we talked, something strange happened: I found myself bringing up the angel show.

"Now, when you hire that executive producer," I said, "make sure he portrays angels as loving, joyful beings. And remember," I emphasized, "don't give the audience the option of believing in them."

Again and again, I raised points that I felt should be considered. Even outside the restaurant, I continued talking about the show. As I finally left, I rolled down my car window and said, "If you need any ideas, give me a call."

Andy smiled and waved good-bye. As I pulled away I felt I was leaving something important behind. But I had another possibility: NBC had offered me a courtroom drama series. Not only did it promise to be a success, it would also earn me more money than I had ever made before.

My deadline to accept this offer was the Friday before Memorial Day weekend, less than a week away. But during the next few days, no matter what I did—driving, reading, cooking—my thoughts kept turning to angels. Every time I prayed, I kept hearing the word *angels*. Each time I gave thanks over a meal, angels came to mind. Finally, I had to believe the Lord was speaking to me. I called Andy Hill at CBS. "Andy, is the angel job still open?"

"No, not exactly," he said. "We've made appointments to interview other producers." My heart sank. "But," he added, "why don't you come in? The earliest we could see you would be Wednesday after Memorial Day."

After Memorial Day?

"Well . . . yes," I agreed. "I'll be there."

I slumped onto my sofa, my stomach tightening. I had to give my answer to NBC this coming Friday. But I wouldn't know about the angel show until the following Wednesday. Should I risk giving up the best offer I had ever had for something that might not even happen?

For two days and nights I wrestled with my decision. Friday morning I woke still in a quandary. Finally, with only hours left, I did what I should have done earlier: I called a prayer partner.

"Greg, please pray for a decision I must make today," I said. "I'm not going to tell you what it's about except that in a few hours I have to accept or turn down a good job opportunity. I just want you to ask the Lord if I should say yes or no."

An hour later my phone rang. "Martha," said Greg. "I've been in prayer since you called and all I keep hearing is no."

This was my confirmation, for I had been getting the same answer. I hung up the phone and was about to call NBC when something made me hesitate. Was it wise to turn down a sure thing? Then I remembered one of my favorite Proverbs: "Trust in the Lord with all your heart and lean not on your own understanding; in all your ways acknowledge him, and he will make your paths straight" (Proverbs 3:5).

I called the NBC people and told them I was sorry, but I couldn't do the courtroom show.

On Wednesday I went to CBS Television City in Hollywood. How ironic, I thought, as I got out of my car in the parking lot. Here I was interviewing for a job I had had in hand just two weeks ago.

I was ushered into a large conference room where a host of CBS executives waited—Peter Tortorici, president of CBS Entertainment, Andy Hill, four vice presidents and others. I prayed quickly for guidance and started my presentation.

"You know I'm a Christian," I began, "and, though this is not a religious show, there are standards I feel we must follow.

"If I do a show about angels, it must be true to what I know is true," I continued. I looked around at the impassive faces, took a deep breath and went on.

"I'll be responsible for providing you with one hour of quality entertainment," I said. "But we cannot do a show about angels if we don't respect God.

"Every successful show has rules that are never broken without consequences. Look at *Little House on the Prairie*. No one failed to love the other. No one betrayed the other. The family had rules. If a character broke one, there was a price to pay. By the same token, God has rules and they do not get broken without consequences.

"I think one of the problems with television today," I went on, "is that so many rules get broken. I believe what makes a series long running is when the audience knows the rules are inviolate. So I want to go to the Scriptures to make sure what the angel rules are and still come up with something an audience can enjoy."

The room was silent. Finally someone asked, "So, do you think you can fix the pilot?"

I thought a moment and said boldly, "No, I want to start all over. I'd rewrite completely and keep just the angels Monica and Tess."

No one said a word, but I felt a strong sense of peace. Then Peter Tortorici said, "Okay, Martha, please wait in the next office and we'll let you know."

It was the longest wait I ever spent. *Have I blown it?* I wondered.

The door opened and Peter appeared. He pointed to the room behind him. "Everything you just said in there? Write it!"

My challenge was just beginning. I was asking the network to throw away a pilot that had cost two million dollars to produce. The responsibility fell heavy on me.

It was now June and the show was to air in September. Normally, it takes four weeks to write, shoot and fine-tune a pilot, plus come up with new episodes to follow right away. On top of that, I had to hire writers and producers and move to Salt Lake City, where we would be filming.

But I believe God bends time to his purpose. I wrote the pilot in three and a half weeks, and began shooting on time in Salt Lake City.

Though the CBS hierarchy was supportive, I didn't think anyone felt optimistic. One day an executive told me, "Look, Martha, we know you've been asked to do something impossible. When this show bombs, nobody is going to blame you."

That only increased my commitment, and we made our deadline. On Wednesday, September 14, 1994, I sat at home alone, once again on my living room floor, watching the first episode of *Touched by an Angel*, starring Della Reese as Tess and Roma Downey as Monica. It was about a grief-stricken mother who had lost her baby to sudden infant death syndrome.

Monica comes to console her. But the mother snaps, "You're an angel? So what. Where was the angel when my baby died? Why didn't an angel call 911 for me? Why didn't the angel drag me out of my bed into that nursery? Where was the angel then?"

Monica drops to her knees and says, "There was an angel with your baby when she died. And it's the same angel who is with your baby now. God loves you more than you can possibly imagine."

Tears streamed down my face. I couldn't believe I had had anything to do with those words, or that they were being spoken on network television. And today, after two successful years of *Touched by an Angel*, I still feel that way.

As far as I'm concerned, God is the show's true executive producer.

BILL PUGIN

From Singing to Signing

It was a strange comment in an odd place and it took me aback. I had just finished singing "Oklahoma!" in the lounge of the *Pacific Princess* cruise ship when a stranger stepped up to the stage and called to me, "Don't hide your light under a bushel!" I wondered what he meant.

At the time I had been fulfilling my lifelong ambition of being an entertainer. For more than five years I had sailed the seas aboard Princess Cruises' ships, singing and dancing in Broadway show routines. It was a wonderful life, from mixing with passengers to standing at the rail at night under a Caribbean sky wild with stars.

Then, within a month, I found myself flat on my back in a hospital. Though I was only in my twenties, years of dancing had taken their toll. Lifting female dancers and doing acrobatic routines while balancing against the roll of the ship had injured my back to the point where I was in constant pain.

An orthopedic surgeon in Los Angeles removed two ruptured disks. When I asked if I would be able to dance again he shook his head. "Son, you are fortunate to be able to walk."

I didn't feel fortunate at all. After eight days in the hospital I faced a long recuperation in a small apartment I shared with a friend in Los Angeles. No job, savings gone, no future.

Most of all I missed my family back East, especially my older sister, Mary Anne. I knew she prayed for me, and I pictured her touching her left palm with her right middle finger and reversing this with her other hand. This indicates nail prints, and means "Jesus" in sign language. My sister is deaf.

Doctors believed she had lost her hearing from an early childhood illness. My family never realized it until one night when Mother prayed with us and Mary Anne said, "Mommy, please turn on the light. Jesus lets me see your lips, but he doesn't let me hear your voice."

It was difficult for Mary Anne growing up in a hearing family. As we laughed and talked at the dinner table, I knew she felt excluded. She was always the first to finish and go off by herself to read.

Finally, she started bringing deaf friends home and I watched as they conversed in sign language. Their graceful movements reminded me of ballet or jazz dancing. I thought it was a secret language; there were those beautiful gestures, a burst of laughter from her friends, and I wondered what they had said.

Soon I was learning sign language from Mary Anne. When we signed something humorous and laughed, Dad asked, "What was that all about?" I started to reply, "Oh, it's not important" until I realized that was how we used to respond to Mary Anne's questioning looks in earlier years.

She earned high honors in the classroom and a purple belt in judo, which impressed me to no end. After completing two master's degrees at Gallaudet University for the deaf in Washington, DC, she stayed on to work there. Gallaudet was the best place to learn sign language, so I went there too, delighted to be close to my sister.

After several years I moved to Los Angeles to work with the National Captioning Institute, which provides closed captioning so the deaf can enjoy television, movies and other media. In 1980, I joined Princess Cruises as a performer.

Now, after the operation, I lay in my small apartment in deep depression. With my career in ruins, I had lost heart. One day while moodily watching a rerun of *The Love Boat* on television, I was overwhelmed by nostalgia for my shipboard days. And I thought of that stranger who had shouted up to me on the stage: "Don't hide your light under a bushel!"

I knew he was quoting from the Bible, when Jesus asked, "Who ever heard of someone lighting a lamp and then covering it up to keep it from shining?" (Luke 8:16). But I had never understood why that man made his comment. I picked up my Bible and turned to that passage. While holding it, I realized my hands had formed the sign for "book."

It had been a long time since I had signed. I remembered some deaf passengers on the ship; when they discovered they could communicate with me their faces lit up.

The memory of Mary Anne leaving the table as a little girl while the rest of us laughed and talked gave me a twinge of guilt. I wondered, *How many other people feel like she did? What do they do when they visit their doctors? Their banks? How do they buy a car or apply for a driver's license?*

Was signing my light? Was I keeping it under a bushel?

I began calling every local agency that might know of needs for an interpreter for the deaf. Soon I was translating. The salary was modest but the rewards were magnificent.

One of my first assignments was helping an elderly woman who was not only deaf but also blind. She had found a discrepancy in her checking account and I accompanied her to the bank, where we sat down with an officer. I noted his condescending attitude as she lightly felt my hands as I signed his words. But her mind was razor sharp and she knew exactly what she was doing. I enjoyed seeing the officer abjectly apologize to her for the bank's mistake.

A scary time came when I was working in an operating room. A hearing-impaired woman was having eye surgery and she had to remain conscious during the operation so the surgeon could ask her questions. She was under a relaxant and I was concerned that she might slur signs the same way a speaking person might slur words. So I had to make doubly sure I conveyed her answers exactly. I found myself praying for help, and the surgery went well.

It was most traumatic when I translated for a young man in therapy. I acted as a communicator between the psychiatrist and the patient, who was suffering deep emotional pain from unresolved problems with his father, who had died some years earlier. My interpreting brought a breakthrough for the patient, who had kept his anguish bottled up for years.

As I walked out of the doctor's office that day, I had a feeling of being used by God for something special. I now realized what my light was, and felt a self-esteem and worth I had never experienced before. I went on to translate for weddings, funerals, Yom Kippur services, and even interpreted for the minister Robert Schuller.

Then an agent submitted my name for *Reasonable Doubts*, a new television show starring Marlee Matlin, the Academy Award-winning actress who is hearing-impaired. I auditioned with eight other aspirants and left the studio putting everything in God's hands, as I had now learned to do. Three days later I got a phone call that I was hired for the role of Ben Douglass, Marlee Matlin's interpreter on the series. It was exciting working in television, and when the series ended after two years I wasn't depressed—I knew God would have something else waiting for me.

Why did that stranger call out to me on the stage of the *Pacific Princess*? Whatever the reason, I believe he got his cue from the Holy Spirit.

MARLEE MATLIN

Changing Roles

All I wanted as a kid in Morton Grove, Illinois, was to be like everyone else. But I wasn't. I'd lost virtually all my hearing at eighteen months of age, after a bout of roseola. My parents were determined not to let my deafness hold me back, though. They got advice from a psychologist at Northwestern University's Clinic for the Deaf, and I started speech classes at the age of three, lipreading and sign language at five. Mom found a synagogue with services that were both spoken and signed. I loved going to temple and being with other people who "spoke" the same language I did. There in God's house, I felt like I really belonged.

Nowhere else did I feel truly a part of everything that went on, not even at home. I'd see my older brothers singing along with the radio, but I couldn't hear the music without the volume cranked up so high it would have blown out the windows. I wanted to talk on the phone with my grandmother, but I couldn't make out a word she said. It was hard for me to follow stuff on TV, except cop shows, where there was little dialogue and lots of action. I loved cop shows.

At school there were interpreters, teachers who knew sign language. Even without them, I could read lips and speak well enough to get along with most of the other students. But I got tired of sticking up for myself with the kids who laughed at the way I talked, and of being the only one my age who signed.

Sometimes when I got home I'd be so frustrated I'd rip out my hearing aids and throw them across the room. (The technician who fixed them claimed I set a record for repairs.) "I hate asking for help. Why can't I do all the things everyone else does? It's not fair!"

"We all have some things we just can't do," Mom would patiently tell me. "But God gives us other gifts that more than make up for that."

What was my gift then, the thing that I was really good at? At services I'd ask God to help me find it. But before I did, I found something else just as wondrous. A new girl my age came to temple one day. The girl, I noticed, was signing. I went right up to her. "Hi, I'm Marlee," I finger-spelled my name.

"I'm Liz," she replied. "I'm deaf."

"Me too!" I was so excited my fingers flew. "I think we should be best friends."

For a second, she was too surprised to respond. Then she nodded and broke into a big smile. Our friendship was sealed from that moment on.

Then the summer I was seven I discovered it—the gift Mom had talked about. One afternoon at day camp the counselors showed me a stage and said, "If you want, you can get up there and perform." I must have looked puzzled because they explained, "We're going to teach your group a song. The other girls will sing the words, and you can sign them."

I will never forget being on that stage at summer camp, signing my heart out to the beat of the music, and seeing all those people looking back at me, smiling and clapping. This is it! a voice deep inside told me. This is where you belong! The rush I got was like that incredible sense of connection I got in temple, when I felt closest to everything and everyone else in God's world.

At home I'd stand in front of the bathroom mirror and make believe an entire audience was looking back at me. Then I'd pretend to be a camp counselor, a teacher, a mother, a cop like on TV. I would playact for hours . . . until my brothers complained, "Marlee's hogging the bathroom again!"

That fall Mom took me to the newly opened Center on Deafness, where the psychologist from Northwestern directed children's theater programs. The day we visited, they were putting together a musical, *The Wizard of Oz*, which I knew from television, so I asked, "Who's Dorothy?" The director told me they didn't have a girl for the part yet. I didn't hesitate. "How about me?"

That was the first of many roles I played in their productions over the years. By third grade my friend Liz, too, had become a regular at the Center. Onstage, it seemed the usual barriers to communication fell away and I had a direct connection with the people watching, like a conversation that went deeper than words. "You have a real gift for reaching the audience," the director remarked one day when I was twelve. I hadn't thought of a gift being something I could share; that struck me because I had been studying for my bat mitzvah, the Jewish girl's coming-of-age ceremony, and learning about my place in the greater community of God's world. Could acting be what I was meant to do?

"That's not very practical," some of my relatives tried to dissuade me. I would have let them, too, if not for one evening in 1977 when my friends and I performed at a benefit for the Center. I couldn't believe who came up to me afterward. The Fonz from the TV show *Happy Days*. Cool! He shook my hand. "I'm Henry Winkler," he said. "You were great. I hope you keep acting."

I couldn't help myself. "Do you think I can work in Hollywood someday, like you?" I asked.

He didn't have any trouble understanding me. He looked me right in the eye and said, "You can be whatever you want to be." He even asked me to keep in touch and to look him up any time I was in Los Angeles.

In high school, though, I got caught up in being a teenager and put acting aside. I did stay in touch with Henry, but Hollywood seemed so far away compared to the immediate excitement of cars, parties, boys. For once, my deafness didn't get in the way of the things that mattered to the other kids—I could drive, dance, and yes, I'll admit it, flirt. I reveled in being just like everyone else. After graduation I studied criminal justice at a local junior college (maybe it was all those cop shows I'd watched growing up), but I dropped out when I found out being deaf drastically limited my career options in law enforcement.

The spring of 1985 my brothers told me about auditions for a Chicago production of *Children of a Lesser God*, an award-winning play with a number of deaf characters. I hesitated. After all, as I said to Liz, I hadn't been onstage in years. "What are you waiting for?" she exclaimed. "You love to act! Try out!"

As soon as I stepped onstage for my audition, I felt right at home. I won a supporting role in the play. Things happened fast after that. Movie producers cast me in the lead role in the film version. There I was, a nineteen-year-old who had never lived away from home, starring in a Hollywood movie and moving to New York City to pursue an acting career. At the same time, I found my first serious boyfriend. No wonder I was overwhelmed. Fortunately I also found a skilled interpreter, Jack Jason, a graduate student in film and the son of deaf parents, who stuck with me through all the interviews after the movie premiered in the autumn of 1986.

Never did I imagine that six months after my twenty-first birthday I would be accepting the Academy Award for Best Actress. Afterward I made sure to stop by and see my old friend Henry Winkler. He opened his front door, and I just held up the golden statue, my own personal sign language for "Thank you for encouraging me to follow my dreams."

I should have been on top of the world. Instead, I nearly got crushed in a maelstrom of negativity. Did I truly deserve the award, critics asked, or was it a sympathy vote? One magazine dismissed me as a one-hit wonder. People in the movie business predicted I'd never work again. It was true, opportunities didn't open up for me as I had hoped. So many times I was told, "You're a wonderful actress. But you're deaf. What else is there for you, really?" I started to wonder myself. I could have handled it if I tried out for roles and got turned down, but I wasn't even considered to begin with . . . all because I was deaf. Just like when I was a kid, I felt left out of a world I longed to be part of.

And just like back then, I was too proud to ask for help. My parents and Liz could tell I was unhappy and visited from Chicago often. They'd already given me so much support; I was afraid to let them down. I didn't want to burden Jack, my only real friend in New York, who worked hard enough as my interpreter. Worst of all, my relationship with my boyfriend was falling apart.

I felt as if I were falling apart too. Don't I belong in acting? Can something that feels so right be all wrong for me? I kept asking myself.

From inside me, a voice spoke, a voice I heard clearly. The same voice that had introduced me to the joy of connecting with an audience way back in summer camp. This time I knew who it had to be.

Only God could reach past the anger and frustration and pain and answer the questions deep in my soul. *If you aren't happy with your life, change it. If the roles aren't coming to you, go to them. Make the most of what you've been given.*

I made a break with everything that had been dragging me down, including my unhealthy relationship with my boyfriend. I decided to start over in Los Angeles, where the movie and TV studios were. Surely there would be more roles for me there. Luckily Jack, eager to find more opportunities in film, joined me.

"Marlee, where are you staying?" Henry asked when I told him I was in town. "A hotel on—" He didn't let me finish. "Forget it. Stacey and I have plenty of room. You're staying with us."

"Only until I find my own place," I said. "A weekend, tops."

I ended up living with the Winklers for two years. I needed that time to grow up. To see that turning away help from the ones who cared for me most, like Liz and Jack, Stacey and Henry, was like turning away God, who also wanted the best for me. To learn that really connecting with people, deaf and hearing, onstage and off, meant both opening up to them and being open to what they had to share with me.

I stuck with acting, finding small parts in a few movies. Then in 1991, at twenty-six, I landed the starring role in the television series *Reasonable Doubts*. Much as I enjoyed playing a fully drawn character whose deafness was only part of who she was, the best thing about the show for me was meeting the love of my life.

When you shoot on location on the streets of LA, police officers are there to direct traffic. One day on the set I noticed a cute new man in blue. Really cute. There was just something about him. I asked one of the other cops who he was. "Name's Kevin Grandalski."

"Is he single?"

He sure was. From our first date, we clicked. My fascination with cops, his ability to sign (he'd learned in order to fulfill his language requirement in college). Not to mention the healthy balance he brought to my life—Kevin's athletic to my artistic, shy to my outgoing, laid-back to my intense. When he proposed, I exclaimed right along with the voice inside me, "Yes!"

The first people we shared the news with, besides our parents, were Henry and Stacey. "You're having the wedding here," Stacey announced. On August 29, 1993, on the Fonz's front lawn, with my family and Liz and Jack looking on, Kevin and I were married.

All I'd wanted as a little girl trying to come to terms with my deafness was to be like everyone else. I feel so blessed to have ended up exactly where I belong—being me, an actress, wife and mom, guided through my deepest struggles by the one voice I always hear.

TIMOTHY JOHNSON, MD

Have a Long and Happy Life!

A lot has happened in medicine in the thirty years I've been covering health issues for ABC News. Extraordinary new drugs, amazing machines that can see deeper than ever into the human body, the mapping of the human genome, as important a journey of discovery as we humans have ever undertaken. Treatments have turned many cancer sufferers into cancer survivors. Revolutionary surgical procedures prolong our lives. A century ago the average life expectancy was slightly more than half of what it is today. And yet when I think about the basis for a healthy and happy life, the underlying principles don't seem so new. In fact, most have been around for thousands of years, since Hippocrates and Moses at least. Let's start with this medical fact: Research shows that people who attend religious services regularly—it doesn't matter what your faith is—live longer, healthier lives. Such people are less likely to indulge in self-destructive behavior. (Think of the greatest risks to health: smoking, drug abuse, unsafe sexual practices.) They remember what I learned as a boy: "The body is the temple of the Holy Spirit."

Before I became a doctor I went to seminary. One of my classes was in pastoral education. I was required to visit people in the hospital. I was fascinated by the similarities between the way a good pastor ministers to his parishioners and the way a good doctor ministers to his patients. Could I do both? I felt called to try, so after seminary, I went to medical school and became a doctor. Maybe this gives me a unique perspective on healing. What I've found is this: Body and soul are a single entity, and what's good for one is usually good for the other. Here are some basic examples.

MOVE IT.

Take a guess at what the second biggest killer in America is (after smoking). It's obesity. The Surgeon General's office estimates that obesity is responsible for some three hundred thousand deaths a year! Of course, there are sometimes underlying physiological and genetic reasons for being overweight, but there are two things almost anyone can do: diet and exercise. If I had to choose between the two, I'd go for exercise.

Surprised? Sure, cutting back makes sense. And yet it's almost impossible to maintain a weight loss if you don't also walk, run, swim, dance, lift weights or do something—anything—vigorous several times a week. Consistency, that's the key. Statistics on long-term weight loss back me up. God did not create us to sit in front of the TV stuffing our faces. That's why, once you get into an exercise routine, you will naturally feel renewed and more at peace.

What do I do? I walk. Thirty minutes a day. I even walked from our ABC studios in New York in Times Square to the Guideposts offices on 34th Street for this interview. It felt great!

GIVE OF YOURSELF.

My mother was blessed with good health, and her regimen isn't something you'd normally find in a medical textbook. But it's a prescription I'll give anyone.

As the old saying goes, "If you help someone up a hill, you're that much closer to the top yourself." My mother was always helping people. Baking a casserole. Collecting winter clothes for a family. Calling on a shut-in. Serving others was the same as serving God.

It was different for her, you might protest. She lived in a different era. Nonsense. There are always people in need. Ever since I've been on television they call me with their problems. It would be easy to pass those calls on to an overworked intern or claim that I'm no longer a practicing physician. But I don't. Whenever possible, I take the call. I listen and make suggestions. I do it because of Mom's example, but I also do it for myself. People who help others have a more positive attitude, and people with positive attitudes live longer, happier lives. Helping others is exercise for the soul.

Make It a Point.

Nobody likes to be poked and prodded, but you must visit your doctor regularly. Fortunately, testing procedures are much more intensive than they used to be, and a lot more accurate. Have your cholesterol and blood pressure checked as often as your doctor thinks is necessary. High cholesterol and high blood pressure are "silent killers." They damage your heart and arteries without producing any telltale symptoms until it is often too late. There's only one way to find out if you have a potential problem: Get tested.

If you are over fifty, have a colonoscopy (younger if you have a family history of colon cancer). Colon cancer is usually pretty easy to stop if it's caught soon enough, and a colonoscopy is an accurate test. If you're a man over fifty, you should also have your PSA [prostate specific antigen] levels regularly checked. Prostate cancer is potentially lethal, and just as easy to stop if detected early. For women, Pap smears and mammograms are musts in the battle against cancer. The point is, make an appointment! God gave you your body, but you have to take care of it. So if you have been putting off that medical exam, promise me you'll pick up the phone today.

Got to Have Friends.

Do you know what I think the most devastating disorder in our society is? Loneliness. I'm stunned by how many people, even successful people, don't have really close friends. The best friends are the ones you develop over a lifetime, the people who really know you, warts and all. They'll take you out of yourself, and out of preoccupations that can truly be unhealthy: worry, stress, fear. The first treatment for anxiety I always advise is to get together with a good friend. It's hard to feel anxious when you're with someone you trust and love. And make no mistake about it, mental stress is physically toxic. And there is no more fertile breeding ground for negative emotions than loneliness and isolation.

Where do you find friends? Volunteer groups where you'll meet people with similar interests. Or a church or synagogue. Not long ago I met an older fellow who was feeling out of sorts with life. He started volunteering at the local swimming pool and made a whole new set of friends. Friends can save your life as surely as any medical breakthrough.

Rest Easy.

Mom was right. A good night's sleep is like medicine. Maybe better. If you're sleep-deprived over a long period of time, your body becomes vulnerable to a host of diseases. Try to maintain a regular bedtime schedule, get some exercise during the day, avoid caffeine and alcohol at least three hours before bedtime.

Vacations are as necessary for our bodies as sleep. I like bird-watching. There's something about being outdoors, searching the sky for a glimpse of fleeting color. Take up meditation. Not only is there a good biblical basis for this, but tests have shown it can have a positive effect on blood pressure.

MAKE YOUR MOVE.

Follow your heart and you can't go wrong. That's how I ended up doing what I do.

I was a senior in med school. One evening I saw a snippet of news. Huntley and Brinkley were doing a report on the controversial appointment of a new assistant secretary of Health, Education and Welfare. I felt strongly about it and the next day I wrote a note to the appointee, John Knowles, MD, then head of Massachusetts General in Boston. I got a nice note back. "If you're ever in Boston," he wrote, "look me up."

We became friends. At the time he was part of a group setting up a local talk show on health and medicine. One day he said, "Timothy, why don't you host it?"

I went on from that show to join the cast of *Good Morning America* and have been reporting on medicine ever since. I have loved it from the start. But I wonder what would have happened if I hadn't given in to my passion and written Dr. Knowles?

A force greater than ourselves points us in the right direction, but it is up to us to move. Always do something that you love, that you are moved by in the deepest part of your being. It's the best health advice I know.

ED ASNER

My Turning Point

My heart was pounding as I stood in the shadowy wings of the University of Chicago's theater. It was summer term, August 1951, and the intermission for our student production of T. S. Eliot's *Murder in the Cathedral* was nearly over. I could hear the sound of the audience returning to their seats. Nervously, I tugged at my belted costume. The musty purple garment was unlined and scratchy.

I was playing the lead role—Thomas à Becket, Archbishop of Canterbury in the year 1170. Becket was a Christian martyr, a man who lived and died in twelfth-century England, in loyalty to his faith. So far, the play had gone well—but I was more than a little nervous about the upcoming final act.

Back in high school in Kansas City, Kansas, I had performed in many radio dramas, but this was my first try at stage acting. Since I'd been in college, I had dabbled in a lot of subjects, but acting was the only thing that held my interest. For this reason, more than any other time in my life, I wanted to do a good job.

Restlessly, I tapped my foot.

Don't worry, I told myself. *You know your lines. You'll do fine.*

But the anxiety I was feeling ran deeper than the usual case of opening night jitters. From the first rehearsal, I had felt unsure about the Becket role. There was a part of his character—the essence of the man—that I couldn't grasp. His relationship with God seemed so intense, so personal. I couldn't understand it.

Hey, I told myself again, *take it easy.* But I couldn't stop worrying. Amid the confusion of backstage activity, I mentally reviewed the script, considering the events leading to the big final scene—Becket's martyrdom in Canterbury Cathedral. Under my breath, I murmured his final words of faith, hoping that this time I might somehow experience firsthand what Becket felt. It was my last chance.

"For my Lord"—I paused dramatically, waiting for inspiration—"I am now ready to die."

But nothing happened. As usual, the words came out flat and empty. In the silence that followed, I flinched with the bitter realization that I would probably never be able to put myself in Becket's shoes, no matter how hard I tried.

But, I asked myself, how could I be expected to? I was a twentieth-century American Jew. What could I possibly have in common with a twelfth-century Christian martyr?

The more I brooded about it, the more discouraged I became. This wasn't the first time my faith had seemed a stumbling block to my hopes, dreams, desires. Memories of growing up in Kansas City as one of less than one hundred Orthodox Jewish families in a city of 120,000 came flooding back. . . .

It was 4:00 PM on a gray and muggy afternoon. I was a chubby little kid, waiting after school for the city bus (which was late) that would take me to the streetcar, that would take me to another city bus, that would finally drop me off at Hebrew school.

All the other kids were having fun playing football or basketball, and visiting each other's houses and eating peanut butter and jelly sandwiches. The sound of laughter caused me to look up as a group of classmates approached, grinning and joking and taking playful punches at one another. When they saw me, they waved hello, and stopped for a minute to talk. Then they moved on. I liked them a lot—and I think they liked me, too. But they knew I was different.

As I watched them walk away, I tried to ignore the hollow pit in my stomach. My fingers reached deep into my jacket pocket and curled around the soft, flat yarmulke that had been tucked there since morning. I would put it on this afternoon before entering the synagogue for lessons with the rabbi.

Sometimes I wondered what it would be like not to be Jewish; to be able to play with the other kids after school; not to have to wear a skull cap; to worship on Sunday instead of Saturday.

But then I chased away such thoughts with warm recollections of home and family behind the red brick walls of our two-story house on Oakland Avenue . . . the sweet aroma of fresh-baked challah wafting from Mama's always bustling kitchen; the candlelight magic of sundown seders; the mystery and wonder of shared prayers and songs around the dinner table on High Holy Days.

Still, I had to face the fact that when I was away from home, I was lonely. Sometimes a deep fear gripped me—a cold, hopeless feeling that I would never have friends, never be accepted, never be "normal."

At moments like this, my best friend was my imagination. While waiting for the bus to Hebrew school, I entertained myself by lapsing into fantasy about my favorite biblical characters. Like a mighty army of superheroes on parade, they thundered past the reviewing stand of my mind. First came Abraham, wise and faithful patriarch. Then came his son Isaac, with grandson Jacob—who later became known as Israel—and great-grandson Joseph. Fearless Samson followed, his spectacular mane blowing in the wind. Daniel was there, too, flanked on either side by a pride of protective lions, like so many loyal dogs. All passed by in glorious procession. Then, finally, came Moses. His face shone brilliant with the light of the Lord. His eyes were ablaze with his vision of the Promised Land—the land he would safely lead his people to, but would never reach himself. Truly, I wondered, these were all great men of God; men who lived and died in loyalty to their faith . . .

"Ed!"

I jumped, startled. It was the stage manager.

"Five minutes to curtain," he said.

"Thanks," I acknowledged.

At the thought of going onstage, my old anxiety returned with staggering force. I felt like a little kid again—afraid of failing, afraid of being rejected. Suddenly—and quite unexpectedly—I heard myself saying, "Lord, help me do a good job. Take away my fear. Let me live this role; let me be this man, Becket, who died so bravely so long ago. Don't . . . ," I hesitated. "Don't let our differences stand in the way."

As I took a deep breath and walked onstage for Becket's final scene, my heart was racing.

Why, I thought frantically, should this time be any different from the rehearsals?

But this time, something was different.

God must have heard me, because suddenly I understood that the God Becket prayed to and died for was none other than the same God of my childhood—the same God Who spoke to Abraham, the same God Moses saw face-to-face. The differences between Christianity and Judaism were great, certainly. Yet there was this tremendous heritage that we shared: faith in one Father, Creator of us all. Where once it seemed that Becket and I were strangers, now I knew what we had in common. Finally, I understood the man.

"For my Lord," I heard my voice ring out with newfound conviction, "I am now ready to die!"

The words shot out like blazing arrows into the darkened theater. They must have hit their mark; the performance earned good reviews. From that night on, I knew I was destined to be an actor.

Most importantly, I knew that never again would my faith be a stumbling block to my hopes, dreams, desires. Rather it would serve as a mighty bridge to meet them.

Rachael Ray

What's Cooking?

There are two things I can't do in the kitchen: bake or make coffee. You laugh, but it's the truth. So how did I end up with two popular shows on the Food Network? Well, it's like they say, you've got to work with what you've got. With what you've been given. It's true in cooking. It's true in life. Here are a few lessons I learned about both along the way.

Keep It Simple.

Baking, to me, is like conducting a science experiment. All those precise measurements and exact times and temperatures. I don't have the patience for it. I don't even own a set of measuring cups. Not being able to bake doesn't bother me. (Besides, my sister is a fantastic baker, so if I want some apple and cinnamon cake, I know where to go.) But coffee? I break out in a sweat at the mere thought of making a pot. Is it two spoonfuls or one? Table or teaspoon? Per cup or per pot? I can never remember. I make the lousiest coffee in North America!

All that coffee-making trauma has taught me something. What might be a breeze for one person can send someone else into a panic. So I try to stick to the basics when I'm writing a recipe. I want to make sure even an inexperienced cook can pull it off. See a way to save time? I'll put in a tip. Catch myself including too many ingredients? I'll pare down the list. Don't overload your brain. Keep it simple. Focus on the essentials and you'll get results, in and out of the kitchen.

CHOOSE HAPPINESS.

My Grampa Emmanuel always said, "You can laugh or you can cry. Just be sure to choose what you're going to cry about carefully." Grampa didn't cry about much, though he didn't have the easiest life. He grew up in Sicily, one of fourteen children. They all worked in a pottery yard. Then one of his brothers was killed on the job. Grampa came to America and became a stonemason. He settled down in Cape Cod.

Grampa's real passions were gardening and cooking. Every Sunday he'd pick fruits and vegetables and cook up a storm for the family. There were too many of us to fit in the house, so he set up a big table outside. Pasta, meat, salad, melon, ice cream. Oh, what a feast! Grampa's dinner table was where I first saw—I guess I should say, tasted—the power of cooking. It can fill you up. With food and with contentment. Think of how you feel after a good dinner. Is there any more peaceful feeling?

That's why I think one great way to happiness is cooking. Say you're worn out from a long day at the office, frazzled from juggling your kids' activities. Sure, it's easy to hit the drive-through or get take-out. But you've got another choice. How about putting on some music and making dinner? Nothing complicated. Just good fresh food. Try that one night. I think you'll be surprised at how satisfying it is.

BE REAL.

My mom, Elsa, is only four feet ten. But don't let that fool you. She has a big personality. Everything I know about cooking I learned from her. She's a brilliant businesswoman too. At one point she ran nine restaurants simultaneously. Whenever she talked to employees, she'd stand in front of them on a milk crate. Why? So she could look them straight in the eye, really connect with them.

These days my mom is my business manager, my researcher, my morale officer and so much more. Sure, we fight sometimes. Besides, my family is Italian and Cajun—not exactly the quietest people. I think it's terrific to be open and honest and let things out. If you have the senses God gave you, then you're going to have opinions and, of course, they're not always going to agree with everyone else's.

One day a woman named Vicky was helping me prepare caponata, an Italian eggplant dish, for a cooking class. "You forgot the sugar and vinegar," Vicky pointed out. They're ingredients in most caponata recipes, so I explained, "In my family, we don't add sugar and vinegar to our caponata." She said, "We do in my family. And our caponata is good." "Yeah? Well, ours is great!" I shot back. Back and forth we went. We both got so worked up we burst into tears. What are you doing? I asked myself. You're practically coming to blows over a recipe! Shouldn't you be happy that Vicky feels as passionate about food and family as you do? I grabbed Vicky and threw my arms around her. She hugged me right back. We've been best friends ever since. If we'd been stingy with our words or our emotions, we would've missed out on a wonderful friendship.

Be real. Make connections with people. Look them in the eye. Tell them how you feel. Don't be afraid to say what you mean. When you let go of the stuff you hold inside, you'll be amazed at what comes back to you.

SAVOR LIFE.

Okay, no one really likes school cafeteria food. Me, I couldn't stand it. I cried at having to eat it. I was brought up on squid and sardines and anchovies and garlic. All those good Italian things. To me, school food had no taste. So Grampa made me a sack lunch. The smell of it cleared the cafeteria. But I didn't care. I was too busy savoring every bite.

I think we're born with our minds open to everything the world has to offer. Too bad sometimes we learn to close them. One day I was doing a cooking demonstration in a grocery store. A Cajun specialty. That time jambalaya. A woman pushed her shopping cart past me. A little boy was sitting in the seat. "What's she cooking, Mom?" he asked. "Can I have some?" They came back and stopped in front of me. "It smells yummy, Mom." The woman peeked into the pot and crinkled her nose. "No, you don't like that," she told her son, and wheeled him away. *She wouldn't even let him have a taste,* I thought. And he really wanted to. It made me sad.

Try new things. Not just foods, but experiences. Travel to that faraway country even if you're scared of flying. Take a different route home from work. Stop to talk to your neighbor. Don't waste time worrying about what you might be getting yourself into. God has packed life full of interesting flavors, ideas, people. Savor it all!

A LITTLE GOES A LONG WAY.

That goes for lots of things. Spices. Success. Think you're not up to the task, whatever it might be? There's a way you can knock those feelings of inadequacy right out of your head. How? Make dinner. Really! It's the greatest therapy I know. Just give it a shot. Cooking is easier than you think. Plus, it gives you an incredible payoff.

You take a pile of raw ingredients and—presto, chango—turn them into something that appeals to your senses. Oh, that looks good, you'll tell yourself the first time you make a nice dinner. And then you'll be like, Wow! I did that. What else can I do? That's how I felt the first time I helped my mom make lasagna. There's nothing we can't do if we set our minds to it. Well, except maybe make coffee. Which gets me back to where I started.

Work with What You've Been Given.

I grew up in restaurants—Mom would hold me in one arm and stir the pot with the other—but I didn't set out to be in the food business. My majors were literature and communications. After college I took a job managing a candy counter at the marketplace in Macy's. Not because I had a great love for candy. I needed to pay the rent, and it isn't cheap to live in New York City. Then the guy in charge of the fresh foods department got fired. "Can you sit in?" I was asked. "It'll only be for a little while, till we find someone qualified." The manager of the marketplace took a liking to me. He taught me all about cheese, pâté, imported this and exported that. I took to it like a fish to water. They let me keep the job. A job I was supposedly unqualified for.

I left Macy's to become a buyer for a gourmet supermarket uptown. But I missed Mom and home. I moved to the Adirondacks and—wouldn't you know it?—kind of fell into a job at a supermarket. The store did a good business in prepared foods, but regular groceries just weren't moving. The manager came up with an idea: Give cooking classes using fresh produce and meat. People would buy more if they knew what to do with it.

Great idea, but every chef we talked to demanded an outrageous salary. I could do this myself, I thought. Why not? That's where my thirty-minute meals got their start. A local news report landed me on the *Today* show, and that led to my own show on the Food Network.

I really believe there are no such things as accidents, only opportunities. God gives everyone the ingredients to a good, happy life. It's up to us to make the most of them. So, tell me, what do you put in your caponata?